BANDIT HEAVEN

BANDIT HEAVEN

The Hole-in-the-Wall Gangs and the Final Chapter of the Wild West

TOM CLAVIN

ST. MARTIN'S PRESS
NEW YORK

First published in the United States by St. Martin's Press,
an imprint of St. Martin's Publishing Group

BANDIT HEAVEN. Copyright © 2024 by Tom Clavin. All rights reserved.
Printed in the United States of America. For information, address
St. Martin's Publishing Group, 120 Broadway, New York, NY 10271.

www.stmartins.com

Endpaper credits: Wyoming map, circa 1883 © THEPALMER/Getty Images;
horse riders © Jules Frazier/Getty Images; gunfighters © Weerachai pattala/Shutterstock;
gunfighter1 © Qazi Umar/Shutterstock; gunfighter2 © AnaLysiSStudiO/Shutterstock;
gunfighter3 © loesak pakdeeto/Shutterstock

Maps by David Lindroth

The Library of Congress Cataloging-in-Publication Data is available upon request.

ISBN 978-1-250-28240-8 (hardcover)
ISBN 978-1-250-38260-3 (signed edition)
ISBN 978-1-250-28241-5 (ebook)

Our books may be purchased in bulk for promotional, educational,
or business use. Please contact your local bookseller or the Macmillan Corporate and
Premium Sales Department at 1-800-221-7945, extension 5442, or by email
at MacmillanSpecialMarkets@macmillan.com.

First Edition: 2024

10 9 8 7 6 5 4 3 2 1

To Stewart and Susan Kampel

CONTENTS

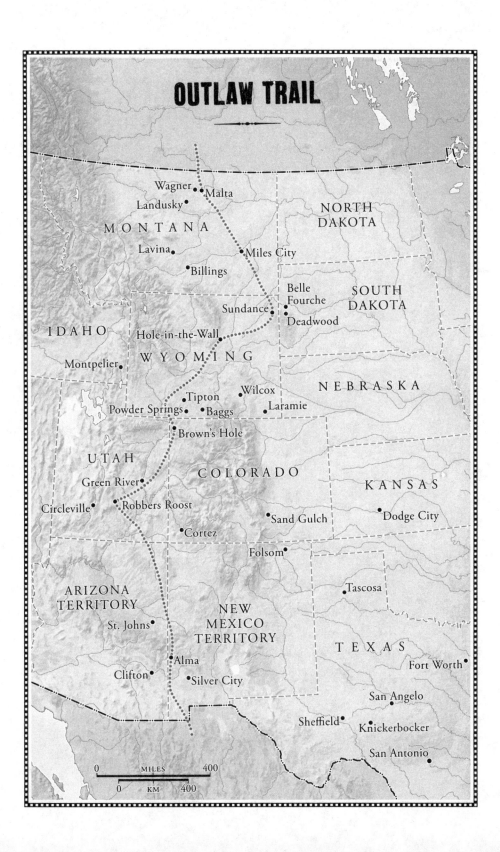

OUTLAW TRAIL

MONTANA
Wagner • Malta
Landusky •
Lavina • Miles City •
Billings •

NORTH DAKOTA

SOUTH DAKOTA
Belle Fourche
Sundance • Deadwood

IDAHO
Hole-in-the-Wall •
WYOMING
Montpelier •
Tipton Wilcox
Powder Springs • Baggs • Laramie
Brown's Hole •

NEBRASKA

UTAH
Green River •
Circleville • Robbers Roost
Cortez •

COLORADO
Sand Gulch •
Folsom •

KANSAS
Dodge City •

ARIZONA TERRITORY
St. Johns •
Alma •
Clifton • Silver City •

NEW MEXICO TERRITORY

Tascosa •

TEXAS
Fort Worth •
San Angelo •
Sheffield • Knickerbocker •
San Antonio •

0   MILES   400

0   KM   400

WILD BUNCH ROBBERIES

Wagner ■■ **Malta**
July 1901 *December 1892*

NORTH DAKOTA

M O N T A N A

• Miles City

Belle Fourche
June 1897

SOUTH DAKOTA

Sundance • • Deadwood

I D A H O

Hole-in-the-Wall •

Montpelier
August 1896 ■

W Y O M I N G

Wilcox
June 1899

Winnemucca
September 1900 ■

Rock Springs • ■ **Tipton**
August 1900

NEBRASKA

Salt Lake City •

Brown's
Hole

Castle Gate
April 1897 ■

N E V A D A

U T A H

C O L O R A D O

Beaver •
Circleville •   • Robbers
Roost

Telluride
June 1889 ■

• Cortez

Folsom
July 1899 ■

ARIZONA
TERRITORY

NEW MEXICO
TERRITORY

• Alma

• Silver City

0   MILES   400

0   KM   400

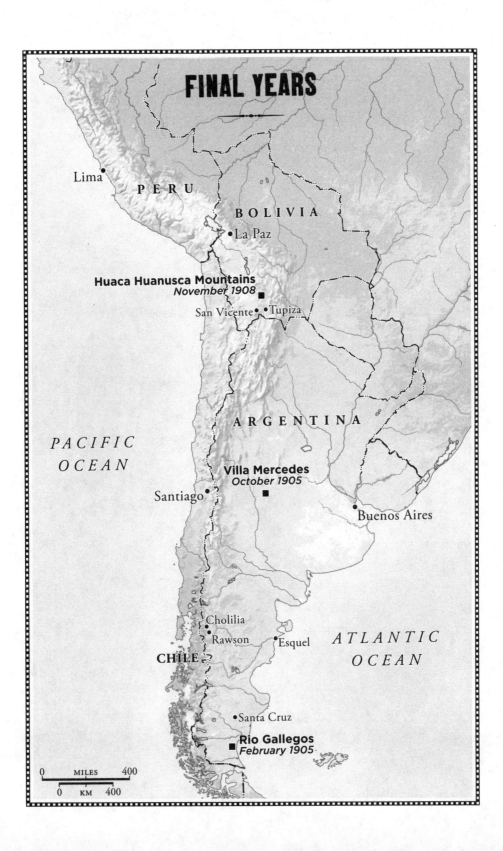

FINAL YEARS

Lima •

PERU

BOLIVIA

• La Paz

Huaca Huanusca Mountains
November 1908 ■

San Vicente • • Tupiza

ARGENTINA

*PACIFIC
OCEAN*

Villa Mercedes
October 1905 ■

Santiago •

• Buenos Aires

Cholilia •
• Rawson • Esquel

*ATLANTIC
OCEAN*

CHILE

• Santa Cruz

Rio Gallegos
February 1905 ■

0 MILES 400

0 KM 400

PROLOGUE

The train station in Wilcox that served the Union Pacific line was in the southern half of Wyoming, ninety-five miles west of Cheyenne. Early in the morning on June 2, 1899, a gang that newspaper accounts had christened the Wild Bunch planned to rob the Overland Flyer No. 1 as it approached the station.

And that was what happened—but not exactly as the perpetrators planned.

It was 2:18 A.M. when W. R. Jones, the train's engineer, spotted a man standing beside the tracks waving a red lantern. For a moment, Jones, who had earned the nickname "Grindstone" because of his serious work ethic, hesitated. Bandits were known to do this as a trick to get a train to stop unnecessarily. But if there was a legitimate reason to stop, such as track damage ahead, and the engineer did not, the result could be catastrophic. Jones was not one to take chances.

He ordered the train to halt. For the right reason, he made the wrong decision. But it turned out not to matter. He would have stopped the train anyway when he caught sight of the man crawling over the coal tender and into the engine compartment. He held a pistol pointed at Grindstone. This was infinitely more persuasive than a lantern of any color.

To emphasize that, the man said, "Do what I say, you son of a bitch, or I will put light through you." Grindstone would later learn that the bandit was Butch Cassidy.

Immediately after the train stopped, four other men appeared trackside. One was George "Flatnose" Currie, a kick from a horse having earned him that nickname. The other three were related: Bob Lee, and his cousins, the brothers Lonie and Harvey Logan. The latter was more familiar to lawmen as Kid Curry. The man who had been swinging the lantern would be identified as Harry Longabaugh, who also had a juvenile nickname—the Sundance Kid. All six men, Grindstone noted, his dismay deepening, had long masks covering their faces, and each carried a Winchester rifle in addition to a Colt pistol.[1]

The plan, so far, was working perfectly. It would soon dawn on the passengers that the train stopping short of the Wilcox station might mean a robbery was in progress, and to be on the safe side, they would stay glued to their seats. The wild card in the Wild Bunch was always Kid Curry. He had a hair-trigger temper and could be unpredictable. Cassidy had to keep him on a short rein, and usually, the Kid followed the plan.

As Cassidy had rehearsed with his crew, Grindstone Jones and his fireman were hauled down from the engine compartment and escorted along the tracks to the mail car. This was where the first deviation from the plan occurred: the men inside refused to open up. The mail car door remained fixed and locked even after Cassidy shouted that they had two hostages and the gang fired bullets into the car.

The second deviation caused even more consternation to Cassidy:

---

1 At the time, there was a chain of restaurants that had been founded twenty-three years earlier by Fred Harvey to cater to the growing number of train passengers. Most likely, before the robbery, members of the gang had dined there because their masks were cloth napkins pilfered from a Harvey House.

the lights of another Overland Limited train came into view, traveling in the same direction. Now what?

Cassidy was not keen on giving up just yet. He ordered his men to hop back on the train, and Grindstone Jones and the fireman were pushed back up into the engine compartment. Cassidy knew this section of track and that about a mile ahead was a gully over which a bridge had recently been built. He had the train travel to the other side of it. Then, as the engine idled, billowing smoke disappearing into the dark sky, Cassidy ran back to the bridge. A minute later, an explosion of ten pounds of gunpowder turned the bridge into a precarious structure that no train should risk crossing.

Thus far, Butch Cassidy had been such a cool customer that no one would have guessed this was his very first train robbery.

Cassidy told Jones to get the train rolling again. This Jones did, but the engine struggled a bit on an upgrade. As he nervously adjusted the controls, the engineer heard one of the men say, "I'll fix you!" With that, Kid Curry clunked Jones on the head with his Colt pistol. He went to strike again, but this time, Jones deflected the blow with his hand. There would not be a third time—Cassidy told the Kid, "Calm down or you'll kill someone." So far in his criminal career, Cassidy had avoided doing that, and he did not want to start now.

Several miles later, the train stopped. With the entire event taking too long, Cassidy and his crew had to forget the mail car and get into the express car, which contained two safes. They could not know that the plan would go awry in another way, one that would result in a death. Worse, the dead man would be Josiah Hazen, the sheriff of Converse County. He would receive one of the largest funerals the area had ever seen, presided over by J. DeForest Richards, the governor of Wyoming.

News of the sheriff's murder and burial in the Pioneer Cemetery made headlines across America, which in turn inspired a push by lawmen to once and for all round up the gangs who called Bandit Heaven home. The famous Pinkerton National Detective Agency was part of that effort. It assigned the best man it had, Charlie Siringo, to track down Butch Cassidy, Kid Curry, the Sundance Kid, and the others.

For now, though, the thieves had no idea what lay in store. They had a train to rob. Cassidy ordered the man inside the express car to open up—and received another refusal. There was no time for persuasion. Instead, it was time for more dynamite. The explosion sounded especially loud in the dark night. Maybe the darkness combined with smoke explained why, when the dazed messenger was pulled out of the express car covered in soot and debris, it looked like he was covered in blood.

ACT I

HEAVEN ON EARTH

1

MAVERICKS

Many people might view the "creation" of the pre–Civil War American West—though to the Indigenous residents, of course, it had been created a long time ago—as the steady and relentless migration of people looking for land west of the Missouri River on which to settle and raise crops and livestock. However, this was not true for most of the first half of the nineteenth century.

The Lewis and Clark Corps of Discovery expedition that set off from St. Charles, Missouri, in 1804 was, as its name indicates, about finding what was in the 828,000 square miles that President Thomas Jefferson and the U.S. government had purchased from France the year before. For decades, there had been tales that the land beyond the Missouri River was inhabited by fantastic creatures, such as woolly mammoths and giant sloths, and some maps labeled much of the vast, uncharted territory the Great American Desert. Some people believed that it was all one big, lush garden, a utopia to be enjoyed. In any case, when Lewis and Clark returned to "civilization" in 1806, their extraordinary tales only intensified curiosity.

But those who ventured forth after them were not looking for a place to live. There were mapmaking forays, the most prominent one led by the army lieutenant Zebulon Pike. And then there were the fur trappers. Adventure and discovery were inevitably part of the journeys to the Rocky Mountains and beyond, but the main impetus was money. Beaver was the prize, with prices for pelts soaring thanks to the fervor for fur hats and garments back east and in Europe. From 1822 until 1840, when a combination of falling prices and depleted stocks ended the era, the trappers scoured the plains and mountains and valleys for beaver and any other animals that would provide food or cash. For these restless men, wearing viscera-stained buckskin and toting long rifles and blood-flecked knives, the end of one expedition was an invitation to begin the next one.

Following the fur trappers were those who viewed much of the American West as not a destination but a route. The Oregon Trail and the Santa Fe Trail were ways to get from here to there. As they lumbered along, the columns of covered wagons left behind hastily dug graves, decaying buffalo carcasses, and discarded furniture and other litter. The Mormons changed that equation. When Brigham Young and his followers aimed their wagons west, it was to find a place to dig in and farm. They found it in the Salt Lake Valley. Very soon after stopping there in July 1847, they found that farming would not work, at least not on a scale to feed them all.

The dry land of the West would not sustain some of the crops grown back east. However, the land did grow grass that was good for grazing. Gone was the dream of raising an array of crops; it was replaced by the practice of raising livestock, which could be done pretty much year-round. Over the years, when a landowner prospered, it was not from farming but from having expanding herds of horses and cattle.

There were pockets of communities, such as the Mormon one, before and during the Civil War, but four years after Lee surrendered to Grant at Appomattox, there was a dramatic change in the American West. On May 10, 1869, at Promontory Point in Utah, the last spike was pounded in to complete the transcontinental railroad. The iron horse made it much easier for thousands of men and women to seek new homes a thousand miles or more away from their old ones. Some of them went to work at ranches or brought along enough capital to start their own.

There was a great demand for cattle, and Texas ranches were happy to meet it. Tens of thousands of livestock were sent by trail and rail to Wyoming, Utah, and Montana. After fattening up sufficiently on the sweet grasses, the "beeves" were pushed into railroad cars and shipped east for slaughter. There would soon be so many cattle barons that they would routinely fight over grazing land and fresh water. And like the dwindling Indian tribes had done with ponies, the ranch owners would steal stock from each other. The size of the herds bestowed wealth and power. And that is where cowboys came in.

The occupation was originally spelled "cow-boy." The initially derisive name referred to someone who tended cattle while on horseback and was derived from the Spanish *vaquero,* with *vaca* meaning "cow." One might think the American West created the cowboy, but the word first appeared in print in 1725, written by Jonathan Swift, the Irish essayist and author best known for *Gulliver's Travels. Cowboy* was also used in the early 1800s in Great Britain to describe the youngsters who managed cattle belonging to their families or the community.

In the United States, *cowboy* was being used as early as 1849, and two years later, there was a reference in print to a "cowhand." It took almost thirty years for another, similar name to be used—*cowpoke.* It referred specifically to the men who used long poles to persuade cows to get up into railroad cars. Other variations of the occupation were cowpuncher—mostly in Texas—and buckaroo.

As the ranches proliferated in Wyoming and its adjacent territories in the 1870s and 1880s and the population of cattle swelled, more and more cowboys were needed. There was no cowboy academy, of course, and many who filled in the ranks were raw easterners seeking adventure.[2] The ones who survived did so against a lot of odds—extremes in weather, resentful fellow cowboys, stampedes, and many lonely nights—and the lifestyle offered little chance to improve oneself.

"Almost as nomadic as Indians, they moved from one big outfit to another as their fancy dictated, unhampered by family," writes Charles Kelly in his indispensable *The Outlaw Trail,* first published in 1938. "If some misguided cowpuncher with a few months' pay in his pocket planned to start a ranch of his own on a small scale, he found his efforts violently opposed by the large ranch owners, who had claimed all public domain, under the theory that it had been created and reserved for their special benefit."

According to Kelly, "The cowboy-outlaw era began about 1875, reached its climax in 1897, and ended about 1905."

While in the employ of the ranch owners, cowboys routinely collected and branded "mavericks"—loose cattle that had wandered off from their owners. This was a sort of rustling because, with very few cattle being born free, they had to belong to someone. And at times, the mavericks already had brands on them, ones that were altered after the beasts drifted onto the property of their new owner. As long as this did not become blatant theft, it was tolerated, and the numbers pretty much evened themselves out anyway.

But the equation began to change with the increasing number of cattle and the rising number of cowboys who wanted to make money for themselves, more than or in place of the wages doled out by the large landowners. As Kelly notes, "From branding mavericks to genuine rustling was but a short and easy step. A generation of cattle thieves sprang up within a very short time, the like of which was never seen before [and] the largest gang of outlaws the West ever saw was organized in the Utah-Wyoming-Colorado section."

---

2 For a pretty realistic (for Hollywood) portrayal, watch the 1958 feature film that is simply titled *Cowboy,* with Glenn Ford as the leather-tough trail boss and Jack Lemmon as the greenhorn.

It could be difficult for the big ranchers to keep the rustling to an acceptable level. Many of the sworn lawmen in the region were poorly paid part-timers with limited jurisdictions and little motivation to risk their lives to protect the stuffed pockets of high-handed ranch owners. In turn, an owner could not completely rely on his own employees to protect the ranch's interest because as many as half of them, or more, could be rustlers themselves.

And so, thousands of cattle (and some horses) were being stolen from ranches—a dozen here or there or sometimes a hundred or more. Early on, though, the thieves did not have what the owners did, which was a place to keep the cattle that offered enough food and water until they could be sold or shipped. A big bonus would be if the location was impervious to posses.

When one such place was found, the first "bandit heaven" was born.

2

BROWN'S HOLE

There would ultimately be three main hideouts, and they would be connected by what came to be known as the Outlaw Trail. It extended from Canada to Mexico, and unlike other such trails elsewhere in the U.S., this one, according to Charles Kelly, "was provided with better hideouts, was used by more outlaws, and continued in use for a longer time than any other. Men who used it operated on a large scale; their banditry was bold and spectacular, and their hideouts were practically impregnable."

The first of its kind on the Outlaw Trail was initially known to most as Brown's Hole. It would come to be called Brown's Park, but to the old fur trappers, a "hole" was a valley enclosed by mountains. One of the distinctions the valley on the Green River in the Uintah Mountains had was it included territory from three states: the eastern boundary of Utah, the southern boundary of Wyoming, and the western boundary of Colorado. This could come in handy for bandits evading lawmen in one jurisdiction by escaping into another.

The "hole" or bottom of the valley could be reached only by descending a narrow, rock-filled trail. The entire valley was thirty miles long, east to west, and five miles wide. In June and sometimes into early July, the Green River, which runs along the southern wall of Brown's Hole at the foot of Diamond Mountain, flows with some violence thanks to the melting snow above. When trappers first came to Brown's Hole, they found it filled with game because of all the grazing land the valley provided to antelope, deer, and sheep. Once settlers arrived, some of the land was farmed or sprouted orchards.

Who was the man for whom the "hole" was named? He was Baptiste Brown, a French Canadian trapper working for the Hudson's Bay Company, which had been founded in London in 1670. Men like Brown trapped as much beaver as they could find and, though not especially well compensated personally, by doing so helped to make the company by the early 1800s a powerful rival to the emerging American outfits led by Manuel Lisa, William Ashley, Andrew Henry, and Jedediah Smith.

After an argument with Hudson's Bay Company representatives, Baptiste Brown decided to strike out on his own—well, not completely on his own; in 1827, as he made his way down the Green River, probably in a dugout canoe, he was accompanied by an Indian woman. In the valley, they built a rough shelter as a base for hunting. Over the years, sensibly, given its dimensions and his presence, it became known as Brown's Hole.

He lived there into the 1840s, at times venturing out, such as when he was recorded having attended a fur trappers rendezvous hosted by the celebrated mountain man and scout Jim Bridger on Henry's Fork in 1842. Brown's last appearance in a written record was five years later when he was in Santa Fe, serving as a juror in the trial of Pueblo Indians accused of murdering Charles Bent, the first civilian governor of New Mexico Territory.[3]

What helped hunters and trappers—and, later, bandits—was that

---

3 In January 1847, Bent and several others were killed during the Taos Revolt, an uprising by Hispanic residents and Pueblos against their treatment by U.S. soldiers. His wife survived the attack on their home in Taos. Her sister later married the renowned frontiersman Kit Carson.

Brown's Hole provided some refuge from the worst that a winter in the mountains could offer. The peaks themselves surrounding the valley were a barrier against the strongest of icy winds. And instead of having to brave fierce blasts of snow to find food, the animals came to them, down from the mountains to forage for what they could find on the valley floor.

Other men took up residence in Brown's Hole. In 1837, a year after being killed at the Alamo, Davy Crockett had a "fort" named for him there. It was really only a trading post, a hollow square of one-story log cabins, constructed on the bottoms of the Green River in northeast Colorado near the border with Utah. The increasing number of white men and their Indigenous neighbors lived peacefully until Philip Thompson, one of the men who had built Fort Davy Crockett, built another structure, this one at the mouth of the Uintah River. Included in the effort of stocking it that December 1837 was stealing horses from the Snake Indians.

Wisely, the Snakes did not take up weapons. A delegation trekked to Fort Davy Crockett to plead their case as victims. One of the occupants of the fort was Kit Carson, whose job was to hunt enough game to feed the fort's inhabitants. Grasping that in such an isolated area, peace was preferable to war with a tribe that far outnumbered the whites, Carson recruited fellow frontiersmen William Craig, Joe Meek, and Joe Walker.

This posse proceeded down the Green River to Thompson's outpost, stole the horses that had been stolen from the Snakes, and presented them to the delegation. After the satisfied Snakes left, the residents of Fort Davy Crockett celebrated Christmas in mountain man style, cracking open a keg of whiskey.[4]

---

4 In the spring, Kit Carson left the fort to go on an expedition with fellow trailblazer Jim Bridger. Joe Meek would push on to Oregon and would later be appointed the territory's marshal by President James Polk, whose wife, Sarah, was Meek's cousin. Joseph Walker would, like Carson, log a lot of miles in various expeditions, including establishing a segment of the California Trail that would be used by gold seekers after the discovery of the precious metal on Johann Sutter's farm in California in January 1848.

As would happen decades later across the plains with buffalo, in the mountains and valleys of the West in the late 1830s, the beaver would be thinned almost to extinction, and hunting parties did not earn enough to pay off their creditors. There were fewer and fewer trappers using Brown's Hole as an escape from the harshest winter weather. The locale was not abandoned, though, because some men chose to settle there, often marrying Indigenous women. These families farmed and foraged for themselves and cared little about the doings back east, including a war between northern and southern states.

Jim Bridger reenters the story after the Civil War because he had shown the railroad builders a route through the mountains that would help them finish off the transcontinental tracks. When the railroad reached Rock Springs in Wyoming, suddenly Brown's Hole was not as far off the beaten path as it had once been. And a major figure in bringing civilization closer was John Wesley Powell.

Born in upstate New York in 1834, Powell became one of the most intrepid explorers of nineteenth-century America. Barely out of his teens, he participated in explorations of the Mississippi River valley, spent four months walking across Wisconsin, and rowed the length of the Mississippi from Minnesota to the Gulf of Mexico. Because of several Midwest adventures, Powell was elected to the Illinois Natural History Society at only age twenty-five.

A fervent abolitionist, just weeks after the bombardment of Fort Sumter, he enlisted in the Twentieth Illinois Infantry. A few weeks after that, he was commissioned a lieutenant. And by the end of 1861, he was a captain in the Second Illinois Light Artillery. During the especially bloody Battle of Shiloh the following year, Powell lost most of his right arm when struck by a minié ball while in the process of giving the order to fire. The raw nerve endings in his arm caused him pain for the rest of his life.

He could have sat out the remainder of the war but that was not his nature. As soon as he recovered sufficiently, Powell was back in battle, including the successful siege of Vicksburg in 1863. By the time of the

Atlanta campaign in the summer of 1864, he was a major commanding an artillery brigade. After the Battle of Nashville, he was promoted to lieutenant colonel, but Powell would always prefer to be called "Major."

After the war, it was back to wandering the West. Though essentially one-armed, Powell led several expeditions into the Rocky Mountains and on the Colorado and Green Rivers, collecting specimens and drawing maps along the way. He and six others became the first white men to scale Longs Peak, in 1868. The following year, with ten men in four boats and packing ten months' worth of food, Powell led an expedition that further explored the Colorado River as well as the Grand Canyon. The participants did not get to eat all that packed food because the journey that began on May 24, 1869, was completed by the end of August.[5]

It was during his 1869 travels that Powell hiked through Brown's Hole, which he renamed Brown's Park. Two years later, he was back, encountering two Texas cattlemen named Harrell and Bacon, who had wintered there with their herd. Over time, this became a common practice. Cattle ranches proliferated in Texas after the Civil War, and some of the owners drove them north to Wyoming and Montana where it was not so hot and there was plenty of water and range land for grazing. Some herds would be late leaving, and rather than risk getting the beeves caught in early snowstorms, they would be sheltered in Brown's Hole.

As Charles Kelly informs, "Previous to arrival of the Texas herds, horses were the only form of property in the country worth stealing, and all pre-railroad outlaws were horse thieves. The arrival of immense herds of cattle, however, changed all that; thereafter, Brown's Hole became principal headquarters for the more profitable cattle-rustling business."

_____

5 Among Powell's legacies, Lake Powell, a man-made body of water on the Colorado River, is named after the intrepid major. He would go on to publish books about his experiences in the American West, work for the Smithsonian Institution, and become director of the U.S. Geological Survey. Powell died at sixty-eight in 1902 in, of all places, Maine and was buried with full military honors in the Arlington National Cemetery.

Some cowboys, either because they were budding entrepreneurs or just plain thieves, would cull a few head here and a few head there from the large herds grazing in and around Rock Springs. There were also beeves that had wandered off and could be captured. A good place to hide the cattle until it was safe to sell them was Brown's Hole.

There were also legitimate ranchers in the area. Through the 1870s and 1880s, much of the surrounding range became occupied by large cattle outfits, with some of them having moved full-time from Texas. Their herds grazed on thousands of acres, and to their mind, there was no room for small operations with only a couple hundred head. Not satisfied with enough, they wanted it all. The small-spread ranching families, referred to as homesteaders or "nesters," had just as much right to be there . . . but not the might.

In some instances, enough pressure was applied that homesteaders realized they had no future in the region, so they picked up and moved on. Less subtle methods were to set a nester's barn on fire or to poison his cattle. Sometimes, the only way to get rid of the truly stubborn residents was to kill them and leave their bodies in remote spots. Thus originated the term *dry gulching*, with ravens and vultures benefiting along with the big ranchers.

For the homesteaders who managed to stick it out, stealing cattle was seen as self-defense, though sometimes it was not quite stealing. As Charles Kelly notes, "With so many thousands of cattle roaming the country there were always some who managed to escape round-ups and carried no brand. These mavericks, according to the law of the range, belonged to the man who first put his mark on them." The beeves could be driven into Brown's Hole, branded, and then pushed back out onto the open range.

Word got around that Brown's Hole was a good place not only to conduct secret cattle collecting and branding but also for humans to hide out. A man did not necessarily have to be a criminal to find his way there; he might just want to find some sanctuary from troubles back east or south and think about starting over. But in the 1870s and 1880s, there were men who committed a variety of crimes, including bank and train robberies, and if lawmen were on their trail, the isolated beauty of Brown's Hole was a safe haven. Marshals, sheriffs, and their deputies were not brave or foolish enough to enter the sheltered valley. To gain entry, there were two trails from the north and one from the south—all of them perfect for an outlaw ambush.

One government agency that did maintain access to Brown's Hole, even through snow and sleet and rain, was the U.S. Postal Service. The hole may have seen no tax collector, elected government, or school system, but the mail got through. A man named Parsons owned a store in the Utah section of Brown's Hole, a portion of which was used as a post office. During the winter months, the mail was brought in and out from the Mormon town of Vernal, which was fifty miles over Diamond Mountain, and the rest of the year, it came and went via the Green River.

Otherwise, if you did not have a stamp (but maybe a bounty) on you, you stayed clear of Brown's Hole. By the mid-1890s, while much of the American West was being settled and was tamer than in previous decades, with the more famous criminals dead or in prison, the remote valley had become one of the three main stops on the very busy Outlaw Trail.

3

HOLE-IN-THE-WALL

If one were searching for the legendary Hole-in-the-Wall today, the trip could begin in Casper, Wyoming. Go north to Sheridan, crossing the Powder River at the town of Kaycee, so named because it was the site of the K-C Ranch. From there, go thirty miles to the west. There is a canyon surrounded by black rock that, as one continues, becomes red sandstone. Hereabouts was the settlement of Barnum.[6]

Centuries of erosion were responsible for the narrow opening in the red wall just wide enough to allow a wagon to pass through. Only a couple of riflemen needed to be positioned there to provide a strong defense against an approaching posse. Several miles south of this opening was a small valley, and entrance to it was gained through another hole in a wall, this one V-shaped and big enough for only a horse and rider. Here, over time, a ranch was created by outlaws, consisting of a

---

6 Nearby is the site of what was dubbed the Dull Knife Fight, which took place on November 25, 1876. The Fourth Cavalry, commanded by General Ranald Mackenzie, raided the winter camp of the Northern Cheyenne. All the tribe's supplies were destroyed as were 173 lodges and some five hundred ponies were captured. The Northern Cheyenne were forced to seek shelter with the village of Crazy Horse, a Lakota Sioux, to survive the winter, which they barely did.

half dozen one-room log cabins. This location would be known as the Hole-in-the-Wall Ranch or the Outlaw Ranch.

White people could be found in the area after the Civil War, but it was not until the late 1870s and into the 1880s that settlers in any significant numbers arrived in Big Horn country, being reasonably confident that the Indian tribes who had resided and hunted there had been sufficiently subdued. Soon, the settlers and ranchers had more to worry about from outlaws than Indians, most of the surviving ones having been confined to reservations.

During the mid to late 1870s, Deadwood, to the east across the South Dakota border, was a booming mining town. According to Charles Kelly, it was "a magnet attracting the country's worst characters. When things got too hot in Deadwood, the bandits rode west toward the Big Horns and camped along the Powder River, a fine game country." To enhance a diet that relied on meat, these miscreants, without permission, took advantage of what was in the larders of surrounding ranches.

Some accounts contend that a precedent of using the Hole-in-the-Wall area as a hideout was established by Frank and Jesse James in 1877. While this is possible, what is known is that in the aftermath of the disastrous attempt to rob a bank in Northfield, Minnesota, in September 1876, the brothers rode hard and fast to leave the area behind and hide out under assumed names in the Nashville, Tennessee, vicinity. Still, by the early 1880s, there was no lack of less infamous outlaws there. One who represented the caliber of bandit who helped make the Hole-in-the-Wall home was another man known for a particular facial feature, George "Big Nose" Parrott.

Though born in Montbéliard, France, in 1834, by the late 1870s, Parrott—who also sported the nickname "Big Beak"—was a veteran American West bandit. Perhaps his most profitable hunting ground was the Oregon Trail, especially along the Sweetwater River, where he took from travelers who were not about to challenge his six-shooters. Even better was picking off the occasional stagecoach or pay wagon. It was getting ambitious that did him in: he aspired to be a train robber.

In 1878, following an attempt on a Union Pacific train near Medicine Bow River, Parrott and his gang hid out in a camp in Rattlesnake Canyon, near Elk Mountain. On August 19, a lookout warned that two men were approaching—Robert Widdowfield, a Wyoming deputy sheriff, and Tip Vincent, a detective working for Union Pacific. The bandits stamped out their campfire and got set for an ambush.

Right after the two lawmen entered the camp, Widdowfield kneeled and felt that the ashes were still hot—so hot that he became alarmed that they had walked into a trap. They had, and it was too late to escape it. Parrott and his gang opened fire, and they stopped shooting only when it was evident that both Widdowfield and Vincent were dead. After the victims' guns were taken and the bodies were covered with some brush, the gang took off, stealing one of the lawmen's horses too.

When the bullet-riddled bodies were discovered, the news spread quickly. Friends and colleagues of the two victims were outraged and railroad officials responded by offering a reward—$10,000 initially but that was doubled when Big Nose Parrott and his men continued to elude posses by hiding out in the Hole-in-the-Wall interior. The outlaw's confidence rose to such a level—plus some boredom had set in—that by the following February, Parrott thought it time for another brazen heist.

The gang rode to Milestown, Montana, for some discreet drinking and gambling, but soon Parrott learned that a prosperous local merchant, Morris Cahn, would be taking money back east to buy stocks of merchandise. Parrott and his gang carried out a daring daylight robbery despite Cahn traveling with a military convoy containing fifteen soldiers, two officers, an ambulance, and a wagon from Fort Keogh, which offered the additional bonus of a U.S. Army payroll.

The convoy made it easy for the thieves. Approaching the coulee over a five-mile plateau and ten miles from the Powder River, the soldiers, ambulance, and wagon became strung out, creating large gaps between the groups.[7] Parrott and his pals fixed masks on their faces and positioned themselves at the bottom of the coulee, at a turn in the trail. Once again, their trap worked: The gang first surprised and then captured the lead element of soldiers as well as the ambulance with Cahn and the officers. They waited and likewise corralled the rear element of soldiers with the wagon. The outlaws rode off with over $10,000.

This event, added to the killing of the two lawmen, turned up the heat on the Big Nose Parrott gang. In 1880, he and a sidekick, obviously overconfident, eschewing the safety of the expanding Hole-in-the-Wall compound, were back relaxing in Milestown. Two local deputies, Lem Wilson and Fred Schmalsle, were alerted that Parrott and "Dutch Charlie" Burris were drunk in a saloon and boasting about killing two Wyoming lawmen. When the two deputies entered the saloon with guns drawn, it was the bandits who were the trapped ones; the deputies subsequently arrested the outlaws.

Both outlaws would hang for their crimes, but Parrott's demise was more entertaining to those who enjoy the macabre. He was tried and found guilty and was housed in the jail in Rawlins, Wyoming, awaiting his execution, which was scheduled for April 2, 1881. Unwilling to make it easy on the hangman, Parrott, using a pocketknife and a piece of sandstone, was able to wedge and file the rivets of the heavy shackles on his ankles. He removed his shackles and hid in the washroom. When the jailor, Robert Rankin, entered, Parrott used the shackles to bash Rankin over the head. Though the jailor's skull was fractured, he managed to fight back, at the same time managing to call out to his wife, Rosa, for help. Producing a pistol, she persuaded Parrott to return to his cell.

News of this gambit circulated through town, and citizens decided enough was enough. Groups of people started making their way to the

---

7 Achieving an unhappy form of immortality, this site has since been known as Cahn's Coulee.

jail. A few wearing masks burst into the calaboose and accosted poor Robert Rankin, who was lying on a cot being bandaged by the plucky Rosa. She was no longer packing a pistol and so was unable to prevent the masked men from taking her husband's keys. Parrott was dragged from his cell into the street and presented to the mob, who now numbered some two hundred angry men and women.

George "Big Nose" Parrott suffered the same fate his sidekick Dutch Charlie had months earlier—hanged from the crossbeam of a telegraph pole. However, his contribution to Western lore was not over. This is where the macabre part comes in.

Two physicians, Thomas Maghee and John Osborne, carted Parrott's body off with the intention of studying his brain to see if there was any indication of why he was a criminal. After the top of the outlaw's skull was sawn off, it was gifted to Lillian Heath, who though only sixteen years old, was Dr. Maghee's assistant.[8] A death mask of Parrott's face was created and skin from his thighs and chest was removed. The skin, including the dead man's nipples, was sent to a tannery in Denver, where it was made into a medical bag and a pair of shoes.

Parrott's dismembered body was stored in a whiskey barrel filled with a salt solution for about a year while the experiments continued; then he was buried in the yard behind Dr. Maghee's office. The shoes must have been an attractive and durable enough pair because Dr. Osborne wore them to his inaugural ball when he was sworn in as Wyoming's first Democratic governor in 1893.

The executed outlaw's bones proved to be durable too. On May 11, 1950, while working on the Rawlins National Bank, construction workers unearthed the whiskey barrel. Still inside were the skull with the top sawed off and other remains. Heath, then in her mideighties, was contacted, and she sent her skull cap to the scene. It was found

---

8 Apparently unscarred by the experience, Lillian Heath went on to become Wyoming's first female physician and reportedly used the skull cap as an ash tray.

to fit the skull in the barrel perfectly. DNA testing later confirmed the remains were those of George Parrott.[9]

Parrott's grisly fate did not deter others from riding the Outlaw Trail and using the Hole-in-the-Wall territory as a safe haven. As Kelly notes, it was "only one hard day's ride from Casper and the Overland Trail, and it soon became headquarters for an organized gang of horse thieves operating from Minnesota to Oregon. Stolen horses passed from one station to another were wintered behind the Red Wall and sold in the spring."

Beeves soon joined the bounty of stolen flesh. As the Powder River country to the east became filled with cattle from Texas, it was easy pickings for rustlers. There simply were not enough cowboys to guard all the herds, which grew larger every year, and some of the low-paid cowboys themselves moonlit as rustlers. The stolen stock was well hidden then driven to railroad stations, such as the one in Casper, where they could be sold. Initially, possession was sufficient proof of ownership, but over time, when there was more scrutiny by lawmen and stock detectives, rustlers became adept at changing brands. To the eager representatives of beef-processing plants, the cattle could not be purchased and loaded on the railroad cars fast enough.

With more cowboys possessing an entrepreneurial spirit, small ranches sprang up in that north-central section of Wyoming. The operators still worked off and on for the big cattlemen while they did some rustling, or they were rustlers who did some ranching. This was, as Kelly wryly puts it, a "distinction without a difference."

Early on, what few envisioned was that this scenario would lead to a civil war—one featuring an actual invasion.

---

9 Today, Governor Osborne's shoes, as well as the bottom part of the outlaw's skull and his earless death mask, are on display at the Carbon County Museum in Rawlins. Alas, the medicine bag has never been found.

4

"A PERFECT SMASHUP"

As the 1880s progressed, in north-central Wyoming the prospering cattle barons were becoming increasingly disgruntled. In several ways, Johnson County—founded in 1880 and named for E. P. Johnson, an attorney in Cheyenne—represented what was happening across the Wyoming Territory and spreading into Montana. The owners of the large herds who were building big ranch houses believed that they ruled the ranges. A certain amount of rustling and the existence of the small ranches did not really impact them in a serious way. It was more the principle of the thing—they wanted it all and had made a substantial investment to have it.

Cattle prices peaked in 1882, drawing more money to the business and more cattle to the land. Soon, the consequence of such success was a beef glut. Prices began to fall, yet even so, all the cattle barons could think to do was business as usual—drive more cattle north. Not only did prices fall even further, but also all those beeves depleted the available natural resources, especially good grazing land.

Mother Nature responded in 1886: first, with a drought and, second, with one of the worst winters in American history—so bad, it would become known as the Big Die-Up.

The summer had been unusually hot and dry, with numerous prairie fires, and already strained water sources often dried up. In the fall, signs of a harsh winter ahead began to appear. Birds flew south earlier than usual, beavers were seen collecting more wood than normal, and some cattle grew thicker and shaggier coats. The snows came early in November and were reported as some of the worst in memory. Extreme cold killed humans and animals. Some people left their houses and did not return, later found frozen to death only a few feet from their front doors.[10]

Many of the major cattle operations in Wyoming, Montana, and the Dakota Territory—some belonging to absentee owners, living as far away as Scotland and England—had not allowed for such a weather calamity and hence had not stored nearly enough hay. As a result, estimates were that up to 90 percent of the cattle on the northern ranges perished. The spring thaw revealed the true horror—millions of dead animals, dotting the plains to the horizon, damming the rivers and streams, and raising a stench that wafted over thousands of square miles. Even the cattle that had survived were thin and weakened, and some would not recover enough to be sold.

That cruel winter of 1886–87 finished many of the stock growers outright. And with that, the role of the cowboy changed. Most were driven out of work and took to what was called "riding the chuck-line" for meals and shelter. Some cowboys, more desperate than ambitious, took to making their way with a long rope and a running iron, rustling the cattle they had once been paid to herd.

The ranch owners who managed to continue raising cattle did so with smaller herds. Bowing to necessity, they became farmers too, growing their own fodder and erecting miles of barbed-wire fences

---

10 The winter weather even reached the West Coast, with snowfall of 3.7 inches in downtown San Francisco on February 5, 1887, setting an all-time record.

to keep their cattle from ranging too far from their food supply. The wide-open spaces of the Old West had become buried along with millions of head of cattle beneath that brutal winter's snow and ice.

A familiar figure in American history was one of the typical victims of the Big Die-Up. Fleeing a family tragedy in New York, Theodore Roosevelt had wound up establishing a ranch near Medora in the Dakota Territory. He was hit as hard as any cattle owner. In a letter to his friend Henry Cabot Lodge of Massachusetts, Roosevelt remarked, "Well, we have had a perfect smashup all through the cattle country of the northwest. The losses are crippling. For the first time I have been utterly unable to enjoy a visit to my ranch. I shall be glad to get home." After a valiant effort to keep his ranch going failed, the future president sold off what he could and returned to New York.

In Johnson County, the newspapers reported that one result of the Wyoming cattle industry being in awful financial trouble was that the remaining owners of the big herds deeply resented those who might challenge their unfettered right to run their cattle on public land. More than ever, small ranchers were at risk of being run off or worse, as two homesteaders—Jim Averell and a woman known as "Cattle Kate"—found out. Their fate demonstrated how lawless the region could still be.

Ellen Liddy Watson was born in July 1861 in Ontario, Canada, the oldest of ten children. When Ella, as she was called, was sixteen, the family moved to a farm near Lebanon, Kansas. There she had the misfortune to meet and marry William Pickell, who turned out to be a drunk and abuser. Ella filed for divorce and began to travel the frontier.

She lived in Nebraska and Colorado, and at age twenty-four, she was hired as a cook and housekeeper at the Rawlins House in Rawlins, Wyoming. In February 1886, Ella met James Averell, who had a homestead sixty miles to the east near the Sweetwater River. The youngest of seven children, he had also been born in Ontario, in March 1851. He had served in the U.S. Army where he had found some trouble, shooting and killing a man in Buffalo, Wyoming. It was determined he had acted in self-defense as the victim, Charlie Johnson, was known as mean and violent when drinking, as he had been when he confronted Averell.

By the time he met Ella, the industrious Averell, back in civilian life, was a widower. In addition to a small ranch, he operated a general store and a tavern that benefited from being close to the Oregon Trail. On top of that, in June 1886, he became the local postmaster as well as a justice of the peace. Averell persuaded Ella to move in with him and to own a piece of land right next to his. Soon, she acquired cattle and built a log house on her property.

She applied to obtain a brand registered for her cattle but was refused because of what was known as the Maverick Law: Unbranded calves, found on the open range, could not be removed from the range but were to be branded on the neck with an "M." Such beeves then became the exclusive property of the Wyoming Stock Growers Association. This was a powerful group of men who controlled the cattle industry. The association had also appointed itself the official law enforcement agency for the cattle industry.

The law essentially prevented the smaller ranchers and homesteaders from competing with the resurging large cattle operations. It required that those young calves be auctioned off to the highest bidder only by appointed representatives of the Stock Growers Association and that the proceeds go toward covering the costs of policing the range. And no one could brand calves except those receiving registered brands from the state. Further, small cattle ranchers were not permitted to bid on mavericks, unless they had a registered brand. It also put their own calves at risk if they were to stray too far from their own property. The association could round them up and sell them.

To make matters worse for homesteaders like Ella Watson and Jim Averell, the larger operators began to illegally file claims to much of the still-available land. By placing movable cabins on their claims, they could state that the property had been "improved," a requirement of the Homestead Act. After the claim was filed, they would then place logs under the cabins and roll them to another property, repeating the process over and over again.

Ella and Averell came to the notice of the Wyoming Stock Growers Association when, writing as a justice of the peace, Averell composed letters that were published in newspapers in Casper protesting the association's tactics. They gained more notice in March 1888, when Ella filed her official homestead claim with the Land Office in Cheyenne. Combined, Ella and Averell owned more than 320 acres. She continued to improve her property by building corrals for the livestock and fencing much of it. Aided by the attention Averell's letters were garnering, the lobby in Casper representing smaller land and cattle owners pressured Thomas Moonlight, who had been appointed governor of the Wyoming Territory in 1887. He presided over a successful effort the following year to loosen the big owners' stranglehold.[11]

Beginning in the fall of 1888, Ella bought cattle to stock her modest ranch and she was able to use an LU brand. She also acquired young helpers, first by adopting an eleven-year-old boy, Gene Crowder. Also working at the ranch was John DeCorey, a fourteen-year-old, and the twenty-year-old Ralph Coe, who was a nephew of Averell. Lending a hand from time to time, such as to mend fences, was Frank Buchanan, a neighbor. Ella's hard work and growing brood earned her the nickname of "Cattle Kate" and the enmity of another neighbor, Albert Bothwell.

Before Ella had arrived, Bothwell, a member of the Wyoming Stock Growers Association, had used the property, as well as other large sections of open range, as pastureland for his cattle. In fact, Bothwell was in the habit of running his cattle through the entire Sweetwater Valley, spreading out some twenty miles. Whether he actually believed it or not, Bothwell acted as though he owned all that land.

Initially, he took the high road, approaching Ella several times to

---

11 Understandably, this did not endear Moonlight—who had been born in Forfarshire, Scotland—to the large ranch owners, many of whom contributed to political campaigns. This could explain why Moonlight was a one-term governor.

purchase her property. However, she declared she was here to stay. Bothwell's anger increased and then soared when Averell threatened to rescind the right of way through his property so that he could irrigate his pastureland. Enough was enough: Bothwell was determined to run Ella and Averell off their land.

There was some simple harassment at first, such as having cow-hands keep the couple under surveillance and placing skulls and cross-bones on their doorways. Then in July 1889, he had a stock detective named George Henderson ride through Ella's pasture in the early morning. He returned claiming that the LU brand was illegal. Though probably knowing this was untrue, Bothwell convened a meeting of other cattlemen and convinced them that Ella and Averell had to go. Six ranchers volunteered to take action: M. Earnest McLean, Robert "Captain" Galbraith, John Henry Durbin, Robert Conner, Tom Sun, and, of course, Bothwell.

The men rode to Ella's homestead, and seeing the brands on the cattle—and *not* bothering to confirm their legality—they began tear-ing down a barbed-wire fence to release the beeves. Ella and her ad-opted son, Gene Crowder, were forced into a wagon and told she was being driven to Rawlins after a stop by Averell's place. There, Averell was told by the ranch owners that they had a warrant for his arrest. When Averell demanded to see it, Durbin and Bothwell drew their guns. He was forced into the wagon with Ella and Gene.

The group began to travel north. Gene was allowed to get down off the wagon and dashed back to the Averell place, where he ex-plained to the others what was going on. One listener was Frank Buchanan, who quickly got on his horse and began to follow the vigilantes. They headed toward Sweetwater River and Independence Rock. They stopped at a gulch on the south side of the river. As Buchanan watched, Bothwell tied a rope to a tree and wrapped the other end around Averell's neck. McLean did the same for Ella. See-ing this, Buchanan opened fire on the vigilantes, but when the group returned fire, he turned and raced for the Averell ranch.

By the time he arrived there and sent out pleas for help, Ella and Averell were dead. Their bodies were allowed to hang in the July heat for more than two days. When a local reporter visited the site, his account included, "Side by side they swing, their arms touching each other, their tongues protruding and their faces swollen and discolored almost beyond recognition. Judging from signs too plain to be mistaken a desperate struggle had taken place on the cliff, and both man and woman had fought for their lives until the last."[12]

A coroner's inquest confirmed that Ella and Averell, who were twenty-seven and thirty-eight (respectively), met their deaths at the hands of John Durbin, Tom Sun, A. J. Bothwell, Robert Conner, Robert Galbraith, and Earnest McLean. The victims were buried at the Averell ranch, and the six killers were arrested. Bail was set at $5,000 each, which was paid immediately.

A grand jury was convened for August 25, but before the witnesses could testify, they began to mysteriously die or disappear, such as Gene Crowder, who was never seen again. John DeCorey was said to have gone to Steamboat Springs in Colorado and was never summoned for the hearing. Frank Buchanan also disappeared before the hearing. Years later, it was reported that he had wandered all over the country for the next year or two, hiding from the powerful cattlemen and fearing for his life. Ralph Coe died on the very day of the scheduled hearing, possibly from poisoning.

With no witnesses to testify, all charges were dropped against the six cattlemen. No attempts were ever made to investigate the death of Ralph Coe or the three disappearances of the primary witnesses against the six ranchers. Rumors abounded that Albert Bothwell had some of his cowboys ride to the different homesteaders and small ranchers telling them if they testified against the accused men that they would be burned out or worse—such as ending up like Cattle Kate and Averell.

---

12 The lynchings soon made national news too. One of the more lurid as well as alliterative headlines read, "Blaspheming Border Beauty Barbarously Boosted Branchward."

Before the year was out, both Bothwell and Tom Sun had been made members of the Wyoming Stock Growers Association executive committee, and Robert Galbraith had been elected to the legislature. And a few years later, Bothwell finally acquired both Ella's and Averell's homesteads. He moved his house onto the former's property. He would ultimately retire to Los Angeles, where he died in March 1928 in his seventy-third year.

This time, the big ranchers got away with murder. That would not happen next time, when a war broke out.

5

THE INVASION

To add insult to grievous injury, in the aftermath of the lynchings of Cattle Kate and Jim Averell several sensational articles were published portraying Ella Watson as a prostitute who accepted cattle for her favors. However, it was soon discovered that the articles had been written by an employee of one of the Cheyenne dailies owned by cattle barons.

This revelation was just one indication that things were beginning to change in Wyoming and specifically in Johnson County. There was a wind blowing from a different direction, eroding some of the power of the large ranchers. A stronger indication was that local juries were often acquitting suspects in cattle theft cases. The big barons angrily stated publicly and in private correspondence that the acquittals proved it was impossible to present evidence to a Johnson County jury—no matter how compelling—that would produce a conviction. Why? Because there were now more homesteaders, which meant more of them on juries, and they were more inclined toward rustlers (like themselves, in some cases) than the rich overlords.

And the outcomes of the trials were often the correct ones. Many of the prosecutions were deeply flawed, seemingly motivated by huge reward money and a frantic determination by owners of big herds to punish owners of small herds who claimed rights to grazing on public land.

This pot of antagonism simmered for two more years, with both sides digging in. In one of those years, of the 180 arrests for rustling in Johnson County, there was only one conviction. Finally, in 1891, the larger ranchers once again lashed out.

With generous offers of bounty money, they recruited employees of the Wyoming Stock Growers Association to create a squad of assassins. Evidence of the legal turmoil of the time was that one of those who signed on was Frank Canton. Born Josiah Horner in Virginia in 1849, he was still a child when the family moved to Texas. As a teenager Horner became a cowboy, escorting cattle to Kansas for the Texas rancher Burk Burnett. From 1871 to 1878, he engaged in a variety of illegal activities, becoming a fugitive from justice. Jailed in 1877 for robbing a bank in Texas, Horner soon escaped and helped drive a cattle herd to Nebraska.

Seeking somewhat of a fresh start, he changed his name to Frank Canton and continued north. He accepted a position with the Wyoming Stock Growers Association. In 1882, he was elected sheriff of Johnson County, serving for four years before returning to the Wyoming Stock Growers Association, where he was eager enough to do the barons' bidding.

One assignment had been to arrest a man named Tom Waggoner in Newcastle. He was a horse trader believed to be selling stolen stock. "Arrest" was only a euphemism because when they found Waggoner, on June 4, 1891, they took him to a remote area and hanged him. Why risk putting him in front of a jury who were most likely stealing stock themselves?

To make the murder more shocking, over two weeks passed before anyone found his body. Waggoner's feet were resting on the ground and his legs were bent, as the rope had stretched before rigor mortis set in. "The rope had cut through the flesh after it became rotten, and maggots held high carnival over the lifeless body," the *Newcastle Journal* reported. His face had turned black, half his mustache had sloughed off, and his eyes had swollen and burst.

Next on Canton's list was Nate Champion. He was a bantam of a man with a reputation as a formidable fighter. He ran a herd of about two hundred cattle on one of the forks of the Powder River. Champion's stock grazed on public land, exactly as did the animals of the big cattlemen. He insisted that his cattle had as much right to grass on the public range as did the herd of any cattle baron. He was quite right, and that made him a target—and the unwilling instigator of a new civil war.

A native of Round Rock, Texas, the thirty-three-year-old Champion spent a few years as a cowboy before deciding to run a small ranch in Johnson County. In addition to his grazing philosophy, the large ranchers were upset by Champion's support of a new group calling itself the Northern Wyoming Farmers and Stock Growers Association. The notion of farms taking root and erecting barbed-wire borders was a nightmare for the cattle kings.

The Waggoner lynching had been the prelude. The attempt to administer the wrong kind of frontier justice to Nate Champion became the first salvo in what made national headlines as the Johnson County War.

Early on the morning of November 1, 1891, five members of the assassination squad arrived at the Champion ranch fifteen miles from what would become the town of Kaycee. They tried to force their way into the cabin where Champion and a ranch hand were sleeping, but the narrow doorway allowed only two in. Guns drawn, they told Champion to "give it up."

Keeping calm, Champion stretched and yawned while reaching under a pillow for his own revolver, and the shooting started. Though the intruders fired shots at point-blank range, so close that powder burns were left on Champion's face, all their shots missed. Champion's return fire, however, did not. One of the squad members was hit in the arm and the other was shot in the belly, a mortal wound. The assassination squad fled but not before Champion got a good look at one of them: Joe Elliott, a detective for the Wyoming Stock Growers Association.

During the ensuing investigation, one of the assassination squad members was forced to admit the names of all the members before two witnesses, local ranchers John Tisdale and Orley Jones. Johnson County authorities filed attempted murder charges against Joe Elliott, and newspapers not controlled by the barons pushed for charges against the wealthy and prominent cattlemen behind the assassination squad. A setback to those efforts occurred on December 1, when both Tisdale and Jones were murdered. The killings created an uproar and intensified efforts to indict those responsible.

On February 8, 1892, a preliminary hearing was held in the case of *State v. Elliott* for the attempted murder of Nate Champion. Champion gave dramatic testimony, and Elliott was bound over for trial in the district court on the attempted murder charge. Johnson County attorneys had amassed a great deal of evidence against Elliott and, with Champion's testimony, seemed likely to convict him when his case came to trial. The big cattlemen promptly resolved, in early March, to invade and subdue Johnson County.

Over the next several weeks, dozens of men were recruited—many from Texas—and they gathered in Denver. Their "commander" was Major Frank Wolcott from Kentucky, a Union army veteran who was an experienced enforcer for the Wyoming Stock Growers Association. These southern vigilantes were not used to the weather in that part of the country, and that first week of April they were stopped in their tracks by snow. When they were able to ride again, the first name on their list was Nate Champion.

On the morning of April 9, as many as fifty-five men, including Frank Canton, arrived at the KC Ranch. Champion and three other men were in the main cabin. Two of those men were trappers who had been offered a place to sleep, and as they set off from the cabin, they were arrested. When a third man, a cowboy named Rueben Ray, exited, shooting began, and he was killed. Now alone in the cabin, Champion was besieged by bullets.

However, the stubborn rancher, expecting trouble, was well-stocked with ammunition and he fired back. Champion managed to not only hold out for several hours but also kill four of the attackers and wounded others. Finally, someone had the idea to simply set fire to the cabin. Champion had no choice but to flee, and when he was out in the open, he was gunned down.

This small victory would be a very fleeting one. News of the shoot-out had spread, and men from all over the area rushed to confront the invaders, who holed up south of Buffalo at the T. A. Ranch. There, they were surrounded by a posse that eventually grew to more than four hundred men. The posse conducted a formal siege, perhaps reviving memories for the grizzled Union army veterans among them.

During the next few days the posse slowly closed in on the invaders, whose supplies and courage dwindled. Then things got medieval—fourteen posse members started moving toward the T. A. Ranch house using a ponderous movable fort called a "go-devil" or "ark of safety" made of logs on the running gears of two wagons. The game plan was to get close enough to the invaders' fortifications to use dynamite and force the occupants out into the open.

But the posse never got the chance to use its new weapon because just before they could, soldiers from nearby Fort McKinney arrived. They surrounded the ranch house, and the rather abashed invaders were much relieved to be taken into custody.

The cavalry had arrived in the nick of time thanks to the governor Amos Barber. He did not have an honorable motive, however. Barber was in the pocket of the cattle barons, and he feared that if the invaders were to surrender to the posse, some of them might seek mercy by identifying those who were behind the invasion, a group that included Barber. The alarmed governor had telegraphed President Benjamin Harrison in Washington, DC. Harrison was quickly convinced that there was an "insurrection" in Wyoming and agreed to call on Fort McKinney troops to suppress it.

Would Frank Canton get his comeuppance? Even in the last days of the Wild West, there could be a thin line between lawman and outlaw. Canton survived the siege and would survive subsequent violent events in Johnson County. In 1894, he moved to Oklahoma Territory and served as undersheriff in Pawnee County and as a deputy U.S. marshal. The former assassin played a role in subduing the Oklahoma outlaw gangs, partly by killing the bandit Bill Dunn in Pawnee in 1896. After working in various law enforcement capacities, he was appointed in 1907 by Governor Charles Haskell as adjutant general of the Oklahoma National Guard. Over the next decade, the now General Canton built up the organization. He died in September 1927, at age seventy-eight, and his funeral was a major event in Oklahoma City. He was buried at Fairlawn Cemetery in dress uniform with Masonic rites and military honors.

Governor Barber continued to cover his tracks. Once the invaders were taken into custody, he assumed control over them and refused to allow them to even be questioned. Further aggravation for local authorities was that the costs for feeding and housing the prisoners had to be paid by Johnson County, not to mention the substantial expenses for the preparation of the criminal cases. The territory provided no financial assistance whatever. The invaders were represented by Willis Van Devanter.[13] Eventually, the charges against all the invaders had to be dismissed because a jury could not be seated to try their cases and the county did not have the funds to pay the continuing costs of prosecution.

There would be little time for the governor to enjoy his victory over the justice system. That changing wind in Wyoming blew Barber out of office. The Republican Party was closely associated with the

---

13 In the next century, Van Devanter would serve for twenty-five years on the U.S. Supreme Court. He would be known for his conservative, small-government views and anti-Semitism, which was apparent (among other indications) from the fact that he refused to speak to three of his fellow justices because they were Jewish: Louis Brandeis, Felix Frankfurter, and Benjamin Cardozo.

cattlemen and the Wyoming Stock Growers Association, and an increasing number of voters were disgruntled by that. The 1892 election was a landslide in favor of the Wyoming Democratic Party, which was bad news for Barber. In addition to Barber being voted out of office, enough Democrats were elected to the Wyoming state legislature that Republican senator Francis Warren lost his seat.

Perhaps most significantly, according to the Wyoming historian John W. Davis, in *Wyoming Range War,* the organization primarily responsible for the Johnson County War, the Wyoming Stock Growers Association, was changed forever: "Plagued by continuing economic woes, the cattle barons in the association permanently altered this organization in 1893 when they opened their group to all the stock growers in Wyoming. In what was a galling but necessary action, the small cattlemen of Wyoming, vilified such a short while before, were invited to join. This action abruptly halted the overwhelming hostility of the big cattlemen toward the smaller operators."

After 1893, a measure of peace descended on the Wyoming range. Ironically, that peace included a tolerance for bandits who could easily find hideouts after committing crimes. Some bandits also saw the thwarting of the ambitions of the cattle barons as a call to arms. As one of them, Matt Warner, later reflected, the attempt "to exterminate cattle rustlers and put an end to cattle rustling seemed to us like the final blow to the Old West. We . . . grabbed our Winchesters and rode out to defend and preserve the Old West. Our peculiar way was to get a good rough outfit of horses together and plenty of artillery, make a fast dash up into the Belle Fourche or Johnson County country, take a big herd of cattle right from under the noses of the cattle kings, and show 'em they couldn't get away with their game of murdering and exterminating rustlers."

With that extra effort and manpower, it is no wonder outlaws needed a third solid hideout in Bandit Heaven.

6

ROBBERS ROOST

Joining Hole-in-the-Wall and Brown's Hole on the Outlaw Trail was what came to be called Robbers Roost. It was in southeastern Utah, three hundred miles south of Brown's Hole. It is a plateau bordered on the east side by the Green River, and its elevation was the reason it was a safe haven: no posse could approach without being spotted.

Outlaws could also post lookouts on any of the three narrow trails that led to the hideout—one from the town of Green River, one from Hanksville, and one from Dandy Crossing. Also dissuading most lawmen from visiting was that Robbers Roost and its surroundings were, with the exception of the Green River, arid country. With water scarce, the trails rough and winding, and knowing they were visible from miles away, peace officers preferred to let robbers roost on their high-up hideaway.

Fittingly, it is believed that the first white men to explore the area were on the run from a murder charge. Dr. J. King Robinson had worked as a surgeon with the California Volunteers. The unit arrived in the area early in the Civil War to help guard overland routes. Robinson noted the location of a warm spring, and when he was discharged in 1865, he determined to build a hospital to treat his patients; while he was at it, he established Utah's first bowling alley. He chose a piece of property and constructed a shack on it. But the local law tore it down and set fire to the debris. Union soldiers and non-Mormons were not popular in the area, and Dr. Robinson was both.

The good news was that this had not been the medical man's main residence; the physician had a home and office in Salt Lake City. The bad news began with a knock on his door on the night of October 22, 1866.

When Dr. Robinson opened up, he saw a young man who told him that his brother, a supposed "John Jones," was injured and help was needed right away. The physician grabbed his bag and went out into the night. He did not get very far. After following the young man for a minute, Dr. Robinson was attacked with a club, and then for good measure, he was shot.

The assault took place at a corner near Main Street—not an obscure location, yet other than a report that there were several attackers, no witnesses could relay any identifying information, and there were no officers near the area. Dr. Robinson was finally discovered, but there was no other physician to adequately treat him. Not that it mattered—he succumbed to his injuries a couple of hours later.

As news of Dr. Robinson's murder spread, opinion was quickly split between the Mormon population, who believed it to be a crime of opportunity, and other community members who pointed out that the valuables on his person had not been stolen; this latter faction believed the murder had been motivated by his having offended church officials. Subsequently, Mormons feared that Dr. Robinson's dramatic demise, according to a newspaper account, would "doubtless be used as argument for the necessity of a larger military force being stationed in or near this city." Carved into his tombstone was, *"In Memory of Dr. J. King Robinson who was assassinated Oct. 22, 1866, Aged 50 years, Vengeance is mine: I will repay, saith the Lord."*

No one was ever arrested for the killing. However, there were four men who were subsequently viewed as suspects. They were advised by the Mormon leader Brigham Young to leave the city and hide out for a while. They soon found themselves in the bottomlands of the waterway called the Dirty Devil, which would become the town of Hanksville.

Eph Hanks was not only one of the men who had followed Brigham Young to Utah in 1847 but also a member of a radical wing of Mormons known as the Destroying Angels. Among other things, they were ardent polygamists as well as possible assassins. Being viewed as one of the suspects in Dr. Robinson's murder, he thought it prudent to take Brigham Young's advice.

He and a cousin, Ebenezer Hanks, first traveled to Pleasant Creek, where Eph remained, and Ebenezer and his wives pushed on to found the settlement unimaginatively named Hanksville. Over time, non-Mormons arrived, and two large cattle ranches were established.

The remote location with a town nearby made it appealing to thieves, especially those who coveted cattle. According to Charles Kelly, "Rustlers knew every foot of country and had no difficulty in eluding pursuit. Those who sold the cattle and took the greatest risk made their headquarters in Robbers Roost. It was a No Man's Land. No sheriffs ever went there looking for rustlers, and because of its safety as a hideout it rapidly grew in population and reputation."

Stolen beeves were collected in the nearby Sevier River valley, driven to the Henry Mountains, spent the winter in Robbers Roost, and found buyers in the spring. By 1883, the plateau was becoming home to outlaws.

One reason why the hideout was so hospitable was Jackson Moore. The Texan had gotten into some hot water at home, and he and his wife, Ella, thought that up north might offer new opportunities. A good hand with horses, Jack Moore found a job working at a ranch twenty-five miles southeast of Hanksville owned by J. B. Buhr. The Englishman was in the American West in the hopes that the dryer climate might ease his asthma. Before long, Jack and Ella Moore were taking care of most of the ranch operations as well as Buhr.[14]

What the trusting Buhr did not count on was the Moores being so accommodating to outlaws. According to Pearl Baker, whose family knew many of those who called Robbers Roost a home or a haven, thanks to the Moores, "The Roost became the southern hideout for the same men who used Hole-in-the-Wall and Brown's Hole, and here they bunched up ten to fifteen at a time during off seasons."

Jack Moore had an itinerant background that included being known as Dee Jackson in southeastern Colorado. Pearl Baker describes him as "a striking-looking cowboy, six feet three inches tall, extremely thin, with black curly hair, a black moustache, and swarthy skin. He was about thirty-five, quick and active, well able to take care of himself among his rough companions; his black eyes snapped, he was witty and fond of a joke, roaring with honest appreciation of his own humor."

Moore once told Neil Hanks, the young son of the man who had founded Hanksville, that "outlaws are just fellows, some of them good and some of them no-good. But there's one thing about them—they are usually better-looking than in-laws and a hell of a sight easier to live with."

Unless they were solidly of the "no-good" variety, visitors, including bandits, to the Buhr ranch could find a bed and a meal, sometimes ones cooked by Mrs. Moore. She was much appreciated, Baker recalled, for her ladylike ways: "She made a home for the cowboys of the 3B. She was cultured and pleasant, had good taste, and softened the harsh cabin with pictures, sofa pillows, and other luxuries. She wouldn't let the boys smoke or swear in the house, but they didn't seem to resent it. They ate their meals in the kitchen and sat in the parlor to read and visit."

---

14 Rather unkindly, the locals referred to the Englishman as Wheezin' Buhr. He later became a character in the novel *Robbers' Roost* by Zane Grey.

There were cowboys in the early days of Robbers Roost who fell somewhere in between the good and no-good categories. Such was the gang formed by the McCarty brothers.

A Tennessee man, William McCarty had been a surgeon in the Confederate army; then after the war, he led his wife and seven children out of the South to far-off Montana. Because there were a lot more stock animals than patients there, he traded in being a physician for being a rancher. McCarty and his sons rode down to Utah to buy stock from the Mormons and escorted them back to Montana to be sold. Eventually, he relocated his family to Utah. When old enough, two of his sons, Tom and Bill, were novice ranchers living in Grass Valley. Without looking for one, they almost began a war.

As Charles Kelly tells it, in the fall of 1874, four young Navahos rode onto the ranch the McCarty brothers and a few friends operated and, after killing a calf, burst into the main cabin, ate the occupants' breakfast, and stole a horse as they were leaving. The Navahos were wrong to think that the McCartys would be too intimidated to do anything about it.

The brothers took off after them and shot all four. Three died, but the fourth managed to return home. Outraged, the tribe retaliated by raiding Mormon ranches and making off or sometimes just killing cattle. Thanks to the intervention of Jacob Hamblin—known as the Buckskin Apostle for his missionary work with Indian tribes—a larger conflict was avoided.[15] Still, the McCarty brothers thought it was a good time to give Nevada a try.

Some years later, they were back in Utah, taking over the ranch owned by the restless Dr. McCarty, who had moved on to Oregon. Both brothers married; Tom to the sister of Matt Warner (more on him later), Teenie. They were joined by their brother George and his wife. Through their efforts, the ranch prospered.

---

15 Thanks to having several wives and adoptions, the rambling Hamblin was father to at least two dozen children.

It is unclear why the brothers sold the ranch and pursued other interests, including banditry. In an alleged autobiography, Tom McCarty wrote, "My downfall commenced by gambling" and that he came "in contact with the wrong kind for teaching honesty. After losing all I had I commenced to cast around for something else."

For the next several years, that "something else" was cattle rustling and horse stealing, often accompanied by one or both brothers. They cut a swath of banditry from Montana to Oregon to Arizona and back again. Tom McCarty even ventured east to Iowa, where with some rustling profits he bought racehorses. His original idea was that such swift animals would enable the McCarty brothers to successfully flee from any posse.

But then Tom had another idea—there was good money in horse racing. It sure had its shady side, but it was a mostly legal and popular form of entertainment in the mining and cowboy camps. For a time, the McCartys stayed out of trouble. It would not last.

Most of the cowboys who rustled on the side or who spent more time on the Outlaw Trail did their mischief elsewhere; Robbers Roost, like Brown's Hole and Hole-in-the-Wall, was for hiding out only. With Jack and Ella Moore, who pretty much had free rein on the ailing Buhr's ranch, providing grazing and grooming services as well as home-cooked meals, it was a comfortable arrangement for years. But then Jack got himself into trouble.

It was already an unsettling time because Buhr had announced that he was leaving the area, and he asked Jack to help round up and sell his stock. One day while doing the collecting, Jack found a calf on the San Rafael Desert. It was unbranded, meaning it would be easy pickings, but it was following a cow bearing the brand of Hebe Wilson's ranch. Maybe Moore was feeling reckless that day because he roped the calf and dragged it away. He was unaware that this act was observed by two other ranchers, who swore out a complaint against him.

Moore chose not to show up at court the day he was supposed to be there. By a circuitous route, which included skirting Hanksville, he was heading back to the Buhr ranch when a couple of boys spotted him and ran to tell the sheriff, a man named Rufe Stoddard. He and another neighbor, Jack Cottrell, who was also a part-time deputy, set off in pursuit.

They found Moore and a friend named Aikens as they were corralling more cows they had collected. The latter was not wanted for anything but Moore certainly was, so upon seeing the lawmen approach, he jumped on his horse and took off. Aikens did not wait around asking questions; he quickly followed. The chase was on.

It continued until dark. Aikens had veered off on his own by then, and Moore was hiding behind a big rock on the other side of the Dirty Devil River. Along the way, while doing hard riding, Moore had lost his pistol. Stoddard and Cottrell were stymied because from what they could see in the starlight, the stick Moore displayed could be a rifle. In any case, when it was full dark, Moore slipped away. He found a camp of sheepherders who lent him a horse.

Apparently, Stoddard and Cottrell gave up and Moore was able to return to his roundup chores on the Buhr spread. His next foray off the ranch was to escort some two hundred head of cattle to Green River, where they were to be sold. He was accompanied by friends and good hands known as Silver Tip, Blue John, and Indian Ed. After that mission was completed, the quartet decided against returning to Robbers Roost and instead detoured up into Wyoming. There, they intended to round up a bunch of horses and sell them across the border in Colorado.

They were near a small town named Baggs when they got into more mischief. They spotted some horses ripe for the taking and acted on it. But the owner of the horses, a man named Spicer, observed the theft and expressed his displeasure by firing his rifle as he chased the rustlers.

Annoyed, Moore got off his horse and trotted to the top of a knoll to fire back at the rancher and scare him off. In doing so, however, he left himself exposed, and Spicer was a good shot. The .30–30 slug found Moore. He lingered a few days before dying.

Robbers Roost wasn't quite the same without the accommodating presence of Jack and Ella Moore. And eventually, the widow and the ailing Buhr left the area, reportedly driving Buhr's remaining stock south to Texas. But Robbers Roost was too valuable a hideout for bandits to abandon it. Plus, beginning in the mid-1880s, one of its attractions was the peripatetic presence of Butch Cassidy.

ACT II

LEADER OF THE PACK

7

THE MORMON PARKERS

Today, of the men who rode the Outlaw Trail in the mountain states and territories in the 1890s, the most famous is Butch Cassidy. Of course, this is because of his portrayal by the handsome screen idol Paul Newman in the successful 1969 film *Butch Cassidy and the Sundance Kid*. Most of the time, the reality does not match up to the movie version. But the real outlaw was indeed the charismatic and, for the most part, lucky leader of the wide-ranging bandit gang dubbed the Wild Bunch.

Given the bandit king's occupation, this may seem odd, but most likely, there would not have been a Butch Cassidy without Brigham Young, and before him, Joseph Smith. The latter had organized the Church of Christ at a meeting on April 6, 1830, in Fayette Township, New York. Smith's visionary and prophetic leadership attracted followers. That same year, the Book of Mormon was published.

There were several reasons why this new religion attracted unwanted attention, chief of which was the practice of polygamy. Smith was viewed by many of the townsfolk as a dangerous man, and his Mormons were barely tolerated. In 1844, Smith and his fervent followers were in Carthage, Illinois, where they were no more popular than they had been in upstate New York. He and his brother Hyrum were tossed in jail. On June 27, a mob dragged them out of their cell and lynched them.

Clearly, the future of the Church of Jesus Christ of Latter-day Saints did not lie in Illinois. Sometimes referred to as "handcart pioneers" because of how they trundled along pushing their possessions, the members of the Mormon church began their sojourn west two years after the murder of the Smith brothers. Their 1,300-mile trek was like a biblical exodus.

Without having to be too persuasive, the new head of the church, Brigham Young, had convinced his flock that they had worn out their weak welcome not just in Illinois but in the entire Midwest. The first wave of about three thousand people left in early February 1846. This was not a wise time to travel, and their suffering was intense. When they crossed the Mississippi River, it was frozen. On one evening during the trip, nine babies were born, with their parents barely able to provide any shelter from the elements. Wagons collapsed, and people died from exposure.

After 131 days, the pilgrims had traveled only 310 miles, but they reached the relative safety on the banks of the Missouri, where the river divided Nebraska and Iowa. Throughout their myriad tribulations the church members had managed to persevere; if anything, the seemingly relentless hardships forged an even more solid core. When he found that the Indians in the area near Omaha were friendly, Brigham Young decided they would remain there through the winter of 1846–47.

During that winter, an outbreak of scurvy claimed as much as 15 percent of the camp members—one of Young's sons would later call their settlement the Valley Forge of Mormondom.[16] No doubt relieved

16 This is not an exaggerated comparison. During the Continental army's rough-hewn encampment at Valley Forge in the winter of 1777–78, two thousand of the twelve thousand soldiers perished, mostly from malnourishment as well as disease, which calculates to just under 17 percent of General Washington's command.

that they had survived, the Mormons, though Young himself was ill, pushed out of their winter camp at the first signs of spring and began the second thousand-mile portion of their journey.

The Mormons traveled along the Platte River, creating a new route on its north bank rather than risk encounters with other settlers on the Oregon Trail. The first half of the journey was along the plains and easier going than what was expected in the mountains that loomed up past Fort Laramie, Wyoming. Through these peaks and valleys the hardy souls pressed on, plodding all day yet still having enough energy in the evenings for dancing and singing around the campfires. But there was also plenty of sickness to go around, including for Brigham Young, who came down with "mountain fever." On July 24, 1847, after a total 111 days of travel westward, a wagon carrying the prostrate Young reached the valley of the Great Salt Lake. Looking out on the terrain, he declared, "It is enough. This is the right place."[17]

Over the next two decades more than sixty thousand Mormons would journey to the Utah Territory. Some had the means to come by wagon, while others pushed handcarts across the harsh terrain. Many died, but those who made it established roots around the lake, including the founding of Salt Lake City. Along the way, they had to sweep aside the area's established Indigenous peoples, sometimes in merciless ways. One of the more notorious events occurred in April 1866, when thirty members of the Paiute tribe were murdered.

Part of the Mormons' motivation was having felt victimized themselves. During the 1856–57 Utah War, fearing an attack, the Mormons abandoned their Salt Lake City homes as the U.S. Army approached. However, the so-called war, or Utah Expedition, featured very little actual fighting. Most Mormons would return to their abodes unscathed and would never again be forced to flee for their lives and abandon everything they knew—they had indeed found a permanent home.

---

17 The first white man known to have encountered the Great Salt Lake was the legendary Jim Bridger, in 1824. Initially, the awestruck twenty-year-old thought he had reached the Pacific Ocean.

One of the Mormon men who came to call Utah home was Maximillian Parker, the father of Butch Cassidy himself. In England, Maximillian had been one of six children (two died as infants) of Robert and Ann Hartley Parker. The former had been baptized in the Church of Latter-day Saints in 1840. The expanding and unfortunate family managed to scrape by, but Robert Parker did not see much of a future for them. They were living in Preston when he learned of a mission of Mormons leaving for America—534 of them, to be exact. The Parkers sold everything they had and were on board when the clipper ship left Liverpool in March 1856.

This was not the best time of year to cross the Atlantic Ocean, but the ship arrived safely in Boston after a five-week sail. The journey was far from over, though. Next was eleven days of riding the rails until the Mormon emigrants stepped off the train in Iowa City. And after that, the two hundred or so men and women and children who had chosen this particular path constructed handcarts and began walking west. By the time the Parkers reached Fort Laramie in Wyoming, they were out of food as well as breath.

After hocking their wedding silver to replenish their small larder, Robert, Ann, and their children, including their son Maximillian, set off again. Toiling under the glare and heat of the sun as they continued their trek, the couple took turns collapsing. Finally, the Parkers arrived, staggering into Salt Lake City in late September. The entire exhausting trip had taken six months.

It had almost been a tragic trip. One of the Parkers' other sons, Arthur, just six years old, had vanished during a rainstorm. Frantically and accompanied by other adults, Robert and Ann searched for their son, to no avail. Finally, the troupe of travelers had to move on. Robert remained behind to keep looking for Arthur. Five days later, on July 5, while gazing back from a small rise, Ann spotted two figures hurrying to catch up. Miraculously, Arthur had been found by his father, and the two had managed to locate the Mormon pushcart train.

Two months after the Parkers' clipper ship had berthed in Boston, another one bearing Mormons—this time some 850 of them—arrived. Among those getting off was a child, Ann Campbell Gillies. Eight years later the teenager would meet Maximillian Parker in Beaver, Utah, when they both acted in a church play. Their romance advanced quickly to the altar.

Maximillian and Ann's first son, Robert LeRoy (Bob), was the first Parker to be born in America. That happened in April 1866—specifically, Friday the thirteenth—a little more than a week before and twenty-five miles to the west of what would become known as the Circleville Massacre. Maximillian and Ann did not practice polygamy or, apparently, any method of birth control, having married nine months and one day before their first child's birth. At the time, the twenty-two-year-old Maximillian was serving in the Mormon militia, so was not home to greet his son. Choosing a name for him had been easy, with both grandfathers' names being Robert.

Maximillian and Ann were hard workers, but the growing family barely scraped by—young Bob Parker would eventually be one of thirteen Parker children. Taking whatever jobs he could find, Bob's father was away a lot, with some employment found at other ranches or involving long trips, like guiding a gaggle of new Mormon settlers to Utah from the Missouri River. As the oldest, Bob was often tasked with looking after and entertaining his brothers and sisters. This had much to do with forming his outgoing personality.

"A natural-born ham, he often cast himself as the master of ceremonies—but acted mostly as an impresario who conceived and staged crowd-pleasing events, a regular little Buffalo Bobby," writes Charles Leehrsen in his biography of Cassidy. "His greatest, or at least his most often-recollected, moment of frontier showmanship came when he supposedly tied sticks to katydids—Mormon crickets, they were called—and staged races of the pests, shrinking the sport of kings down to cabin-floor scale, in the manner of the then-popular flea circuses."

How did Robert Leroy Parker become Butch Cassidy? The "Butch" part is obscure, but it is believed that he took on or was given that nickname several years later when he worked for a while as a butcher. The origin of his adopted last name is more certain.

Bob Parker was still a youngster when his father purchased a ranch south of Circleville. It was hoped that this gambit would bring some stability to the family, with parents and children occupying the same (crowded) space. That proved mostly true, though Maximillian was not a good or fortunate farmer. On top of that, he might not have been aware that the brief history of what would become the family homestead included it being a hideout for horse and cattle thieves. One of them was a man the former owner, Jim Marshall, had employed as a cowhand known as Mike Cassidy. Once the place became Parker property, Mike Cassidy stayed on.

Well, that is the conventional story, and there is some truth to it. But Bob Parker's outlaw days began—albeit unintentionally—well before he became Butch Cassidy.

He was just twelve years old when one day he rode to Beaver to buy a pair of overalls. The general store was closed, but he figured a way in, found overalls that fit him fine enough, and then left after writing an IOU note to the owner. Instead of waiting for the stealthy customer to redeem the IOU, the owner went to the sheriff, who in turn rode out to the Parker place. Rather than be ashamed and apologize for what had been a theft, Bob was both irritated and puzzled. All his life, he would "have a peculiar and (of course) rather adorable little blind spot about his relationship to authority," Leehrsen comments, "seeming not to understand why he wasn't allowed to do what he pleased, even when that was clearly a crime. Although he sometimes empathized with individual police officers who were hot on his trail, he always seemed baffled and annoyed by their preoccupation with him."

Probably to keep an eye on him as well as to increase the family's earnings, when Maximillian was hired to work at a ranch eighty-five miles away owned by Pat Ryan, he took his oldest boy with him. Bob enjoyed the work of being a ranch hand, especially taking care of the racehorses that Ryan was breeding. When that job ended, he returned home and apparently stayed out of trouble.

In 1881, when Bob was turning fifteen, it was Ann's turn to supervise her son when she took him along to a job at the Marshall ranch twenty-five miles away. While she worked in the dairy barn, Bob was helping take care of the stock. The number of cattle rose and fell, depending on how successful the brothers Jim and Joe Marshall were with rustling. This was not the best environment for a teenager, but the Parkers had to take work for wages where they could get it.

Bob was still at the Marshall ranch a year later when Mike Cassidy showed up there. He was an engaging scoundrel who made an impression on the adolescent Bob. This was not necessarily a bad thing because from an expert like Cassidy, the boy further improved such useful skills as riding, roping, and how to brand cattle, skills that by themselves did not make one a rustler but an employable man in Utah in the 1880s. Cassidy also taught Bob Parker how to shoot, and he took to it well enough that he was viewed as the best marksman in the entire Circleville area.

"[Cassidy] and Bob immediately struck up a friendship, much to the dismay of Bob's mother, who saw in Cassidy a hardened cowboy who had been put on his own too early and no doubt had acquired vices that she did not want to see in her son," writes Richard Patterson, who wrote the first definitive biography of Butch. "Bob, on the other hand, saw in Mike the man he wanted to be—unrestrained and free to drift in any direction."

Cassidy was, at nineteen, only a little more than a year older than Bob, but he was indeed much more experienced in the ways of the West. "Bob Parker was enthralled by stories related by the earthy Mike Cassidy about rough-and-tumble cattle towns, rollicking saloons, painted dance hall girls, and money won and lost at games of chance," writes Thom Hatch in *The Last Outlaws*. "Bob had never ventured outside of Mormon country, where towns, other than isolated mining boom towns, were orderly and law-abiding. Saloons, brothels, and other dens of iniquity were strictly forbidden."

There were other unsavory influences. Maximillian may have been unaware of another aspect of his oldest boy's development into a young man. Some of the men who used to frequent the Marshall ranch as a hideout still came by from time to time and were welcomed with a handshake by Cassidy. According to Charles Kelly, "From them young Parker quickly obtained a first-class education in the fine points of horse stealing and cattle rustling."

Though not routine for youngsters on the frontier, Bob Parker was blessed with good health. He also developed an easygoing disposition. And he was seen as an energetic and handsome young man, a robust five feet nine and about 150 pounds. There was plenty of work on the family spread to keep him busy, and Mike Cassidy had extra chores for him. The ranch hand usually had a small herd of stolen stock that needed tending until they could be sold and Bob helped out when he could. Over time, this life on the thin edge of the law was more appealing than the nose-to-the-grindstone routine of Maximillian and Ann Parker.

After a few months, Cassidy got restless and decided to move on. Bob Parker and a small herd of cattle rustled from the rustlers' ranch tagged along. After traveling west, they sold off the cattle. But then Bob's apprenticeship ended. Details are scarce, but apparently Mike Cassidy got into some serious trouble—with other rustlers or with lawmen who would not look the other way. Without a glance back, the ranch-hand rustler took off for Mexico, alone. Most likely, Bob Parker never saw him again.[18]

Reluctantly alone, and maybe looking for another mentor like Mike Cassidy, Bob paid his first visit to the nearby hideout known as Robbers Roost.

---

18 At some point, Mike Cassidy returned to the U.S. It is believed that he became the owner of a saloon in Fort Worth. If true, the future Butch Cassidy may have encountered him during a famous visit to that city in 1900.

8

THE GRIFTERS

The young rustler wanted to see the notorious place for himself, but once he did, he did not stay long at Robbers Roost. Probably broke, Bob Parker was soon back in the Circleville area, carving out some space for himself in the crowded Parker house.

Along with the arrival of spring in 1884 came a wave of restlessness, which may have combined with some winter-long claustrophobia. Once more, rustling must have appeared to be fun and easy money. It was, if you did not get caught, which was more likely to happen if you stole from a neighbor.

Another rancher in the Circleville area was Jim Kittleman, and one day he discovered a few of his horses were missing. He followed their trail, gleaned a pretty good idea of where they were being kept hidden, and visited the sheriff to swear out a warrant. The sheriff dispatched a couple of deputies who followed the same trail and found Bob Parker with the recently stolen stock.

He went along peacefully with the lawmen, accompanied by the horses that would be returned to Kittleman. Believing the shackled prisoner posed no threat, the deputies did not pay any attention to

Bob when they stopped near a stream for lunch. One went to fetch water while the second one roamed through a collection of cotton-woods gathering firewood. As the latter knelt down to start a fire, Bob pushed him over, grabbing his pistol as he did so. The lawman returning with water found the firearm pointed at him. He soon surrendered his own six-shooter.

Bob located the key he needed to unshackle himself. Soon he was back on his horse, and the remuda he led out of the camp had grown by two because he had the deputies' horses too. However, only a few minutes later, he was back at the camp. It would be a long, dry walk for the lawmen, so the least Bob could do was give them the canteens that had been attached to their now-stolen saddles.

Bob made a clean getaway, but after finding a buyer for the horses, he realized that it was unwise to remain in Circleville. He knew of several Mormon young men who had found work in Telluride, a booming mining town. One more probably would not be noticed. So Bob Parker, this time atop a mule, made his way to the southwest corner of Colorado.

In Telluride, he found a job transporting silver ore down from mountain mining camps. He must have kept his hands to himself because there is no indication that Bob got into trouble. Still, he did not dwell in Colorado long. He began to wander through Wyoming, working for a time at a ranch here, a ranch there, as the seasons passed. It is believed that at one of his stops, the Embar Ranch, he worked with two other restless young men who would later become close friends, Elzy Lay and Harry Longabaugh, the latter to one day be known as the Sundance Kid.

He seemed to enjoy this itinerant and carefree lifestyle. "These were innocent times," writes Charles Leerhsen. "[Bob] at this point was still more interested in battling the crushing monotony of daily existence in the intermountain West than in robbing banks and railroads. He liked to ride and bet on horses in races at the local carnivals; go to Friday-night dances; play poker, faro, and the harmonica; shoot at targets, sip a little Old Crow; chat up the ladies; fool with the children—all while presenting himself to the world as a carefree cowpoke."

His longest layover at a Wyoming ranch was at the Two Bar, which was in Chugwater.[19] But the fall of 1886 found Bob at a ranch in Montana, where he borrowed money from a former coworker so he could go on to Butte. It may have been there that he holed up to survive the Big Die-Up winter. Then he must have done some traveling because the following spring found him back in Telluride. While lounging at a saloon, he encountered another man who would become a close friend and, of course, an outlaw.

Matt Warner had been born as Erastus Christiansen in April 1864 in Sanpete County in Utah. Both his parents, Christen and Christina, had emigrated from Denmark and made their way west as part of the ongoing Mormon migration. They established a farm, and Christen was also active as a bishop in the church.[20] They tried to keep Erastus and his siblings shielded from the banditry in the area, especially that of rustlers, but that was nearly impossible in that place and time, as evidenced by one of their children, Teenie, marrying Tom McCarty as he was honing his bandit skills.

No doubt to his parents' disappointment, Erastus got into big trouble early. When he was thirteen or fourteen, he became smitten with a local girl named Alice. She must have been quite fetching because another boy, Andrew Hendrickson, was equally interested. When the young suitors finally fought over her, Erastus cracked his rival in the head with a rock. Andrew sure looked dead, and Erastus so believed Hendrickson was dead that he fled and never looked back.

Having helped out on cattle drives into the Uintah Basin, Erastus rode that way. By the time he arrived, he had adopted the name Matt

---

19 The first man to receive a patent on land where Chugwater would be located was Portugee Phillips, in March 1876. He was already a hero in Wyoming for his torturous trek through snow ten years earlier to alert U.S. troops about the Fetterman Fight and the endangered survivors at Fort Phil Kearny. Details of this event can be found in the book *The Heart of Everything That Is*.

20 Farmer Christiansen was so active as a church leader that he reportedly had five wives—Christina was the fifth and youngest—and Erastus was one of at least eight children he sired.

Warner. He acquainted himself with surroundings where cattle grazed on the range and farmers irrigated their crops on remote homesteads. There were some small settlements but no churches or towns and very little law enforcement—just the place the newcomer needed. Overlooking Brown's Hole was Diamond Mountain, and on it was a ranch owned by Jim Warren. He gave the stocky teenager a job.

A big reason why Warren's ranch prospered was because of low overhead—that is, more specifically, he was a good rustler; instead of needing to raise and feed all of his cattle, he was able to sell the beeves he stole for pure profit. The impressionable young Mormon now named Matt became an eager employee. He learned so well that he may have been no more than sixteen when, with his boss's blessing, he started his own ranch—with, of course, stolen horses and cattle. He might have become as successful as his neighbor and mentor, but Matt got into a gunfight with a horse thief up from Mexico and killed him. After that, the young rancher had to keep a very low profile for a while.

Next to a deputy sheriff, the last person Matt Warner wanted to see ride onto his property was a member of the Hendrickson family, but Moroni did one day and revealed his brother Andrew was not dead. He might be addled some from the blow to the head, but he was getting by. The former Erastus had no desire to return home, but he did write to his parents to let them know he was okay.

According to an autobiography written many years later, Warner claimed that reconnecting with his Mormon family did not persuade him to go straight, and in fact he added robbery to his résumé. He overreached as a rustler when he joined up with the veteran outlaw Cherokee Bangs, who had a desire to raid the Wind River country in Wyoming. The raid was very successful—perhaps too successful, because a gang that makes off with over two thousand horses attracts immediate attention.

Warner and Bangs got as far as selling most of the four-legged contraband and were divvying up the loot when a sheriff found them. They managed to disarm the lawman and keep some of the money; however, knowing there would soon be more men with badges in the area, the thieves left and, in Matt Warner's case, headed to Arizona.

Greeting him there was Tom McCarty, who by then was his brother-in-law. What better way to celebrate a family reunion than to sneak into Mexico and steal cattle? They were joined by a friend of McCarty's, Josh Swett. It turned out that collecting a herd of cattle was the easy part; it was after crossing from Mexico into New Mexico that trouble happened. They were spotted by federal border patrol agents whose curiosity was aroused. Rather than risk answering questions, the three rustlers took off.

During the running gun battle, the unlucky Swett was hit three times, in the arm, leg, and worst of all, through one lung. He stayed on his horse, though, and eventually the agents turned back to take possession of the herd.

Somehow managing to stay alive, and to ride, Swett kept up with McCarty and Warner as they headed north and west. They stayed off the main paths and when they got to Kanab, north of the Arizona line in Utah (founded by the active Jacob Hamblin), it was decided that they were safe enough to leave Josh Swett there to receive proper medical attention. His companions rode on to the mining town of Frisco, believing that it would be easy to blend in there.

They were wrong. The marshal, Billy Sackett, had heard about the New Mexico caper, and when he saw McCarty and Warner in town, he arrested them. They were housed first in Frisco and then the jail in Milford, where the two in-laws stood trial. The prosecution really did not have much evidence to convince a local jury that McCarty and Warner were guilty, so they were acquitted. An angry Marshal Sackett made the two men walk the fifteen miles to Frisco to retrieve their horses.

In the spring of 1887, Warner was in Telluride with two new companions. One had four legs and was named Betty; Warner, after buying her from a rancher in Brown's Hole, had nurtured and trained her to be a racehorse. The other was Johnny Nicholson, a friend who also doubled as Betty's rider in races. Racing events were welcomed in Colorado and much of the West in mining towns and other communities where gambling thrived and other forms of lively entertainment were scarce.

In Telluride that evening, Bob Parker overheard Warner making a bet that Betty would beat the racehorse owned by a man named Mulcahy. Bob knew of the local horse and warned Warner, who appeared to have wagered everything he had, that he was about to be wiped out. Warner countered that Parker should back up his warning by betting on the Mulcahy horse as well as be the judge of the race. Bob agreed to both. Claiming to be wagering everything he had, he offered three horses and his saddle.

In the race in front of a raucous crowd, Betty won by half a length. When Bob went to turn over his horses and saddle, Warner refused them. What he wanted instead, Warner said, was for Bob to become his partner as they took Betty on a tour of Colorado towns and camps. This seemed a lot better than having to walk everywhere, so Bob agreed. Soon, Nicholson was left behind when it became clear that Bob was the better jockey.

They were what could be called grifters. For all her talents, Betty was not an impressive-looking horse, and Warner and Bob always seemed reluctant to race her. The owner of the other horse always thought he was setting himself up for easy money. Warner had trained the horse so well and Bob was such a good rider that when Betty won it was always by a short length. And no one appeared more surprised with their unlikely luck than Warner and Bob. And they left town quick, before anyone wondered if they had been snookered.

They had been making good money and mostly staying out of trouble when they arrived in Cortez, Colorado, in July 1888. There, Warner was reunited with Tom McCarty. He had traveled farther down the Outlaw Trail, having completed a sentence in a Nevada prison for robbing a train station. He may have been the one to let Matt know that his sister had died and McCarty was now a widower. But it was otherwise a happy reunion spent swapping stories and drinking the saloon dry. McCarty invited Warner, Bob, and Betty to stay at his cabin a few miles outside of town.

When all had sobered up, McCarty proposed that he join in as one of the scheme's partners. Warner and Bob were not enthusiastic about further spreading out their profits but reasoned it would be too impolite to refuse the man more than a decade their senior—and who had offered his home as a safe hideout. Worse, they soon discovered there might not be any profits. Word of Betty's achievements had gotten around the towns and camps and any rivals left out there were scared off or suspicious. With some desperation, the trio led Betty to McElmo Gulch, where there was a Navaho village.

Stories of Betty's prowess had not traveled that far, so members of the tribe agreed to race their half-blind pony named White Face. They did not have much to wager with, so they offered up some blankets they had made themselves as well as White Face himself. If the latter won, the Navahos would own Betty. It was a dumb bet for the white men to accept—what would they do with an impaired pony? And simply winning could cause problems, and it did.

Betty did triumph, dashing across the finish line at such an indiscreet distance ahead of White Face that the Navaho did more than just notice—they refused to pay up. During the ensuing confrontation, a foolish McCarty hurled a Navaho to the ground and struck him with a riding whip. Seeing the angry expressions of the dozens of other Navaho gathering around them, the white men announced that they would not collect on the bet and hurried to bid them goodbye.

However, the Navaho were not that easily mollified. And McCarty had not gotten any less foolish. Feeling threatened, he yanked out his pistol and fired, hitting one of the Navaho. Bob and Warner reached for their guns too. But the Indians were more concerned about the man who appeared to be dying. They took him away, seeming to forget the white men were there. The trio, with Betty in tow, used this opportunity to make a hasty departure.

Soon after this fiasco, the trio split up. Bob had a legal matter to attend to in Montrose, Colorado. Warner and McCarty also had business in Colorado—robbing the First National Bank in Denver. It made some weird sense that if they couldn't make money as grifters, then stealing from banks was a natural next step.

On March 30, 1889, as would be reported in newspapers from New York to Los Angeles, Warner and McCarty, who was dressed like a tramp, entered the bank. The "tramp" displayed a beaker of liquid he claimed was nitroglycerine and threatened to throw it on the floor, with the idea that the subsequent explosion would bring the bank down on the heads of customers and employees alike. Warner went up to a window to collect the cash. When the teller asked if a $10,000 bill could be included, Warner shrugged and said, "Sure." So, the dynamic duo did make off with $21,000, but $10,000 of that was useless because even if any establishment would accept such a bill, it would be a dead giveaway that they had committed the high-profile crime.

A lot less sensationally, Bob Parker was taking care of different business in Montrose. There, he was on trial for stealing a horse named Cornish the previous year. In the lead-up to the trial, Bob had resided in the town jail. Maximillian Parker had traveled from 150 miles away to visit him, to not only offer fatherly support but also persuade his oldest son to return to Circleville. Bob preferred to remain free of farm life, and after being acquitted in the horse case, he was free in general. He would never see either of his parents again.

It being spring and winter on the wane in the Rockies, Bob could have ridden anywhere in search of work or adventure. He chose the latter—unfortunately, that involved reuniting with Matt Warner and Tom McCarty. They had run out of money, and to them the only solution was to rob another bank.[21]

---

21 The ultimate fate of the $10,000 bill is unknown. Presumably, if found and its provenance proven, it would be a coveted auction item.

9

THE BANK ROBBER

It is a mystery why Bob Parker agreed to go along with a bank robbery. While cattle rustling and especially horse stealing were serious offenses, he had yet to be convicted of anything more serious, and becoming a bank robber was a whole other level of banditry. Bob was familiar with Telluride, at least. And he may have reasoned that if done well, a bank job there was easy pickings. In that, he was right.

He came up with an idea to add some fun as well as protection to the enterprise—dress up. The job was planned for a Saturday, June 22, 1889, but then put off for two days; the bandits figured the bank might contain more money after the weekend. On that Monday, they looked almost like three gentlemen. The logic was that if they looked like cowboys coming to town for revels, people would take less notice than if they skulked around looking like dusty trail trash.

Bob, Warner, and McCarty stopped first at a saloon on West Colorado Avenue from which they could eyeball the San Miguel Valley Bank while enjoying several sips of whiskey and puffs on cigars. They knew from previous stakeouts that often during the morning Charles Painter, the bank's chief officer, exited to run errands, leaving only a teller inside the bank. And indeed, shortly before eleven o'clock on that morning, Painter bolted out of the bank and soon turned a corner. It was show time.

The well-dressed cowboys sauntered across the street, nodding and tipping their hats at passersby. As expected, inside the bank there was just one man behind the counter. McCarty, the most brutal of the trio, handed the teller a note and, when he bent over to read it, grabbed the man's head and slammed it into the counter. The younger accomplices, Bob and Warner, jumped over the railing and began grabbing all the cash they could see. Once the cowhide bags were stuffed, the thieves backed out of the bank. The unarmed, battered teller was not the least inclined to attempt to stop them.

Later, over $22,000 of stolen loot would be counted, more than half a million dollars in today's currency when adjusted for inflation. Come to think of it, the trio might have thought, this sure beat horse hustling.[22]

Outside, they hurried to their horses. Bob employed a trick he had practiced of running at his horse and leaping into the saddle—so much for not being noticed. Aggravatingly, in the process Bob's hat fell off and flew away. As the mounted trio urged their horses into a gallop heading west out of Telluride, they fired their revolvers as a warning to any would-be pursuers.

Just outside of town they encountered two local men heading to Telluride on a wagon. They shouted hello as the supposed cowboys flew by. One of the wagon riders was familiar and the bandits had to figure they were recognized. They kept riding, though, and according to Matt Warner's recollections, McCarty later lamented, "Why didn't I think to shoot them interfering coyotes?"

A few miles on, when the bandits crested Keystone Hill, a horse relay was awaiting them. This was the first of several relay points that McCarty had set up that included Hot Spring, West Fork, and Mud

22 The fate of the valiant and deceptively fast horse Betty is unknown. Most likely, intent on leaving this particular scheme behind, the horse was sold to a rancher.

Springs. They were manned by friends who were given shares of the stolen money in exchange for aiding the getaway. This gave the outlaws a huge advantage because they always had fresh horses while the posse men got more tired and slower the farther away from Telluride they rode. This practice learned from McCarty would become a hallmark of Butch Cassidy's criminal career.

Despite the gunshots and the fast horses, a pursuit had gotten underway, led by Sheriff J. A. Beattie. Conspicuously missing, however, was the Telluride marshal, Jim Clark. People in town had to presume that he had pressing business and was away that day. They presumed wrong, because Clark was in on the holdup. The missing marshal confided years later that the robbers had left him $2,200 of the take under a log along their getaway route in exchange for his timely out-of-town trip.[23]

It seemed, initially, that the bank robbers had made a clean getaway. That would not be seen as good news by Warner. Life had changed, and not for the better. He later lamented, "Right at that point is when we broke with our half-outlaw past, became real outlaws, burned our bridges behind us, and had no way to live except robbing and stealing."

Well, maybe lawmen could alter that future after all. Sheriff Beattie was not the sharpest of trackers, but for a couple of days, he and his deputized followers tried to locate the thieves. They were further stymied by the fugitives stopping from time to time to muddle up their trail, including having their horses step across slick rocks with sacks on their hooves, leaving no trail at all. Bob, Warner, and McCarty felt confident enough to stop at a couple of cabins along the way, where they would exchange a few dollars for meals provided by families who saw only three friendly cowpunchers heading to their next ranch job.

Beattie soon gave up, which did not mean that the three thieves

---

23 Marshal Clark got his comeuppance a few years later while involved in another infamous Telluride event. He was shot and killed in 1895 at the corner of Colorado Avenue and Spruce Street, most likely because of his involvement in the labor battles going on in Telluride at the time, and possibly on the orders of a town councilman.

were in the clear. The sheriff's admission of failure left the chase to other posses—as many as four of them—who were more resilient as well as eager to collect the $500 reward. Bob, Warner, and McCarty traveled more slowly thanks to the mountainous geography of going from Colorado into Utah. Their original destination had been Moab, but after spending just one night there the trio was back in the saddle, their confidence ebbing.

Not at low ebb was the Colorado River. The boatman refused to cross them over until the sun was up because, he claimed, the water was still too high and unpredictable from runoff even in early July. However, the offer of a twenty-dollar gold piece made him a less cautious man.

Day after day, the three thieves trudged on, wondering how many lawmen were after them and if—or when—they would encounter them. Bob probably felt particularly aggrieved. After all, they had robbed just one bank, had not hurt anyone (other than the teller's bruised face), and enough was enough. Didn't these posse men have better things to do back home? The day they had come to dread arrived when they were at Whipsaw Flat, well north of Moab.

Warner was scanning the terrain below when he spotted a man with binoculars looking at him. Five other men appeared and the riders set off in the direction of the spooked trio. They turned and rode away, in enough of a panic that they did not notice the line of cliffs narrowing— soon they were stuck in a box canyon with no path of escape. Yanking out his Winchester, McCarty uttered a line that would find its way into hundreds of Hollywood Westerns: "They'll never take me alive!"

All three held Winchesters as they rode back the way they had ridden in. But instead of riding to their deaths, they turned out to be more lucky than stupid. The posse had given them more credit than they deserved and were galloping around to where they thought the outlaws would emerge from the cliffs. Not pausing to wonder about the open trail ahead, the three thieves took off, leaving the puzzled posse miles behind.

They were able to trade their exhausted mounts for fresh ones at a Ute Indian camp. Then they glimpsed yet another posse and took off to the west. About 150 miles later, they arrived in Brown's Hole. Bob, Warner, and McCarty put up there for a while in a borrowed cabin, but when word came that lawmen were sniffing around and asking questions about the Telluride bandits, they took to the Outlaw Trail. This time, they dismounted in Robbers Roost.

There they stayed put for several months. There is a Parker family fable that Bob began a trip back to Circleville with the intention of reconnecting with his parents and however many siblings remained at the farm. Perhaps he could give up the outlaw life before it got an even greater hold on him. However, this seems like a bit of wishful thinking created years later. There is another story that in Milford, Utah, Bob was approached by a younger brother, Daniel Sinclair Parker, who wanted to join him on the Outlaw Trail, but Bob turned him down.[24]

Despite the rejection—or possibly because of it—Dan embarked on a life of crime anyway. In late December, having renamed himself Tom Ricketts, he and a man named Willie Brown held up a stagecoach outside Rawlins, Wyoming. Some months later, both men were caught, separately. They were reunited in the Utah Territorial Prison. Unable to make bail, they lingered there until a trial was finally held at the U.S. District Court in Cheyenne, Wyoming, in 1891. Both were found guilty, and Judge John Riner sentenced them to the Detroit House of Correction "for the term of their natural lives, at hard labor."

Fortunately for Dan Parker, he had not distanced himself from his family, unlike brother Bob, and Maximillian and Ann persistently pleaded for mercy. It was granted three years later in the form of a pardon by the governor. Also, unlike his brother Bob, Dan had learned his lesson, and he was never in serious trouble with the law again.

Bob had another brush with being arrested soon after encountering

---

24 In some accounts, Dan had tried out for the team by being outside holding the reins of the horses while the bank in Telluride was being robbed.

his younger sibling. Without his two accomplices, he was in Green River purchasing supplies. It was to be a quick in-and-out chore, but while in the general store, he was recognized by a former Circleville acquaintance. He relaxed after a few days had passed, but then a posse was spotted riding toward Robbers Roost. There were four men led by a sheriff named Tom Fares. From a high vantage point, Bob and Matt Warner watched them for a while but instead of coming on, they turned toward very rough and dry country where, as Warner put it, "a bird could get lost." It would not take long for the lawmen to be in danger.

As far as most outlaws were concerned, the world would be a better place with four fewer peace officers, but Bob and Warner really did not want them dead. And they could have a little fun. From the top of the craggy promontory, they fired their rifles, got the posse's attention, and gestured toward a source of water. The grateful, already parched posse went that way. As they were kneeling by the spring, Fares and his deputies were confronted by Bob and Warner and their six-shooters. Their own guns were taken, and as a warning to others, so were the sheriff's pants and saddle. Though quite footsore, Fares and his posse arrived back in Green River alive.

Sometime during this period, "Parker" was dropped in favor of "Cassidy" because, according to Thom Hatch, "now that he had abandoned hope of becoming a solid citizen, he chose to honor the man who had taught him the ways of the outlaw." He had used "George" occasionally, and now he adopted it as a full-time first name. Most likely, when Bob began trying out his new name, his fellow bandits shrugged, as aliases were so common among them it is a wonder any of them remembered their original names.

By the end of 1889, Warner and McCarty decided to go one way and George Cassidy another. Interest in the robbers had died down, and they felt free to roam. The former in-laws were looking for a lively town to spend the winter, while George was looking for—well, something. By Christmas, he was quite a way from Robbers Roost, showing up in Horse Creek in southeast Wyoming. There he spent the holiday at the home of John and Margaret Simpson and their six children, who were mesmerized by the handsome and charismatic Cassidy.

The holiday party was for friends and neighbors of the Simpsons, with the forty-three-year-old Margaret perhaps having only maternal feelings for the road-weary newcomer twenty years her junior. Her festive preparations were a way of "helping alleviate the grinding medieval grimness of the upper Wind River, where, until she came along, December 25 was just another day to milk the cows and cross off the calendar," writes Charles Leerhsen. "Her inclination to make the world a lighter, happier, more hospitable place was definitely something George Cassidy could get behind."[25] And as Richard Patterson explains, Margaret "enjoyed having Butch around because he was so cheerful and also helpful, always keeping the water buckets and woodbox full."

Though grateful for the hospitality of the Simpsons and their neighbors, George did not linger in the upper Wind River area. It seems that during the next several years, he did not linger long anywhere. According to several biographers, he spent his midtwenties wandering the West, working at ranches and for cattle outfits as far south and east as Texas and Nebraska as well as more familiar haunts in Utah and Wyoming. It was in the latter state, in Rock Springs, a coal-mining town, that he spent a winter as a butcher. To those who knew him from that season on, Robert Parker and George Cassidy was now and forever Butch Cassidy.

He took that name with him when he went to prison.

---

25 Margaret Simpson was also the area's first postmaster.

10

CASSIDY CONVICTED

The protagonist in the search for and arrest of the newly christened Butch Cassidy was a rancher named John Chapman. Originally from Illinois, he had spent time in Oregon, and then in 1878, he established a ranch of at least 1,300 acres in northwest Wyoming. His operation, which included breeding especially sturdy stallions, was very successful. Owning an abundance of good stock of horses and cattle, Chapman, inevitably, was the target of rustlers. To keep being successful, he was at the forefront of ranchers' efforts to deter such thieving.

From time to time, Chapman had encountered Butch Cassidy. The rancher liked the young man, who seemed more engaging and literate than the average cowpuncher. But the more Chapman's stock disappeared, the more Butch was suspected, along with a friend of his, Al Hainer.

Next to nothing is known about Hainer other than he was probably also a young Utah Mormon turned cowboy and part-time rustler. He and Butch built a two-room cabin on property the latter purchased, probably with money gained from the Telluride robbery. The duo aimed to raise horses, "borrowing" from neighbors to get the operation going.

Over time, Chapman, sometimes with Wyoming Stock Growers Association detectives riding along, set off after Butch, Hainer, and the stolen stock, but he could never catch them. Butch had an uncanny instinct of knowing when he was being followed and where to go to not be found.

But in April 1894, his instincts failed him—even his reservoir of good luck had a bottom to it. Eschewing the harsher environment of their own small ranch, Butch and Hainer had wintered at a ranch with a sawmill at Stump's Creek in the hills above Auburn, Wyoming. When the weather allowed for it, an ad hoc posse headed by Chapman traveled there to follow up on rumors of the rustler duo's whereabouts. Sure enough, when they made an early morning visit to Stump's Creek, there was Hainer standing outside sipping coffee.

A moonlighting member of the posse was Robert Calverly, a deputy sheriff from Uinta County. With pistol in hand, he arrested Hainer, who revealed that his accomplice was still asleep. Hainer was tied to a tree for safekeeping, and the men approached the cabin. Butch was awake by then, and as Calverly came in the front door, he was slipping out the back one.

But not fast enough. Again displaying his six-shooter, the deputy sheriff said, "I have a warrant for your arrest. Come with me."

Butch replied, "I'll be damned if I do."

He eventually did because Calverly was able to lunge and grab him, and soon a second member of the posse, Al Cook, joined the scrum. During it, Calverly's gun fired, and Butch was shot in the head. Not seriously—the bullet grazed his forehead, but that was enough to knock him down and had him seeing stars that were not on the lawman's coat. When John Chapman entered the cabin, it was not to gloat over finally capturing his quarry but to tend to Butch's bleeding head.

Butch and Hainer endured the hospitality of the Uinta County jail in Evanston, 130 miles away, for six weeks, sharing a cell. They could not make bail—in fact, they could not yet see the inside of a courtroom to have their bail determined because the bandits did not have money to pay for an attorney. Finally, they were transferred 200 miles to the north and east to the jail in Lander, in Fremont County. Here the justice system was a tad less rustic and Butch and Hainer were given lawyers.[26]

Butch's representative was Douglas Arnold Preston, a rather reputable lawyer. Why would he bother with Butch? It was another example of the bandit's luck and ability to make friends. Sometime in the recent past, Butch had entered a saloon in Rock Springs where the beleaguered barrister was about to receive a beating for some perceived sleight. Butch's intervention saved Preston's facial features from being rearranged.

Preston had been born and raised in Illinois and passed the bar there. In 1887, he relocated to Wyoming. His practice expanded to include offices in Cheyenne, Rawlins, Rock Springs, and Lander. He sank roots—or piled up IOUs—fast because only two years later, he was one of the Democratic delegates to the Wyoming constitutional convention. After statehood, Preston would serve in the Wyoming House of Representatives, as the state attorney general, then in the Wyoming Senate.[27] With this résumé, Preston could afford to return a favor to a low-level horse thief.

According to an article in the *Rock Springs Rocket,* "members of the bar who have worked with Preston for years relate many anecdotes of the man who was a keen judge of character which he exercised in the selection of juries for criminal cases. His repartee and masterful wit

26 For those wondering, the Legal Aid Society had been founded eighteen years earlier in New York City, but its practice of providing free legal services to those who could not afford them had not yet migrated this far west.

27 In October 1929, when he was seventy, Preston was involved in a car crash. His injuries included a severe skull fracture, and he soon died in a Rock Springs hospital. The following year, his fifth wife, Anna Preston, who had survived the crash, was nominated to become the Wyoming superintendent of public instruction. His fourth wife, Cora, was editor of the *Wind River Mountaineer.*

turned many an imminent defeat into a last minute triumphant victory. To save his client he resorted to every resource known to the legal world. He could skirt the line of contempt to the very fringe to save his slipping case. But he shrewdly went just so far and never over the line."

Things were looking brighter for Butch—and for Al Hainer too. It was promising that his attorney also had three names: Coker Fifield Rathbone. Rathbone was just thirty-one but was gaining a good reputation, helped along by the *Fremont County Gazette,* of which he was publisher. By this time the prisoners could use all the legal help they could get because another prominent rancher, Otto Franc, had teamed up with John Chapman to accuse Butch and Hainer of horse stealing.

The trial got underway on June 20, 1893, with Judge Jesse Knight presiding. In what probably was not a good omen, one of the prosecutors was Willis Van Devanter, who had been a member of the team that had secured the conviction of Dan Parker.

With Judge Knight nodding along, the prosecution presented a straightforward case with witnesses asserting that Cassidy and Hainer were chronic cattle rustlers and should be on trial a dozen times over. The defense was even sparer, providing no evidence or witnesses. The attorneys explained that in that part of wide-open Wyoming, horses tended to wander if not properly attended to, and the ones that had found their way to Butch and Hainer's camp were simply being cared for until winter was fully gone and they could be returned.

In Wyoming at that time, this was often a winning argument. And it was again: the jury was sequestered for two hours and then returned a verdict of not guilty.

There was little time for celebration because it was revealed that Otto Franc had filed a second horse-stealing complaint. Judge Knight scheduled the trial on it for the fall. It would be postponed once and then again, to the spring of 1894. That June, a Lander deputy sheriff found Butch working at a ranch in Meeteetse and, after seizing his guns, escorted him the 130 miles to Lander. Hainer, who had wintered only fifty miles away, met him there. The two defendants felt confident of another acquittal. After all, the horse in question was worth only fifty dollars, so how serious could prosecutors be? And the lead prosecutor was William Lee (Billy) Simpson, who at twenty-six was still wet behind the ears and was almost a stepbrother to Butch, being the eldest son of John and Margaret Simpson.

Billy Simpson, however, saw that his future did not lie with his rural family and their rustler friends but with the well-heeled cattle barons. Though a harsh outlook, he foresaw that the shelf life of bandits like Butch Cassidy, however colorful a character he was, would soon expire. What better way to demonstrate this than to secure a quick and persuasive conviction?

And this he did, with the help of eleven witnesses and a convincing summation. Speaking for the defense, Douglas Arnold Preston repeated the story of wandering horses not knowing their home address. He rested his case on July 2. With alacrity, the jury reached a verdict by the end of the next day but Judge Knight ordered it sealed until Monday and the conclusion of the July 4 weekend. This decision almost cost the chief prosecutor his life.

According to Charles Kelly, who was told by Billy Simpson over forty years later, Al Hainer, not a smart man to begin with, celebrated the nation's birthday by getting drunk and deciding to attack Simpson. Soon after sunup on Sunday, the young attorney was just riding out of a local livery stable when Hainer and two accomplices tried to drag him off his horse and give him a good beating. Simpson resisted with the help of the frightened horse, and when he managed to pull out his pistol, the three assailants ran away. The attack was witnessed by Simpson's fiancée, whose screams across the street attracted help.[28]

Judge Knight revoked Hainer's bail and Butch's, too, because a rumor circulated that the latter's good friend Matt Warner had collected

---

28 Among the children the couple would have was Milward Simpson, who would become governor of Wyoming. A grandson, Alan Simpson, would represent the state in the U.S. Senate for many years. The retired senator Simpson, ninety-two as of this writing, probably got his longevity from this grandmother, who died in 1974 in her one hundredth year.

a gang of outlaws who were going to storm into Lander and bring Butch out. Citizens of the town gathered that evening with rifles and pistols and shotguns. When satisfied that there would not be a raid of desperadoes, a few of the ad hoc militia gathered to guard the courthouse.

Back in court on Monday morning, Judge Knight read from a sheet of paper: he informed all those in the crowded room that the jury had found Hainer not guilty but had found Cassidy guilty. "And the jury recommend the said Cassidy to the mercy of the court."

He could use it. The convicted Cassidy could have received as much as ten years behind bars for horse stealing. True, the nicked nag was worth only fifty dollars, so Judge Knight could have just imposed a fine. However, he decreed that Butch, stunned by the sudden turn of events, would spend the next two years incarcerated. Immediately, Preston requested a new trial, but the implacable judge simply shook his head.

Cassidy was taken away. His new home, the Wyoming Territorial Prison, had opened in 1872 with enough space for about four dozen prisoners. The inmates, however, found themselves with more space than anticipated after nearly a quarter of the prisoners escaped within the first two years of the institution's existence. Eventually, the escapees were replaced with new prisoners. Still, when federal officials went to inspect the prison in the 1880s, the population had dwindled to fewer than a dozen inmates. Instead of closing the prison, the feds expanded the structure with a second cellblock capable of housing another 150 men. A central kitchen, dining hall, and other improvements were also added. There were worse places to spend two years.[29]

But a disoriented Butch had not expected to spend even two minutes there. To him, here was yet another miscarriage of justice and by

---

29 The expanded Wyoming Territorial Prison saw only a little more than a decade of activity as it was transferred to state control and eventually closed in 1903. The property was then given to the University of Wyoming for agricultural and livestock research until 1989. Two years later, the former prison was opened to tourists.

far the worst one to date. It was sure a sad Sunday for the twenty-eight-year-old Cassidy on July 15, 1894, when he arrived to begin his sentence. Even though he did not serve the full two years, it was probably the longest he had stayed in any one place since leaving Circleville.

And when he exited the prison, it was not to start down a new path in life. Butch Cassidy wanted to form a gang.

11

COMPANIONS IN CRIME

If asked who Butch Cassidy's best friend and chief sidekick in the outlaw gangs he led was, most people would say the Sundance Kid. But
the correct answer was someone who did not get prominently portrayed on the big screen: Elzy Lay.

He was born William Ellsworth Lay in November 1869 to a Civil
War veteran and his wife in Vinton County, Ohio. When he was still
quite young the family moved to Wray, Colorado. Elzy's best friend
growing up was Billy Maginnis, whose family had also come from the
Midwest. As teenagers, the two boys concocted a plan to leave the farm
drudgery behind and ride west to become cowboys. When the time
came to sneak off, though, Billy had a change of heart, and Elzy sought
adventure on his own.[30]

He may have had no choice but to get away from Wray. By the time
he went west, Elzy was already no stranger to banditry. He had done
some horse and cattle rustling and may even have robbed travelers on

---

30 Thanks in no small part to continuing his schooling, William Maginnis went on to a career in
public service, eventually becoming the Colorado state treasurer.

roads near the family farm. The lure of wide-open spaces was much more appealing than the more narrow view from a jail cell.

Elzy not only found a fresh start on freedom and a few jobs, he found love too. In Uintah County, Utah, he went to work on a farm owned by Albert Davis, who had a sister, Maude. She and the new farmhand were smitten with each other immediately.

"Elzy Lay would have been the dream man for any girl," writes Pearl Baker in *The Wild Bunch at Robbers Roost,* seeming rather smitten herself.[31] "He was tall, slender, dark complexioned, with beautiful dark eyes, and possessed of an outstanding gracefulness in a land where riding and outdoor activity made every man a demigod. Extremely intelligent, he radiated charm, and everyone mentions his courtly manner and air of easy leadership."

Demigod or not, Elzy was still a young, itinerant cowpoke and farmhand, so the best he and Maude could do after marrying was set off on what was termed a "horseback honeymoon."

In the fall of 1896, it was time for Maude, who had been waiting in Green River while Elzy spent the summer roaming far and wide as a ranch hand (and conducting some rustling and other banditry), to reunite with her husband. Clearly a hardy as well as determined person, she climbed aboard a wagon loaded with supplies and ammunition. It plodded across the desert; made stops in San Rafael, Cottonwood, and North Springs; and then climbed up to the ridge overlooking Roost Flats. Once it arrived there, Maude found Elzy waiting for her. He and another man unloaded the supplies and ammunition, transferring them to packhorses, and the group moved on, finding their way to what was called the Upper Pasture. There, Elzy and Butch Cassidy had set up a camp for the winter.

The two men had first met in the autumn of 1889 when Elzy worked on Matt Warner's ranch. It was Warner who enabled Elzy to

---

31 Baker's parents, Joe and Millie Biddlecome, operated a ranch near Robbers Roost. They knew some of the outlaws who hid out there and passed stories about them down to their daughters and grandchildren.

return to robbery by tipping Elzy off that a shopkeeper nearby had a large sum of cash. Warner, his nephew Lew McCarty, and Elzy robbed the man and split the money.

Elzy took his share and opened up a gambling house in Vernal, Utah. For a time, it was profitable, until it was shut down by Uintah County sheriff John T. Pope (more about him later). Following this setback, Elzy returned to Matt Warner's ranch, where he renewed his relationship with Josie Bassett. He remained there until Butch Cassidy was released from the prison sentence he had been serving in Wyoming. It was around this time that Elzy and Maude met each other.

On another day that fall, a second pack train of supplies arrived at the Upper Pasture and it brought another woman, this one to be Cassidy's companion. There has been much speculation over the years about who she was, with one suggestion being Etta (or Ethel) Place, who would later be the paramour of the Sundance Kid. About whomever it was, Pearl Baker gushes, "A winter spent with Elzy Lay or Butch Cassidy would not have damaged a girl's reputation in my opinion—I *envy* her!"

In March, as signs of spring worked their way upward toward the Upper Pasture, the two women made the return trip downward. The next month would see the Castle Gate robbery (more about that later, too), and that was a turning point for Elzy and Maude. That summer, when Elzy went to fetch his wife, who had been living in Ashley Valley in Utah, Maude was still determined—this time, to have nothing to do with the outlaw life. And she insisted that Elzy not be part of it anymore. Being separated for months at a time and together only in hidden hideouts did not make for much of a marriage. Upping the ante was the fact that the couple now had a daughter named Marvel.

Elzy did not disagree, but he was not ready to quit the Outlaw Trail yet. He ambled off, leaving his wife and child behind. Maude would divorce him and marry Orrin Curry, who raised Marvel as his own daughter. Elzy returned to riding with Butch Cassidy.

And yes, after Elzy in the Cassidy pecking order was the Sundance Kid. His real name was not that of a dime store–novel Western hero (or villain): Harry Alonzo Longabaugh. He was descended from a German man, Conrad Longabaugh, who had emigrated to Philadelphia just in time to participate in the American Revolution. Afterward, Conrad and his family lived just outside of the city. It was in the village of Mont Clare, five miles from Valley Forge, where some contend the battle against Great Britain was reborn, that Harry Alonzo, the youngest of five siblings, was born in the spring of 1867 to Josiah and Annie Place.

According to the biographer (and Longabaugh family member) Donna B. Ernst, "Josiah was not particularly ambitious; he never owned property or held a job for any length of time." During the Civil War, he was drafted into the Union army but was released from service for "general debility," which Ernst explains was "a gentle way of saying he had hemorrhoids. Annie, however, worked hard to make a home for her family; she was very religious and very strict."

Given the father's disinterest in a career and drifting from job to job, it was necessary that all of the Longabaugh children go to work as soon as they were old enough to secure jobs. At age thirteen, Harry found one that not only suited him but also taught him valuable skills. He worked on a farm of over a hundred acres in Chester County that raised horses, and the teenager took to the caring, feeding, and riding of them. To some people in Pennsylvania in 1880, being a cowboy was a romantic notion, and Harry was not immune.

Another influence was the local library. Harry's schooling came in fits and starts depending on where he was living and the hours of whatever job he had, but a constant was the library card he purchased for a dollar early in 1881. The public library provided him with both nonfiction and especially fiction about the American West.

Harry may have envisioned ending up there when he took his first trip of any real length away from home. He accompanied his uncle Michael Longabaugh on a canal boat to look for more promising work. They visited several cities but then returned to where the family was living, in Phoenixville.

But the stay did not last long. In August 1882, at age fifteen, Harry boarded a train to begin a trip that would indeed take him to what was viewed as the Wild West. A cousin, George Longenbaugh, had just traveled by covered wagon to Colorado, accompanied by his young son and pregnant wife.[32] He could use some help getting settled. Harry was happy to provide it.

When he arrived in Colorado, his cousin's family was living on a farm in Cortez, some fifty miles west of Durango. If Harry experienced any homesickness, it evaporated quickly. He relished the big sky, fresh air, and typical tasks of the farm—which included the breeding of horses. Ernst notes that during his stay of over three years with his cousin's family, Harry "became a horse wrangler and learned how to breed good horseflesh, trades he would put to good use in the future."

Less helpful in the overall scheme of things was that Harry probably encountered several men who exerted an outlaw influence. The Longenbaughs supplied Tom McCarty with necessities when he was avoiding the law, with his regular hideout being only a mile away from the family's farm. For business reasons, such as selling horses, Harry and his cousin George would have visited the booming Telluride and rubbed shoulders and bridles with Matt Warner and Bob Parker at the races. In any case, in the mid-1880s, Colorado had no lack of bandits and it must have seemed to Harry that some of the library books had come alive.

Early in 1886, soon to turn nineteen, Harry was ready to move on. He moseyed north from Cortez, working at different ranches that spring, summer, and fall, his enviable wrangling skills always finding him an employer. The beginning of winter found him working at the N Bar N in Montana Territory—not the best place to be once that

32 When Conrad had emigrated from Germany to America, his brother Baltzer accompanied him, and he decided to spell Longabaugh differently in his adopted country.

ferocious season got going. Harry was among the employees who were
discharged for lack of work. He made his way to the Black Hills and
found some employment here and there, including with the Suffolk
Cattle Company in Wyoming. In one account, Harry got into a fight
with other wranglers and, separately, was arrested by a sheriff for robbing an old man of eighty dollars. Somehow he escaped. If this account is true, it could well be the beginning of the Sundance Kid's
criminal career.

Eventually, Harry aimed his horse back in the direction of the N
Bar N Ranch or one of them: the N Bar N operation was owned by
the three Niedringhaus brothers (the third joined after the ranch was
named) who had made their first fortune in silver mining and enam-
elware manufacturing. They now owned ranches from Canada to New
Mexico containing tens of thousands of cattle. The first ranch to which
Harry planned to return was the company's headquarters near Miles
City in Montana. But he never made it.

On his way, he passed by the Three V Ranch in northeast Wyoming.
Like those of more than a few ranches in the area, the owners were a
group of investors who lived in Great Britain. South of the ranch was
a town called Sundance. Located in the valley of the Bearlodge Mountains on the western edge of the Black Hills, it was founded in 1875
as a trading post. The streets were laid out to accommodate freight
wagons and other wide horse-drawn vehicles, and except for that one
disastrous Die-Up winter, its expectations of prosperity were pretty
much met.

Harry Longabaugh was not feeling at all prosperous on his way
to Montana. Especially with his horse giving out, which must have
been the reason why while he was passing through Three V Ranch
land, he stole a horse. This was not a lost, wandering horse but one
that belonged to a ranch hand named Alonzo Craven that not only
was clearly branded but also had a saddle on it. A search for the
missing horse was conducted, and when it did not turn up, Craven
rode into Sundance because it was the Crook County seat and Sheriff

James Ryan could be found there.[33] And thus began an odd series of events.

Word had already spread about the missing mount and Ryan learned that a man had been detained in Miles City for being seen on it. The sheriff traveled there and arrested Harry. For several days, the suspect was housed in the jail in Miles City, and then on April 12, 1887, he and Ryan boarded a Northern Pacific train that deposited them, seven hundred miles later, in St. Paul, Minnesota. There was no discernible reason for this odyssey, other than the remote possibility that Ryan was paid by the mile to bring suspects to Sundance.

The journey became more bizarre. Instead of staying in St. Paul, the duo departed on another train going back the way they had come, stopping in Rapid City, South Dakota. Harry apparently had no interest in visiting Rapid City because while Ryan was using the bathroom, he picked the locks of his shackles and hopped off the train, landing unhurt. By the time Ryan had the train halted, the slippery suspect was nowhere to be seen. When the sheriff got back to Miles City, he offered a $250 reward for the capture (again) of Harry Longabaugh.

Here is where the fugitive's thinking can be questioned. Instead of heading in any other direction, Harry made his way back to the Miles City area. He was working at one of the N Bar N ranches again when, on June 6, he was found and arrested by a deputy sheriff, Eph Davis, and a man named Smith who was a stock inspector. They shackled him to one wall inside a shack on the property while waiting for the next stagecoach to pass by. According to the June 9 edition of the *Daily Yellowstone Journal,* the officers also "handcuffed him with some patent lock bracelets which were warranted to hold anything until unlocked by the key and which the manufacturers offered a premium if they could be opened otherwise."

Harry could have collected that premium: he again picked the

---

33 The county was named not as a commentary on outlaw activity in the area but for General George Crook, who had served in the Civil War and was a prominent commander during the Plains Indian wars.

locks. But he remained where he was in the shack with the two officers, waiting for them to doze off. Smith eventually did, but the wily
Deputy Davis, knowing what the prisoner had managed to do before,
faked falling asleep. Sure enough, the *Journal* reports, "rising stealthily
[Harry] approached the window and raised it and was about to make
a break for liberty when sly old Eph raised on his elbow with a cocked
six-shooter in his hand and said in a quiet tone, 'Kid your [*sic*] loose,
ain't you' and then called to Smith. The kid dropped back as though
he was shot."

Having been picked up and escorted there—by stagecoach, no
doubt shackled even more surely than before—by Sheriff Ryan, on
June 22, Harry was introduced to the new county jail in Sundance.
There he waited for his trial. And it was because of his long residence
behind those bars that Harry Longabaugh would become known as
the Sundance Kid.

His stay lengthened because in August he pled guilty and was sentenced to eighteen months to be served right where he was. Harry's
tolerance for being behind bars ended the following May when he and
another inmate tried to escape, but they were thwarted by the alert
jailer. The *Sundance Gazette* noted that "'the kid' is the slippery cuss
who gave Sheriff Ryan so much trouble."

He wound up serving almost all of his sentence—the "almost" being that, oddly, on February 4, 1889, only a day before he was to be
released anyway, Harry was granted a full pardon by Governor Thomas
Moonlight. He was last seen in Sundance boarding a stagecoach bound
for Deadwood, South Dakota.

However, the newly christened Sundance Kid had not learned his
lesson. Three months later, he was only thirty-five miles south of Sundance and keeping company with a gang that included a man named
Buck Hanby. Because the latter was wanted for a murder in Kansas,
when word arrived of his whereabouts, two Crook County lawmen
were dispatched to a camp on Oil Creek. Hanby was indeed there, as
was Harry, who watched as Hanby went for his gun when the lawmen

approached, but he was not fast enough—the murder suspect was killed.

Harry "Sundance Kid" Longabaugh must have convinced the deputy sheriffs that Hanby had been a stranger to him, because they let him go. This time, he went and stayed gone. New adventures awaited, especially those with Butch Cassidy.

12

THE OTHER "KID"

Ask any adult who was the most notorious "Kid" of the Wild West and the immediate answer will be Billy the Kid. However, while he was the more infamous gunman, almost two decades after William Bonney's death at the hands of Sheriff Pat Garrett, there was another young man who exceeded him in carnage. His misfortune—if it could be considered that—was operating in the shadow of Butch Cassidy. Curiously, Cassidy was not a killer himself, but after the Sundance Kid and Elzy Lay, "Kid Curry" was the gang leader's closest companion.

This was even though, as Charles Leehrsen writes in his biography of Cassidy, Curry "was a fierce and pitiless man, small and sinewy with 'dark, blowtorch eyes,' said one writer. 'He would shoot a man just to see him quiver,' said an agent for the Union Pacific."[34]

He was born sometime in 1867 with the not-so-Wild-West name of Harvey Alexander Logan in Richland Township, Iowa. Previous generations of Logans had been from Kentucky and Pennsylvania. Harvey

---

34 Another curiosity: Kid Curry appears early in the film *Butch Cassidy and the Sundance Kid*, played by the supersized actor Ted Cassidy and about to give Butch a beating.

was one of five sons of William and Eliza Jane Logan, who also had a daughter. When Harvey was still a child, the family relocated to a farm near Gentryville, Missouri.

According to the Logan family biographer Mark Smokov, "The Logan boys were considered handsome, with swarthy complexions, dark hair and eyes, and high cheekbones. Harvey was said to have had strong, even teeth and they lighted up his dark face when he laughed." The Logan boys were, to put it mildly, rambunctious, often getting into scrapes, with Harvey sometimes going that extra yard. When he was twelve, he robbed a man of his revolver (presumably, ammunition too) and took his brothers into the woods for target practice. After dispatching a menagerie of rabbits and other small game, it was determined that Harvey was the better shooter.

In a more disturbing incident, Harvey confronted the town constable, pressing him up against the wall of a shed, and told the petrified policeman that he would be killed if he filed another complaint against any of the Logan boys. No fortune teller would have been surprised that one day Harvey would have one of the thicker files found at the Chicago headquarters of the Pinkerton National Detective Agency.

Like many boys in the early 1880s, he was enthralled by the tales collected in dime novels about famous figures of the American West, including Wild Bill Hickok and Buffalo Bill Cody. Like some boys, Harvey decided he wanted that life for himself. When he was sixteen or seventeen, he and an older brother, Hank, lit out and headed west with the intention of becoming cowboys.

The early fall of 1884 found the Logan brothers in north-central Montana, in a town named Rocky Point. It was a supply hub for nearby ranches, and if the Logans had not done so already, surely here they encountered men who practiced horse and cattle rustling. Somewhere on the way to Rocky Point, Harvey and Hank had undergone a name change—they were now the Curry brothers. Two explanations have been offered, one being that Harvey was on the run from some trouble in Colorado, the other that Hank had heard that the wife he had left behind in Missouri was trying to track him down.

About that possible trouble, all one has to do is ponder Charles Leehrsen's comment that Harvey "had already established himself as a master thief (he once managed to steal the pack of bloodhounds that was pursuing him) and a varmint supreme."

In any case, they were given jobs at the Circle Bar ranch. Soon, because he was the youngest of the hands there, Harvey became "Kid" Curry. Both brothers worked hard and for the rest of that year and into the next—which included cutting firewood in winter to sell to steamboat operators in the spring—they were steadily employed. It is believed that during this time the Currys got acquainted with a rancher, Jim Thornhill, who would play a significant role in their lives.

In the summer or early fall of 1886, a herd of cattle made the now-familiar journey from Texas to Montana. One of the cowboys on the trail was Harry Longabaugh, who was still getting his tender feet wet out west. He would impress the Curry brothers and others working the ranches in the area with his horse-wrangling skills. But getting deeper into the fall, with fewer cattle as well as horses to care for, Longabaugh was not kept on by any of the owners. He drifted off, toward South Dakota. Kid Curry would not see him again until they were members of Cassidy's crew and Longabaugh was also a "Kid."

With assistance from Thornhill, the brothers not only survived the Die-Up winter of 1886–87 but were able to build a homestead complete with a cabin, corrals, and a barn. They were gaining a reputation as expert horse-breakers, and ranch owners would bring them their most ornery horses to be tamed. The brothers acquired some of their own horses and began raising cattle, reportedly none of this via rustling.

And their friendship with Thornhill was further cemented by an incident in the fall of '87. During the seasonal roundup, he and Kid Curry were escorting cattle at the Rocky Point Crossing of the Missouri River. Stuck in the middle of the river's harsh current, Thornhill's horse panicked. It thrashed about, repeatedly spilling its rider into the river, and Thornhill tried to claw his way back toward the riverbank. He was nearly drowned when Curry arrived alongside and hauled him to shore, saving the rancher.

Life in Montana was good enough that it could accommodate more Logan brothers. Hank and Harvey wrote home to invite John and Lonie to come west, and they did—John first and then Lonie in 1889. Though they sometimes worked for surrounding ranches when necessary, the Curry ranch was home base. "Guests were always welcome," Smokov writes, and he quotes a frequent visitor that the four brothers were "being of a kind nature and not disposed to quarrel except when under the influence of whiskey."

This may have been true at home, but over time not all of the brothers—by now, all going by Curry instead of Logan—were on their best behavior. Smokov reports, "There were contemporaries of the young John Curry who describe him as a small man seeking a reputation as a badman by wearing a gun and always hankering for a fight." In July 1892, he got a good one.

The hotheaded youngest brother had previously been rubbed the wrong way by a sheepherder named Olson. One day, after leaving the Curry ranch, John was riding near Rocky Point when he encountered Olson. Apparently, the two men had reached the point of shoot on sight because nearing each other they yanked out and began firing Winchesters. John Curry got the worst of the exchange of lead, with two bullets in his right arm. His horse was killed too. The only damage he inflicted on Olson was to his hat.

Leaking blood, Curry managed to stagger to the nearest farmhouse, and from there, he bounced around in a wagon that transported him to Fort Belknap, where he received some basic treatment. But his arm was in bad enough shape that his brother Hank took him by train to a hospital at Fort Benton. John received further treatment at the better facility. Even so, after a week, doctors realized that it was either lop off the arm or lose the entire patient.

John Curry recovered; however, next it was older brother Hank's turn to visit a hospital, and the outcome was worse. He began to suffer chest pains, and when he started coughing up blood, he was back at Fort Benton. He was diagnosed with the dreaded and almost always fatal disease of tuberculosis. The only treatment, really, was a visit to Glenwood Springs in Colorado and then move on to breathe in the drier air of Arizona.[35]

Hank was for following this advice, but before he could, he was soaked through trying to free steers in a spring, contracting pneumonia as a result. Too late, the brothers began the trip to Glenwood Springs—Hank died on the way.

Kid Curry might have drifted or steered himself into a life of crime anyway, but an abrupt turning point was the killing of "Pike" Landusky. This was not just another death, because up until he was confronted by Curry, Landusky, one of the more colorful characters in the late nineteenth-century American West, was believed to be unkillable.

He was born Powell Landusky, but when he left Missouri in the summer of 1868, he brought with him the Pike of Pike County, where he was raised. He was another member of a generation of young men bent on making it to Montana to prospect for gold. Landusky did get as far as Helena, leaving a line of battered men in his wake because he enjoyed fighting as much or more than anything else. And he was darn good at it. He never did find gold but he found some success as a horse breeder and trader. He and a succession of partners had by 1878 created a compound of log cabins and a corral with a high fence to dissuade bands of Blackfeet and Lakota Sioux from stealing horses.

However, according to the Kid Curry biographer Gary A. Wilson, hunting and trapping for beaver "were probably better occupations for Pike than trading. He had scrape after scrape with the Indian parties, who also came to believe that he was at the least, an evil spirit." In his last confrontation, Pike had a portion of his jaw broken, leaving a large

---

35 A stay at Glenwood Springs had not helped the similarly afflicted Doc Holliday, as evidenced by his grave in the Linwood Cemetery there.

facial scar and some of his teeth missing. After ten days on a whiskey diet, he had the wound dressed by the doctor at Fort Maginnis but later had to have it rebroken and reset by another doctor. None of this helped his disposition, either.

These and other encounters furthered the impression that you could hurt Pike Landusky, but you could not kill him.

He was also known as a man who never overcame a grudge. One time, he was on a hunting expedition and three Lakota Sioux entered his camp site. Two of them, he recalled, had stolen his pelts and trapping gear that past winter. Axe in hand, Landusky slew them and the unfortunate third warrior failed in his escape attempt. They were scalped and their bodies dismembered.

In the early 1880s, Landusky was a little worn down by his various wounds and he relocated to Maiden, a mining town also in Montana. Before long, he was the owner of a saloon and a line of passenger and freight vehicles. He married a divorced woman, Julia St. Denis-Dessery, who already had five children. She would soon have six, when she gave birth to Landusky's daughter, and that total was upped to seven when a son arrived. One of Julia's older daughters was named Elfie, who would have a close relationship with two Curry brothers.

Over the years, Landusky's infatuation with gold was revived. There were reports of gold strikes elsewhere in Montana and in the Black Hills, and over the years he would leave his family for weeks at a time to join other hopeful prospectors. Remarkably, though it took years of what were viewed as foolhardy forays, in August 1893, Landusky and a partner, Bob Orman, struck pay dirt. They had crushed an odd-looking rock and found that it contained gold.

Keeping this encouraging discovery to themselves, they worked the site where the rock had been found and discovered more gold. Landusky and Orman filed claims and eventually realized at least $100,000 from their efforts, which would make them millionaires today. Some of that money was spent creating a town that, immodestly, was christened Landusky.

The successful miners invited Harvey and Lonie Curry to file claims too. The brothers had visited the Landusky home from time to time, often when Julia just happened to be preparing dinner, and Jim Thornhill was a frequent visitor too. There were some social reciprocations, including a barn dance the Currys hosted, during which Elfie and Harvey took more notice of each other.

For several years, life was pretty good. Pike Landusky became a powerful and prosperous man with a large and active family. The Curry brothers (Hank was still alive then) continued their ranching activities, breaking up any boredom with rides into Landusky to see Pike and Julia and enjoy his saloons and other entertainments. And then they fell out over a plow.

Pike had borrowed the implement from the Curry ranch, and after it was returned, one of the brothers noted that a handle was broken. The irritated brothers sent the plow back, and Pike took umbrage. Upping the ante, Pike insulted Hank: the wealthy Landuskys had a live-in schoolteacher named Mary, and when the older Curry brother became smitten with her, Pike paid Mary not to see him. Soon, not wanting to be in the middle of trouble, Mary left the area. The forlorn Hank persuaded his brothers to conduct a raid during which several of Landusky's outbuildings were decorated with bullet holes.

The raid was an aberration because the older brother was usually the steadying influence on the Curry clan. After his death, that too was gone. According to Mark Smokov, the "advice to his younger brothers was to treat Landusky fairly, stay away from him whenever possible, and don't have any business dealings with him. After the death of Hank, this peaceful coexistence was fated to end."

The slightly older Jim Thornhill, in a way, took Hank's place as a stand-up friend and occasional business partner, but it just was not the same. And it did not help that Lonie, not Harvey, was found to be having furtive evening meetings with fifteen-year-old Elfie. Adding to the tension, according to Gary Wilson, was that the "escalating feud also tended to divide the population into two opposing camps: the miners versus the cowboys."

It was in October 1894 that matters came to a head. An alleged assault of a man named James Ross in a Landusky saloon led to the arrest of Harvey and Lonie. The brothers were known as brawlers when whiskey was involved, so few people were surprised when the county sheriff, Jack Buckley, arrived to apply handcuffs. The Currys, however, contended that Ross, at Pike Landusky's urging, had invented the assault. What followed was an indisputably gruesome incident.

Pike held the office of postmaster and had appointed himself to just about every other notable position in the town named after him, including jailer. When Sheriff Buckley moved on to his next assignment, he left Harvey and Lonie in Landusky's custody. He chained them to his milk house, went to the nearest saloon to drink, and when he returned, he was so lathered up that he began beating the brothers.

As Wilson vividly puts it, Landusky "stomped and kicked them until he got tired. He spat tobacco in their faces, calling them all the vile names he could think of, including insults to their mother. Then Pike relieved himself on them. Bored with all that, he took out his knife and threatened to make eunuchs of them."

The durable brothers survived the ordeal, and a worn-out Landusky complied with citizens' demands that they be released. Harvey told his former friend that the next time they met, the outcome would be very different.

That meeting took place on December 27. There had been a two-day celebration of Christmas in Landusky, and during it Pike and the brothers managed to get along reasonably well. Perhaps Pike assumed the feud was concluded. Lonie even played the fiddle during several of the cheerful dances. But on the twenty-seventh, a handful of men, including Pike, were having a postcelebration celebration in a saloon when Lonie and Jim Thornhill entered and then moved aside to let Harvey walk in. He went up behind Pike and tapped him on the shoulder. Without waiting for a reaction, Harvey spun Pike around and punched him in the face. The fight was on.

Given Pike's clear size advantage, the battle was surprisingly one-sided. Harvey's ferocity certainly was a factor. And, of course, revenge was a powerful motivator. While Lonie and Thornhill strongly suggested that no one interfere, Harvey knocked Pike to the floor, straddled his chest, and kept pummeling his face until Thornhill begged him to let the older man be. Having administered enough punishment, Harvey stood up.

Incredibly, Pike managed to get to his feet. Even more of a shock, he reached into his right coat pocket and produced a pistol. He pressed the barrel up against Harvey and pulled the trigger. Nothing happened—a misfire. Harvey was not about to let him try again. He drew his own gun and fired three times. Landusky fell to the floor. As Landusky lay dying, the Currys and Thornhill walked out, found their way to another saloon, and had a drink. Soon, John Curry pulled up in a wagon outside. After the three men got in, they set off for the brothers' ranch.

"There is good reason to believe Kid Curry would not have been convicted of murder at trial," writes Mark Smokov, "but he did not stay around long enough to be served."

It was time for Kid Curry to hit the road—on a path that would lead him to being a full-time outlaw.

13

"WILD" WOMEN

Even outlaws fell in love. Sure, many of them took advantage of the availability of prostitutes in the towns along the Outlaw Trail. However, some of these men had more long-lasting relationships with women who, unlike Elzy Lay's wife, were willing to overlook or at least tolerate the unsavory aspects of their lovers' occupation. As an example, one must begin with the Bassett women.

The matriarch of the family was Elizabeth. She was a native of Arkansas, born in Hot Springs in August 1855. She had the misfortune of having both her parents, Hannah and Ewell Chamberlain, die when she was still quite young. Her mother passed away in 1861, and her father, who was a sergeant in the Confederate army, was wounded in May 1864; despite (or because of) having his leg amputated, he died the following month in Lynchburg, Virginia.

Elizabeth had some good fortune, some of which came from having a wealthy racehorse-raising grandfather, Judge Crawford Miller, who raised her. When she married Herb Bassett, a Civil War veteran who, at thirty-seven, was almost twice her age, one of them had the idea to head west. (Understandably, Herb may have been anxious to leave his job as a federal tax collector, which made him rather unpopular in Norfolk, Virginia.) They wound up in Brown's Hole after visiting Herb's brother Sam Bassett, a U.S. government scout on the Overland Trail. In this new and still-to-be explored setting, Elizabeth could focus on what she wanted to do, which was to establish a ranch and emulate her grandfather. This would allow the less ambitious Herb to do what he wanted, which was to teach school during the week and a Bible study on Sunday.

They were very different people—and in their case, that made for a good marriage. "For the most part, their relationship was complementary— passive Herb married to determined Elizabeth, a woman who insisted on getting her way," observes Michael Rutter in *Wild Bunch Women*. "[They] never dwelt on any frictions between them. Both parents doted on their children and provided a secure and loving, if unorthodox, home environment."

One reason why that environment was unorthodox was Elizabeth's progressive views and practices. Here she was in the American West, she and Herb first arriving there in the 1870s, and she was a strong advocate for a woman's right to vote. Elizabeth was also fine with the female head of the household being the breadwinner, which was indeed her role as she grew the ranch and its collection of horses. And, Rutter notes, she "had a soft spot in her heart for strays: dogs, cats, cattle, horses, and lonely men."

And that was another reason for an unorthodox environment: often, those lonely men were outlaws. As long as they respected the Bassett ranch and its livestock—meaning, especially, no rustling—bandits were welcome there. Among the family's friends were Elzy Lay, Matt Warner, and, eventually, Butch Cassidy, who was a decade younger than Elizabeth. The ranch "was a haven for these men who lived in a convoluted world of violence, lawless acts, confusion, lewd women, and gunplay," Rutter states. "Elizabeth was the center of this haven. She was welcoming, graceful, and charming."

The Bassett ranch was on the north side of Vermillion Creek. That

Herb had asthma and was bedeviled by bouts of malaria contracted during the war could well be the reason why the couple had traveled to the West and at least contributed to Elizabeth being the head of operations. What had begun with two wagons full of possessions turned into a thriving ranch. Herb was not completely idle, however. He served for several years as the Brown's Hole postmaster, and in addition to his teaching duties, he founded the area's first public library. It was seeded by his own bulging shelves of books.

Also a bit unusual for the time, the Bassetts welcomed the local Indians, many of whom were members of the Ute tribe. If hungry men and women appeared on the property, they were fed, their color or tribe did not matter. The Indians fondly called Elizabeth "Magpie" because she evidently enjoyed talking.

The friendship with the Utes may have saved their ranch in 1879. On September 29, in Colorado, members of a band of the tribe attacked the Indian agency on their reservation, killing the reservation's agent, Nathan Meeker, and his ten male employees and taking five women and children as hostages. Meeker had angered the Utes by attempting to convert them to Christianity, to force them to be farmers, and to prevent them from following their nomadic culture.

On the same day as the massacre, U.S. Army troops were en route to the agency from Fort Steele in Wyoming because of reported threats against Meeker. The Utes attacked the Bluecoats at Milk Creek, eighteen miles north of the present-day town called Meeker. They killed Major Thomas Thornburg and thirteen troops. Relief troops were called in, and the Utes dispersed.[36]

When word had first spread of the Ute uprising, Herb had taken the children from the Bassett ranch to Rock Springs in Wyoming to avoid the hostilities. Elizabeth wanted to stay behind to oversee the

---

36 The conflict ended there, but consequences for the tribe began. The Utes lost most of the lands granted to them by treaty in Colorado, there was the forced removal of the White River Utes and the Uncompahgre Utes, and the Southern Utes' landholdings within Colorado were reduced. The expulsion of the Utes opened up millions of acres of land to white settlement.

ranch, but Herb was adamant that she leave with the rest of the family. Sometime later, they returned to their ranch to find it had not been burned down as feared.

When outdoors, Elizabeth was not one to be overlooked. For one thing, she worked the routine chores as hard as any of the male ranch hands. And with the ranch becoming successful in its raising and selling of stock, she could afford to dress well, and she enjoyed it. She could be found roaming the ranch riding side-saddle to accommodate the long, flowing dresses she favored. Elizabeth continued to comport herself as a Southern belle, as though she had never left Arkansas, so it could be a shock that when sufficiently irritated she could curse as fiercely as the next cowboy.

She was a sort of den mother to the young men on her ranch, some of whom were bandits at least part time, though never on her time. "Elizabeth was beloved by her men," according to Michael Rutter. "She was fair with them, but more important, she wasn't greedy or overdemanding like so many range bosses. She allowed her cowboys time to build up herds of their own if they wished."

Two familiar figures in Brown's Hole who Elizabeth Bassett helped get their start were Isom Dart and Madison Rash. Not much is known about the early life of the latter. As Matt Rash, he arrived in Brown's Hole from Texas in the early 1880s, probably with stolen cattle he needed to hide. He met the Bassetts and stayed on, eventually becoming their ranch foreman and, as we will see, the fiancé of one of the Bassett daughters.

Isom Dart became one of the very few well-known African American cowboys in the Wyoming, Utah, and Colorado region in the late nineteenth century. He was also originally from Arkansas, born there in 1849 as a slave. His real name was Ned Huddleston.

Reportedly, his enslaver brought Dart along when the he went off to fight in the Civil War. The end of the war saw him a free man and separated from his enslaver, who had either returned to Texas or died. Seeking adventure or at least a fresh start, the teenage Ned wandered about the countryside. He began earning money wrangling cattle and, for a time, worked at the ranch owned by Charles Goodnight. Setting off again, Ned worked as everything from camp cook to rodeo clown.

Then the lure of a life of crime drew him in, and he joined the notorious but short-lived Tip Gault Gang. He may have changed his name here if he had not already, but in any case, after a failed foray with the gang, Isom Dart chose to go straight. In 1881, he was one of a group of men who drove cattle north to the Wyoming Territory. He decided to stay as a horse wrangler and a cook at a railroad construction camp between Green River and Rock Springs. Two years later, he was a member of a cattle drive to Brown's Hole, and when the rest of the men moved on, Dart stayed, finding a job with the Bassetts.

He was a ranch hand who also cooked meals, washed laundry, cut wood, and performed other household duties. Making him an even more valuable employee, he was fond of children and his turns as a babysitter included playing the harmonica and fiddle, singing and putting on shows, and even teaching them how to ride and rope. Fellow ranch hands recognized Dart as an accomplished and skilled bronco buster and a "top hand among cowboys," according to Joe Davenport, a friend, when interviewed in 1929. "I have seen all the great riders. But for all-around skill as a cowman, Isam [*sic*] Dart was unexcelled and I never saw his peer."

Although it was common for Black people to be subjected to hostility at that time, Dart was well respected. While they sometimes eyed each other as rivals, he and Matt Rash ran their own cattle operations without friction and frequently fended off rustling accusations. In one case, Dart was said to have been arrested by a deputy sheriff, who drove his prisoner toward town and jail in a buckboard wagon. The rickety vehicle slipped off the side of a hill, and the two men were thrown out. Both men landed hard, but it was the deputy who could not get up.

Instead of taking advantage of the opportunity to flee, Dart tended to the injured deputy and then hiked to the sheriff's office, where he surrendered and told the deputies on duty of the injured deputy's location.

The grateful lawman was a character witness for Dart in his trial. As the result of the deputy's testimony, Dart was acquitted of whatever crime had resulted in an indictment.

In addition to continuing to do some work (and play) for the Bassett family, Dart captured, broke in, and sold wild horses. At times, this put him at odds with the more established and larger ranching operations. One of them, J. S. Hoy, was vocal about intending to remove small ranchers, like Dart and Rash, from the area. When Hoy's ranch was burned down, Dart was charged with the crime. He was taken to a jail north of Steamboat Springs, where he awaited the start of the trial for arson in 1890. He escaped from the jail, laid low in Denver for some time, and when he returned to Brown's Park, Hoy had left. No one said anything about arson, and Isom Dart was soon back in business.

Given how busy Elizabeth was with the ranch and the young men who worked on and visited it, it is a wonder she had time for children. She did, though, with her and Herb being the parents of five. Among them were Ann (the first white child born in Brown's Hole, in 1878) and Josie. It was a rare group of youngsters who would have Butch Cassidy, the Sundance Kid, and a few other bandits as something like uncles.

Josie had been born—in 1874—in time to be part of her parents' trek west, riding on and walking behind the two wagons of possessions. Decades later, she would relate to family members' memories of a winter spent in her uncle Sam's cabin on the way to Brown's Hole and of having to flee the family ranch because Indians might burn it down. Thanks to her mother and employees like Matt Rash and Isom Dart, before she was a teenager she could ride any horse on the ranch and kill game with a well-placed rifle shot.

About her and her sister, Ann, Michael Rutter writes, "The West never bred a more colorful or gorgeous pair of sisters. It would be an understatement to say they had the men of Brown's Hole and western Colorado wrapped about their little fingers." They had quick-trigger tempers but "both girls could be kind and downright generous, as well as charming and seductive. These two had the innocence of a schoolgirl blended with a streetwalker's savvy."

Josie Bassett first met Butch Cassidy when he visited Brown's Hole in 1888. Many years later, she claimed that he "was the most dashing and handsome man I had ever seen." Considering that she was only fourteen and in a mostly isolated area, this was likely true. And she would later become more than just an admirer.

Her younger sister, Ann, would one day be called Queen of the Rustlers. Inevitably, as Ann grew up, she knew not only Cassidy but also Elzy Lay, Harvey "Kid Curry" Logan, Tom McCarty, Matt Warner, and others in that outlaw orbit. But Butch, who was still George Cassidy when she met him, was crush material for Ann, who most likely didn't harbor Josie's slightly more mature feelings.

Rutter notes that whenever he helped out around the Bassett ranch in exchange for shelter and food, Cassidy "had a shameless awkward shadow and her name was Ann. She followed him everywhere and made no qualms about how she felt about him. He put up with the little girl, never guessing how pretty she'd turn out."

Many years later, Ann would refer to Cassidy as her "Brown's Park beau." Josie would coyly say that she "didn't let him get bored" when Butch had to stay for a while in the hideout.

A third "wild" woman who was apparently not averse to sharing was Ethel Place.[37] Reportedly, she was involved with Cassidy before (and perhaps during) her relationship and then marriage to the Sundance Kid. Next to nothing is known about her before she showed up in the West. She may have been born there in, it is believed, 1878, though some claim that like Harry Longabaugh she hailed from Pennsylvania. Some accounts contend that she was a schoolteacher. Her real first name was Ethel but was misspelled as "Etta" in the Pinkerton National

---

37 Research published in Utah in 1992 contended that Ethel Place and Ann Bassett were one and the same person, but this has not received much traction among many western historians.

Detective Agency file kept in their Chicago office. Her last name was not Place, but she borrowed Harry's mother's maiden name.

The agency, in a 1906 entry, described her as having "classic good looks, 27 or 28 years old, 5'4" to 5'5" in height, weighing between 110 and 115 lb, with a medium build and brown hair." Etta Place was the name used on the Pinkerton wanted posters after she, Longabaugh, and Cassidy had escaped to South America. The agency noted that she had been born in Texas.

The author D. J. Herda, to write his biography *Etta Place,* includes information that she may have emigrated from another country with her family while she was still a child, in 1884, and by around the time she met Longabaugh, in 1899 or 1900, she was working in a San Antonio brothel.

In any case, the origin story of Ethel Place is not nearly as important as the one created when she became one of the women inducted into the Wild Bunch and its bandit tributaries. Perhaps what distinguishes her most, in addition to her portrayal by Katherine Ross in the famous 1969 movie, is that when the time came, she vanished.

14

THE IDAHO JOB

George Cassidy did not want to be in prison, but he tried to make the most of it—which included learning from the more experienced criminals with whom he was incarcerated. Whatever he had not known before about horse stealing, cattle rustling, and even some of the violent crime he abhorred, he learned during the eighteen months he was in Wyoming Territorial Prison as inmate no. 187.

A valuable friendship was formed with Abraham Stoker, nicknamed "Rocky," a sheep rancher in Wyoming who had resorted to larceny to make ends meet and not gotten away with it. After completing his four-year stretch, he and Cassidy would reunite from time to time, when the latter hid loot on Rocky's ranch.

Another unanticipated benefit of being behind bars was getting into good physical shape. In addition to being away from the saloons and so-called soiled doves, Cassidy's sentence called for hard labor and the prison staff kept him busy. When the Wyoming weather allowed, there were road and prison facilities to repair, crops to grow and harvest on the prison farm, and livestock to tend in adjacent fields under the watchful eyes of rifle-toting guards. Barns and pens had to be cleaned out and indoor workshops turned out a variety of products, from brooms to clothing.

The food was not that nutritious and the cells were small, though worse was committing a serious enough infraction to end up in a windowless solitary confinement cell, shackled, and allowed only bread and water. Still, life in the penitentiary was not nonstop drudgery. Rodeos were organized and baseball games were played, and there could be special entertainments, such as on July 4, 1894 (eleven days before Cassidy arrived), when, of all things, an opera company performed at the prison to help celebrate, ironically, Independence Day.

A minor but routine entertainment was keeping track of who tried to escape, how, and what the result was. When the institution had opened as the Laramie Territorial Penitentiary in 1873, the very first inmate there, Richard Scott, a murderer, managed to disappear. Security had tightened since then and escapes were rare. Often, the outcome of such efforts was to hang in chains from the ceiling, be blasted by a pressurized water hose, or placed in the darkness of solitary confinement.

Cassidy, though having a restless nature, was not going to risk any of that. However, as good an inmate as he was, he was still implicated in a crime: attempted murder. The horse he had been convicted of stealing dwelled on the Big Horn Range ranch owned by Richard Ashworth. He, like many owners of large ranches in Wyoming and Montana, had emigrated from Great Britain. In February 1895, a shot was fired through the window of Ashworth's front room. He was unharmed but rumors circulated that the attempted assassination was conducted by a friend or friends of the convict.

Cassidy was questioned but truthfully knew nothing about it. Ultimately, it was revealed that the perpetrator was Wilfred Jevons, also a Brit, who was the ranch foreman. Both men were infatuated with the same woman, and Jevons, distressed at being rejected or by his poor aim, committed suicide.[38]

Late that year, Cassidy, having indeed been a model prisoner, applied for a pardon. It sure was encouraging when Governor William Richards had the inmate brought to him for a personal interview. Richards explained that an early release could be arranged if Cassidy promised to go straight and forswear anymore outlaw activities.[39]

The governor was both startled and impressed by Cassidy's response: "If I give you my word I'd only have to break it. I'm in too deep now to quit the game. But I'll promise you one thing: If you give me a pardon, I'll keep out of Wyoming."

That was close enough for Richards. Three weeks later, on January 19, 1896, with Richards on hand to observe, Butch Cassidy strode out the front gate of the Wyoming Territory Prison.[40]

With several destinations to choose from, Cassidy headed to Brown's Hole, where he visited Matt Warner at his cabin on Diamond Mountain. His wife, Rose, had left him again, but this time not because of his outlaw activities. She had cancer and had taken their daughter, Hayda, with her to Vernal, Utah, where she could receive medical treatment. Unfortunately for the young mother, the cancer

---

38 The story about Richard Ashworth and Wilfred Jevons is thought to be the basis for a romance novel set in Wyoming called *The Phantom Lady* by Emerson Hough. It features a love triangle between two men and a young woman working on the ranch.

39 Oddly, Richards was already in receipt of a long letter from Judge Jesse Knight, who had sentenced Cassidy to prison, blaming himself and the prosecution for the horse thief's conviction and urging the governor to be lenient.

40 William Richards's postgovernor career included being appointed commissioner of the General Land Office by President Theodore Roosevelt. During his tenure he helped save Native American ruins and other important monuments from further damage and destruction by asking Edgar L. Hewett of New Mexico for a list of sites that should be protected. The resulting memorandum Richards composed led to the passage of the Antiquities Act of 1906, which has been used by American presidents to set aside innumerable national monuments. In 1912, Richards traveled to Melbourne, Australia, to start a new life after the violent deaths of his daughter, Edna, and her husband, Thomas Jenkins. Shortly after his arrival, he suffered a fatal heart attack.

caused the amputation of one of her legs. That did not stop the spread of the disease, and Warner eventually wound up as a widower.

Though he was still avoiding any bandit temptations, Warner was glad to see Cassidy and relieve some of the loneliness in the cabin. And he could use a hand with the routine chores on the ranch. In turn, Cassidy was soon glad to see another familiar face, a visiting Elzy Lay. Before long, the two men were sharing the cabin because Warner, with Rose's condition worsening, went to spend more time with her and their daughter.

While Warner had come to Vernal for a good reason, unfortunately, it was where bad trouble began for him. At a saloon there he found an old gambling acquaintance, Bill Wall, who introduced him to a man named Coleman. He owned a mine he was shutting down and he hired Warner and Wall to help him pack up and remove the equipment to another mine he was about to begin work in.

This seemed like a simple enough job, but then it got complicated. At the mine, the trio was ambushed by two men who claimed title to Coleman's mine. Guns were fisted and fired, and the two men must have been better prospectors than fighters because they were killed. When Warner, Wall, and Coleman returned to Vernal, they were charged with murder and tossed into the Uintah County calaboose. Soon, they were transferred to the jail in Ogden to await trial.

With medical expenses on top of the regular ranch expenses, Matt Warner had no money for a lawyer. No problem, Butch Cassidy assured him when he arrived at the Ogden jail. He vowed to hire Douglas Preston and would provide the $3,500 retainer. How? What made perfect sense given the urgency of the situation was to rob a bank.

Cassidy and Elzy Lay chose one in Montpelier, Idaho. (Cassidy was not about to break his promise to the Wyoming governor.) And they chose a third man to be part of the escapade, Henry Rhodes Meeks Jr., nicknamed "Bub." He was a Utah native, having been born in Provo in 1869. He was a tall horse wrangler who Cassidy had first encountered when he and Al Hainer owned the small horse ranch. That he was being invited to become a bank robber did not seem to bother him.[41]

It was in July 1896 that the planning got serious, with the three men moving to the area and taking jobs at a ranch close to town so they could case the bank and, of course, identify escape routes. On August 13, they were ready to go. Cassidy and Lay, wearing bandannas on their faces, entered the building a little after 3:00 P.M. that day.

Lay went directly to the counter while Cassidy covered the front door, reassuring shocked customers that this caper would be quick and easy and no one would get hurt. Lay shoved a canvas bag into the teller's cage and told the man behind it, Angus McIntosh (obviously, no need to supply his country of origin), to put whatever he had into it. When the assistant cashier hesitated, claiming to be low on cash, Lay cracked him in the head with his gun barrel.

"Leave that man alone!" shouted Cassidy, not only because he disliked violence but also because of what he had just told the customers.

While McIntosh tried to shake the stars out of his eyes, Lay walked behind the counter. He took the contents of the cashier's cash drawer and plucked piles of cash out of the vault; then it was back to the counter to corral all the silver and gold coins in sight. It was a heavy haul of loot he carried outside, where Meeks waited with their horses. Cassidy warned the customers to stay where they were and say nothing for ten minutes; then he exited. On their mounts, the three thieves ambled away from the Bank of Montpelier, barely attracting attention.

However, once the word got out, a posse was quickly formed and gave chase. It consisted of the only law enforcement the town had, a process server named Fred Cruickshank, whose day job was clerking at a local dry goods store. Not owning a horse (or, for that matter, a gun), he jumped on his bicycle and pedaled away. Not furiously enough, however, because the robbers' horses easily left Cruickshank literally in the dust.

---

41 Apparently, other things bothered Meeks more and more over time because he wound up in an insane asylum. He was only forty-three when he died in Evanston, Wyoming.

But there was a proper posse. When the county sheriff in Paris, Idaho, M. Jeff Davis, ten miles away, received a telegram about the bold robbery, he and a deputy swore in a handful of townspeople as temporary lawmen, and they took off. They actually managed to get close enough that Cassidy, Lay, and Meeks halted and shot at the pursuers. The lawmen were more temporary than they had expected to be—they wheeled and aimed their horses back toward Paris while bullets flew harmlessly overhead.

Sheriff Davis and his deputy, Mike Malone, were game, forging ahead, but all they found were abandoned horses. Cassidy had made sure to have fresh mounts waiting and they easily outdistanced the tired horses of the peace officers, who fired off a few shots in frustration.[42]

The law was not quite through with the daring thieves, though. One-legged Rose Warner suspected that Matt was somehow in on the Idaho job—meaning that, despite all his promises, he had returned to his wayward ways. (Apparently, she was unaware that he was already behind bars.) She was furious about it. And with that rogue Cassidy to boot, who most likely had lured her husband to return to the road to perdition. She approached the authorities in Vernal and offered to have word sent to Cassidy at his hideout that she desperately needed to see him and would be most grateful if he quietly came to Vernal to meet her.

Cassidy knew a con when he heard one, so instead of making the trip he sent a letter to her that was published by the eager editors at the *Salt Lake Tribune*. It included: "I can't tell when I can get there. If you have got anything to tell me that will help your Matt, write and tell me what it is, and I will be there on time," which had to have been written with his tongue lodged in his cheek. "I am sorry to hear about your leg. If I can do anything to help you out let me know and I will do it," except, of course, be arrested. He concluded with the assurance, "Believe me to be a true friend to my kind of people"—like the ones who don't try to entrap him.

---

42 After hearing reports of the gunfire and before Davis and Malone arrived back in town, the *Montpelier Examiner*, apparently not confident in their abilities, prematurely prepared an edition reporting the officers' deaths.

While Rose and bank authorities and lawmen stewed over the letter, some of the proceeds of the Montpelier heist was making its way to Orlando Woodworth Powers. Upon further reflection, it was decided that the onetime member of the Utah Supreme Court would be a better choice as a defense attorney than a Wyoming one.

The switch did not end up mattering that much. The deck was pretty much stacked against Warner, and the few character witnesses called by Powers were not of much help. At least, when Warner was convicted, it was for voluntary manslaughter instead of murder. There were reports that Cassidy and his crew were poised to bust Warner out of jail, but nothing came of it.

He was sentenced to five years of hard labor. Unlike Cassidy's experience, Warner's stay in stir made a lasting impression. Also unlike Cassidy, after serving forty months in prison, when Governor Heber Manning Wells made the offer of a pardon in exchange for going straight, Warner took it. His wife, Rose, had died by then, and he moved in with his father and worked as a bartender. He would later remarry.

Warner did live the straight life, so much so that he ran for public office. But he did so under his birth name, Willard Erastus Christiansen, which did not attract enough votes, and he lost. The next time, having reverted to Matt Warner again, he was elected a justice of the peace and was appointed a deputy sheriff. When he and his second wife settled in Carbon County, Utah, he worked as a night guard and detective.

Late in life, with some whitewashing, Warner composed a memoir titled *The Last of the Bandit Riders*. It was published in 1940, but Matt Warner could not celebrate its release, having died two years earlier. He was seventy-four and was buried in the Price City Cemetery.

Being incarcerated, Warner was one of the few in Cassidy's circle of friends who did not gather for a memorable Thanksgiving feast in the Brown's Hole hideout in November 1896. That circle expanded to include Harry Longabaugh. The Sundance Kid had been employing his horse-wrangling skills at a ranch in the Snake River Valley, but when he heard about Butch and others congregating in Brown's Hole, he headed there. He arrived in time for the holiday feast hosted by the Bassett family, with as many as thirty-five people in attendance.

It was more than simply a sit-down dinner; it was a sort of celebration of being safe and among friends in one of the Bandit Heaven hideouts. Butch was not only back from prison but back in action, with guests lauding him and Elzy Lay and Henry Meeks for pulling off the Montpelier heist and predicting that there would be more successful adventures to come.

Where Elizabeth Bassett put everybody remains a mystery—some accounts claim the dinner was not at her place but at the Davenport Ranch—but there had clearly been some preparation for this feast because the men wore dark suits with bow ties fastened to white starched collars. The Bassett sisters and other women wore the best dresses they owned. When all were seated and drinks were poured, it was time for the food to appear.

"The kitchen door flew open with a bang—and Butch Cassidy and the Sundance Kid barreled in," writes Charles Leerhsen. "They were wearing butcher's aprons and balancing large serving platters as best they could. They bowed, they scraped, they proffered nervous smiles. As they moved from guest to guest, drumsticks seemed to drop from the sky, and gravy boats nearly capsized."

What became known as the Outlaw Thanksgiving was a big success. There were plenty of guns and alcohol and mostly young men and women under one roof, but there was no fighting; instead, there was more a sense that the bandit life was not so bad. (Again, Matt Warner was not there to offer his opinion.)

Soon afterward, when rumors floated in that a posse might look for the Montpelier robbers at Brown's Hole, Butch and Elzy and a grown-up Ann Bassett relocated to the even safer Robbers Roost. They would wait out the winter there. Come spring, Cassidy and his friends would return to the Outlaw Trail, on their way to being known as the Wild Bunch, with Butch as head bandit.

ACT III

THE LAWMAN TRAIL

15

DAYS OF THE OPEN RANGE

During the second half of the nineteenth century, the evolution in law enforcement had been especially swift and dramatic in the American West. In the years following the Civil War, frontier justice was often meted out by part-time, inexperienced, and untrained lawmen or by gunslingers wearing badges. A prime example of the latter was Wild Bill Hickok when he was marshal of Abilene, Kansas, until the town leaders could not stomach the body count.

Frontier justice was also administered by the few and far between judges, some of whom rode the circuit from one town or county to another, interpreting the law as best they could. A few of them, such as Judge Roy Bean in Texas, who declared himself the "only law west of the Pecos," had a very personal view of crime and punishment.

By the 1880s, genuine progress could be seen. Law enforcement was becoming more of a system spreading rapidly west of peace officers and courts upholding a consistent set of laws. Many of these peace officers, though still underpaid, took their jobs more seriously. They were professionals, not moonlighting farmers and shopkeepers. They were protecting communities where their own children were growing up. And behind them on the bench were judges with authority, with more of them having legal training. Though known as the Hanging Judge, Isaac Parker ran a tight ship as a federal judge headquartered in Fort Smith, Arkansas, and his example was taking root in Arizona, Colorado, and other states and territories in the West.

Some cities and counties were going beyond having marshals and sheriffs to establishing police departments. Though mostly known as the marshal of Tombstone, Arizona, at the time of the Gunfight at the O.K. Corral in October 1881, Virgil Earp was officially the police commissioner. With telegraph lines crisscrossing the West, lawmen were better able to communicate with each other. A fugitive fleeing a bank robbery in one town could find deputies waiting for him in another. The introduction of telephone service tightened the law-enforcement net considerably.

Being a bandit was quickly going from romantic to risky in the American West.

Perhaps more than any other man at the time, Charles Siringo represented the new kind of peace officer. Though not a trained lawman, he developed a clear view of the law and that it needed to be enforced for the common good.[43] True, he often wore a gun and got into more than his share of scrapes, but for him the right outcome to any case he pursued was the arrest of the perpetrators and then letting the wheels of the justice system grind on. He often went undercover, gathered intelligence, and collected evidence before swooping in with handcuffs. He could shoot it out if he had to, but violence was to be avoided—he did not want to get killed, and he did not want anyone else to get killed either.

So when Siringo was assigned to take on the outlaws who called Bandit Heaven home, it was a sure sign that the days of being an outlaw were dwindling down to a precious few.

---

43 The concept of providing new peace officers with training in basic policing skills was so revolutionary that it was not until 1908 that the first police academy opened, in Berkeley, California. Its founder was August Vollmer, who had been the chief of police in Los Angeles.

Charles Angelo Siringo, mostly known as "Charlie" when not as-suming an undercover identity, was born in 1855 on the Matagorda Peninsula in southern Texas. His mother, Bridget White, had immigrated from Ireland and his father, Antonio, from Italy. The latter died when his son was only a year old. Charlie, his mother, and his sister, Catherine, pretty much fended for themselves, with his first lessons in being a cowpuncher coming when he was eleven years old.

"Charlie Siringo was born on one of liveliest, most historic, con-troversial, and yet established areas in pre–Civil War Texas," states the biographer Howard R. Lamar. "It was no wonder that he himself de-veloped a great ambition to get ahead in a world where he thought the key to success was the cattle industry."

He was not to remain on the Matagorda Peninsula. When his mother remarried, the family resided in St. Louis. That stay was short-lived. Bridget's new husband was a northerner named Carrier who had severe problems with alcohol and a penchant for swindling. Until he mercifully disappeared, Carrier kept the family in poverty, his wife and children sometimes surviving through the kindness of strangers in between whatever jobs Charlie could get, from shoveling snow to coal.

Over time, the call of being a cowboy became irresistible. He re-turned to Texas and found work at various ranches, sending most of his earnings back to his mother.

He learned the most about cowpunching when at age sixteen he be-gan working at the Rancho Grande near Tres Palacious, co-owned by one of the early cattle barons, Abel Head Pierce, nicknamed "Shang-hai." He had been born in Rhode Island, a ninth-generation descen-dant of John Alden and Priscilla Mullins, and he was related to both the poet Henry Wadsworth Longfellow and the fourteenth president of the U.S., Franklin Pierce. He stowed away on a ship out of New York, and when it docked in Indianola, Texas, the teenager slipped off. Beginning as a ranch hand, Pierce acquired a lot of knowledge about cattle and eventually a lot of cattle.

There were two theories as to how he gained the nickname. One was his resemblance to a banty Shanghai rooster, long-legged and with short pants. Another attributes "Shanghai" to his ruthless business dealings. Perhaps the most imposing thing about Pierce was his voice. Siringo would recall that it "could be heard nearly half a mile, even when he tried to whisper."[44]

For the next several years, into his early twenties, Charlie Siringo had various adventures on the trails and in the towns in between. Most of them, in spite of the dust-choking work and sudden shifts in weather and sometimes uncooperative cows and cowboys, he enjoyed. An occupation like detective was unthinkable when sleeping under the stars and sampling the pleasures of the smoke-filled saloons.

Because of an incident in one of those saloons, in Dodge City in 1877, Siringo almost never made it to becoming a detective or anything else. On July 3, he was one of the cowboys who had guided a herd from Texas along the Chisholm Trail and was expected to continue its noisy way north. At that time, though Dodge City counted among its lawmen the likes of Wyatt Earp and Bat Masterson, the railroad hub for herds was still known as the "wickedest town in the West," which could be cat-nip to young and restless cowboys. On this day, one of them was Siringo, who decided to draw his pay and stay on for a while to see how wicked Dodge City could really be.

On Independence Day, he loped into the Lone Star Dancehall, which was co-owned by the moonlighting Masterson.[45] Siringo was accompanied by a cowboy friend, Wes Adams, and the duo enjoyed their refreshments as well as the dancing girls. But then, at 11:00 P.M., the experience became less enjoyable. Adams claimed that one of the buffalo hunters in the saloon had insulted him—which one, he was

---

44 Later in his life, Siringo would pay a visit to Shanghai Pierce's grave in the Bridge-Hawley Cemetery in Deming, Texas, which was adorned with a bronze statue forty feet tall that had cost $10,000.

45 Bat Masterson would have less time for such moonlighting come November, when he would be elected sheriff of Ford County. To keep things in the family, the following year his brother, Ed, would become the Dodge City marshal. Unfortunately, Ed was killed in the line of duty in April 1878, with Bat subsequently gunning down the shooters.

not sure, because the long-haired, bearded buffalo hunters in stained clothing pretty much looked alike.

Unwisely, the two cowboys went and got their horses from the livery stable, tied them to a post outside the Lone Star, and reentered the saloon with their Colt six-shooters. The ensuing fight did not involve gunplay but did feature plenty of fisticuffs and chairs and other objects being tossed about, including Bat Masterson chucking heavy beer glasses at the combatants. One smashed as it hit a wall, sending a shard of glass into Siringo's face. Wounded more seriously was Wes Adams—a buffalo hunter had shoved a skinning knife into his back.

The cowboys fled. Siringo helped his friend onto his horse and they rode off, almost trampling a deputy, Joe Mason, who tried to stop them. Siringo, at least, was not out of Dodge City long. Once they arrived at a shanty at a stockyard outside of town and he could lift Adams's shirt to examine the ugly wound, Siringo knew it would have to be stitched right away or his friend would bleed to death. He took a circuitous way back into town; somehow acquired needles, thread, and other necessities (at that hour, he probably stole them); and returned to the shanty.

Siringo was unaware that Masterson and several other Dodge City and Ford County deputies, expecting the two feisty bar-fighters would return, had set up an ambush. The rifles and shotguns they carried went unused, however, because of the looping route the cautious cowpuncher had used.

Adams tried not to moan too loud as Siringo patched him up as best he could. Once back on their horses, they steered away from Dodge City, at dawn finding a cattle camp. They signed on as trail hands, though it would take a sore and weak Adams ten days to fully recover.

This outfit would be home to Siringo for the next few years. Not as odd as one might think in the 1870s and 1880s, it was owned by two men from Boston who had made some money as shoe manufacturers and decided to spend it on cattle. David Beals and W. H. Bates had established a ranch on the Arkansas River in Colorado but were now on their way to found a new one in the Texas Panhandle. This they did, with Siringo as one of their riders, and the LX Ranch was born a mile east of Pitcher Creek. Eventually, the operation would grow to include at least fifty thousand head of cattle.[46]

According to Siringo's account, which is believed to be true, it was while he was an LX hand that he encountered Billy the Kid. One day in the fall of 1878, the cowpuncher returned in the evening from Dodge City, 225 miles away, after delivering four hundred head to be shipped off to a Chicago slaughterhouse. (Time and distance must have unhardened the hearts of the city's lawmen and he was not tossed in the calaboose.) After the cook rang the dinner bell, Siringo found himself sitting at the long wooden table next to a young man intro-duced as William Bonney, who was visiting with some men from Lincoln County, New Mexico.

They must have hit it off because, as Siringo recalled in his mem-oirs, "During the next few weeks Billy the Kid and I became quite chummy." After the Kid and his colleagues sold the stolen ponies they had brought with them, "he left for the Canadian River country, and I never saw him again."

However, two years later, because of Billy the Kid, Siringo received his first taste of what being a lawman must be like. His boss at the LX Ranch assigned him to lead a posse of cowboys to track down and take back stock Billy the Kid and his pals had stolen from several Panhandle ranches, including the LX. In New Mexico, they were asked to join forces with another posse, this one led by the Lincoln County sheriff, Pat Garrett, and Barney Mason, the sheriff's brother-in-law. Siringo's group preferred to go on their own.

They thus missed out on Garrett's posse chasing the Kid and his gang down to Stinking Springs where two bandits were killed in a gun

46 Beals would become another entrepreneur success story in Texas. Seven years after founding the LX Ranch, he and his partners sold it to the American Pastoral Company of London for what was reported to be $1,650,000. The holdings in 1884 included over 187,000 acres, thirty-four thousand cattle, and more than a thousand horses. Beals counted his money in Kansas City, where he orga-nized the Union National Bank and became an even richer real estate investor.

battle and the Kid was captured.[47] Billy would wind up in jail in Santa Fe. He would later escape custody and quite the manhunt was undertaken. Dangerously, Siringo and Billy the Kid were almost reunited.

In Fort Sumner, New Mexico, Siringo and a few of his hands attended a dance where he met the widow of Charles Bowdre, who had been killed by Pat Garrett's posse during the Stinking Springs shootout. As the dance was winding down, Siringo escorted the pretty, post-mourning Mrs. Bowdre upstairs. Though the attraction was mutual, she refused to let him in her room. Months later, Siringo encountered her again, and she revealed that the Kid had been hiding out in her room.

Overall, the mission was still a success, though, because Siringo, displaying a few detective-like skills, and his posse managed to round up over two thousand head of cattle and return them to the LX and its neighboring ranches.

The memory of that mission and a certain amount of pride at having accomplished it stuck with Siringo. He began to think of a life beyond being a ranch hand. "At one time Siringo thought he had found his métier in being a cowboy and he would always consider himself as such," writes the biographer Ben E. Pingenot. "Yet, he had experienced a new kind of adventure with skills and challenges that were far removed from the prosaic duties he had known as a cowboy on the open range." Another consideration was that Siringo "might have been aware that the days of the open range were nearing an end, and in anticipation of it he could see that his own days as a wild and carefree cowpuncher were also numbered."

Still, in the absence of any more concrete thoughts about his future, Siringo stayed on at the LX Ranch—until marriage intervened. His employer, David Beals, writing from Boston, assigned Siringo to take charge of a farm he had purchased in the vicinity of Caldwell, Kansas, near the border with Indian Territory (now Oklahoma). This

---

47 One of the Kid's companions arrested was Dirty Dave Rudabaugh, a notorious outlaw whose ultimate fate would be to have his head on display on a pike outside a Mexican cantina.

he did through the fall and winter into 1884. After attending church on March 1, he was introduced to the fifteen-year-old Mamie Lloyd. Only six days later, they presented themselves to a preacher.

Siringo continued to lead the owners' cattle and horses to and from the Panhandle until the fall when he decided he was tired of life on the trail. He had moved his mother to Caldwell and Mamie was pregnant. Time for a new life—well, literally, when in January 1885 his daughter Viola was born. But it also meant that he rather boldly tried two occupations. One was storekeeper, beginning with operating a tobacco shop. This did well enough that he ended up having five employees and selling oysters, ice cream, and foodstuffs in addition to cigars.

The other occupation was quite the stretch: author. Though he had had an adequate education, what did Charlie Siringo know about writing a book? Apparently, he did not consider this gap in his experience daunting. He began composing what would be titled *A Texas Cowboy; Or, Fifteen Years on the Hurricane Deck of a Spanish Pony.* Close to immediately after he finished it, the autobiography found a publisher, in Chicago, and it was released in the fall of 1885.[48] This in itself was remarkable, but even more so was the fact that the initial printing sold out—so long to being a storekeeper now that Siringo was a successful author.

In a roundabout way, that led to him becoming a detective. Siringo himself would later assert that that line of work was already ordained. In 1884, a noted blind phrenologist came to Caldwell to give a lecture at the Leland Hotel.[49] Curious, Siringo attended and was both entertained and impressed as the phrenologist placed his hands on the heads of several volunteers and told accurate stories about their lives.

---

48 It is considered the first autobiography of a cowboy to be published. The Oklahoma comedian Will Rogers would declare it the "cowboy's Bible." Between 1885 and 1927, Siringo would have seven books on his résumé.

49 In the late 1800s, phrenology was viewed as part science, part magic. It involved the measurement of bumps on a skull to predict mental traits, based on the belief that the brain, being the organ of the mind, has certain areas with specific functions or modules. Also, if the brain contains different muscles, those that were used more were bigger, resulting in different skull shapes. Phrenologists were experts—they claimed—in feeling and interpreting these bumps.

Finally, it was Siringo's turn. As he reported in his 1912 memoir, *A Cowboy Detective*, he sat down in a chair in the center of the parlor. "The blind man laid his hand on the top of my head and then said, 'Ladies and gentlemen, here is a mule's head.'" After explaining that a certain large bump indicated stubbornness, the phrenologist said that Siringo "had a fine head for a newspaper editor, a fine stock raiser, or detective; that in any of these callings I would make a success."

The following spring, the Siringo family moved to Chicago where he could oversee the second and larger printing of *A Texas Cowboy*. And it was there on May 4 that what became known as the Haymarket Affair occurred, changing Charlie Siringo's life.

16

A PINKERTON OP

The way Charlie Siringo put it in his memoir *A Cowboy Detective,* "The spring of 1886 found me in Chicago with a pretty young wife and a sweet little girl baby on my hands . . . when an anarchist's bomb killed and maimed over sixty of the city's police officers. We went to bed expecting a riot before morning, so we were not surprised when we heard the explosion of the bomb, and, soon after, the shooting which followed."[50]

What would be a turning point for the former cowboy happened to be a pivotal moment for the American labor movement. One of its instigators was Albert Parsons, who was the leader of the American branch of the International Working People's Association (IWPA). The stated goal of this anarchist group was to engineer a social revolution that would empower the working class. Parsons was a paradox—a Confederate soldier who had become a Radical Republican after the Civil War and married a former enslaved person.

Another instigator was August Spies, the editor of the anarchist

---

50 More accurately, the bomb killed one police officer outright, and of those wounded, six later died.

newspaper the *Alarm*. In Chicago, he and Parsons addressed the working-class German community, calling for demonstrations and organizing parades. The IWPA had, at most, only five thousand members, but its tactics were so confrontational that it had a powerful influence. Demonstrators would snake by the clubs and homes of the elite and around the Chicago Board of Trade, shouting slogans and waving fists. Articles in the anarchist newspapers explained how to make bombs with dynamite and editorials supported the assassination of public officials in Europe. On his desk, Spies kept a length of pipe that he claimed was a bomb.

In 1886, the Federation of Organized Trades and Labor Unions organized a May Day general strike to demand an eight-hour day. The anarchists saw an opportunity to increase membership and joined the event. Because Chicago had a sympathetic mayor in Carter Harrison, the nationwide movement focused on that city. On May 1, eighty thousand workers who had walked off their jobs marched up Michigan Avenue, led by Spies. Hundreds of private security and militia groups monitored the march, but the day ended peacefully.

Meanwhile, a strike was on at the McCormick Reaper Works. On May 3, strikers attacked scabs leaving the McCormick building. Immediately, two hundred policemen led by Captain "Black Jack" Bonfield attacked the crowd, swinging nightsticks and firing their guns.[51] Two workers were killed, and as a result, the anarchists called for a protest rally the next night at Haymarket Square. Mayor Harrison, who attended the rally, had Bonfield and his men stand by a block from the square. After Spies and Parsons spoke, rain began to fall, dispersing the crowd. As the mayor left the rally, he told Bonfield that the gathering posed no threat.

Still, once Harrison was out of sight, Bonfield sent in his troops. From

---

51 Bonfield had distinguished himself as a thug the previous July when during a violent transit strike, he and police officers under his command liberally beat the crowd. Bonfield himself was accused of cracking numerous skulls, including that of a seventy-year-old man. While the streetcars did run without incident by the end of the day, the complaints continued to rain down on the police chief and Mayor Harrison. In his own defense, Bonfield said, "A club today to make them scatter may save the use of a pistol tomorrow." Shortly afterward, Bonfield was promoted to inspector.

somewhere in the crowd, a bomb was thrown in front of the columns of police. When the dust settled, six police officers were dead (or soon would die) and sixty were injured, many of them hit by wild shots from fellow policemen. A like number of civilians were killed and injured. Following the tragedy, police rounded up suspicious foreign workers and anarchist leaders.[52]

Siringo was inclined to go see the rioting action, but he acceded to his wife's pleading not to risk the danger. "After the riot the city was all excitement, and I commenced to wish that I were a detective so as to help ferret out the thrower of the bomb and his backers." He recalled the "secret work for Texas cattlemen against cattle thieves in Western Texas and New Mexico. This had given me a taste for the work, and I liked it."

He turned his wish into action when he presented himself to the Pinkerton National Detective Agency. Its office in Chicago conducted operations in the West and was overseen by William Pinkerton, a son of the founder.

The creation of and expansion of this detective agency also represents the evolution of law enforcement in the American West after the Civil War. It had a humble beginning thanks to the humble beginning of its founder. Allan J. Pinkerton was born in the Gorbals area of Glasgow on July 21, 1819, the second surviving son of Isobel McQueen and William Pinkerton. He left school at the age of ten after his father's death, but he self-educated by reading voraciously. He learned to be a cooper but did not learn much about religion, becoming a lifelong atheist.

Pinkerton emigrated to the United States in 1842, and the following year, he settled in Dundee Township, Illinois, fifty miles northwest of Chicago. He built a cabin on the banks of the Fox River and started

---

52 Eight men would stand trial for murder. One of them was Albert Parsons. He had fled the city immediately after the bombing but turned himself in to be tried with his comrades. None of the defendants had been identified as the bomber but they were tried as accessories to murder based on their inflammatory speeches.

a cooperage, and then he sent for his wife, who had been a singer in Scotland. As early as 1844, Pinkerton worked for the Chicago abolitionist leaders, and years later, his Dundee home was a stop on the Underground Railroad.

One day while wandering through the wooded groves around Dundee, looking for trees to make barrel staves, Pinkerton came across a band of counterfeiters who may have been affiliated with the notorious Banditti of the Prairie.[53] After observing their movements for some time he informed the local sheriff, who arrested them. This later led to Pinkerton being appointed, in 1849, as the first police detective in Cook County. His career was launched. The next year, he partnered with Chicago attorney Edward Rucker in forming the North-Western Police Agency, which later became Pinkerton & Co. and finally the Pinkerton National Detective Agency.[54] Its business insignia was a wide-open eye captioned "We Never Sleep."

As railroads followed and spurred U.S. expansion westward in the 1850s, train robberies were one of the unwelcome byproducts. However, this was good for Allan Pinkerton. He came into contact with officials at the major railroads who were willing to try detecting methods as a way to not only catch thieves but also frustrate bandit plans before they could be carried out. It was in this way that Pinkerton was introduced to the attorney Abraham Lincoln, who sometimes represented the Illinois Central Railroad.

He also found time for extracurricular activities. In 1859, Pinkerton attended the secret meetings held by John Brown and Frederick Douglass in Chicago along with abolitionists John Jones and Henry Wagoner. At those meetings, Jones, Wagoner, and Pinkerton helped

---

53 Also known as Pirates of the Prairie, this was a group of loose-knit outlaw gangs during the early to mid-nineteenth century that carried out crime sprees throughout the frontier Midwest. With established law enforcement often overmatched, some of the outlaws were tracked down, captured, and often swiftly punished by vigilante patrols calling themselves Regulators.

54 Though seemingly a relic from the nineteenth century, the agency is still in existence today, operating as Pinkerton Consulting and Investigations, a subsidiary of Securitas AB, a firm headquartered in Stockholm, Sweden.

purchase clothes and supplies for Brown—including the suit Brown was hanged in after the failure of Brown's raid on Harpers Ferry that November.

The Civil War was a boom time for the ambitious founder of the detective agency. When it began, Pinkerton served as head of the Union Intelligence Service. His tenure got off to a very good start when he foiled a plot to assassinate Lincoln in Baltimore while the president-elect was on the way to Washington, DC, to be inaugurated. Pinkerton also provided estimates of Confederate troop numbers to General George McClellan when he commanded the Army of the Potomac. His agents often worked undercover as Confederate soldiers and sympathizers to gather military intelligence. Pinkerton himself carried out several undercover missions as a Confederate officer using the alias Major E. J. Allen. During one such mission, in Memphis, he barely escaped with his life.

Following his services for the Union army, Pinkerton continued his pursuit of train robbers, including the Reno Gang, led by a quartet of brothers who preyed on the railroad companies. He was hired by railroad officials to track down the outlaw James brothers, but after he failed to capture Jesse or Frank, his employers withdrew their financial support and Pinkerton continued to track them at his own expense. However, after Jesse allegedly captured and killed one of Pinkerton's undercover agents, he abandoned the chase.

Recovering from this setback, the Pinkerton National Detective Agency thrived during the rest of the 1870s and into the 1880s, thanks in large measure to being involved in incidents of labor agitation. One notable example was the Great Railroad Strike of 1877, with the agency working on behalf of the employers who, of course, could much better afford high fees than the workers. Another was when Franklin Gowen, president of the Philadelphia and Reading Railroad, hired the agency to investigate the labor unions in the company's mines. A Pinkerton agent, James McParland—who would become an important figure in Charlie Siringo's career—using the alias James McKenna, infiltrated the Molly Maguires, a secret society of mainly Irish American coal miners, leading to the downfall of the labor organization.[55]

By the time Siringo signed on, the agency—which was by now referred to as America's Scotland Yard—had hundreds of operatives in its employ and offices in New York, Chicago, Boston, and Philadelphia. It also had new leadership. Allan Pinkerton had passed away on July 1, 1884, in Chicago. How he died was disputed. One claim was that he slipped on the pavement and bit his tongue, resulting in gangrene. Another was that he succumbed to a stroke—he had survived one a year earlier—or to a reoccurrence of the malaria he had contracted somewhere in the South, perhaps as far back as his undercover Civil War service. In any case, at the time of his death, Pinkerton was working on a system to centralize all criminal identification records, similar to the database created decades later by the Federal Bureau of Investigation.

The detective agency was inherited by his two sons, Robert, based in New York, and William, in Chicago. The latter hired Siringo as an operative. However, while waiting for the appointment, Siringo became involved in an incident that revealed the mettle he would bring to his future assignments. P. T. Barnum's company was in town, and as Siringo was nearing the ticket wagon:

> *a great crowd was scrambling to buy tickets to the circus. A large man, who would have made two of me, tried to be fresh and I called him down. He made a pass to put me to sleep with the first punch but before he could get in his work the weight of my old Colt's 45 pistol had landed on his head. This was followed up by one more lick which buried the sharp pistol-sight into his skull. This brought the blood in a stream. By this time his partner had picked up a piece of board and had it raised to strike me from the rear. I saw him just in*

---

55 The incident inspired Arthur Conan Doyle's novel *The Valley of Fear,* featuring Sherlock Holmes. A Pinkerton agent also appears in a small role in "The Adventure of the Red Circle," a 1911 Holmes story. A 1970 film, *The Molly Maguires,* starring Sean Connery, was loosely based on the Pinkerton investigation.

time. He found a cocked pistol in his face, and dropping the board, begged for mercy. A policeman came running up, but he was so excited that he forgot to take my pistol, so I put it back in my pocket.

Siringo was disappointed not to be immediately assigned to the Haymarket bombing investigation. The event and the subsequent manhunt were breathlessly reported by newspapers across the country as was the trial of the eight suspects who had been distilled from the over two hundred people arrested. They were found guilty and four of them, including Parsons and Spies, were hanged. A fifth man somehow—though fittingly—managed to die by blowing himself up while in jail. The three other convicted men became inmates of a federal prison in Illinois.

Instead, Siringo, after a few menial local assignments, was shipped off to the agency's office in Denver, with Mamie and Viola in tow. After his first mission, one that took him to Cincinnati to investigate an Irish organization (perhaps he did not tell his mother, Bridget), Siringo detected some malfeasance in the Pinkerton Agency itself. He turned in a modest expenses report and was admonished for not charging enough. The assistant supervisor in Chicago, John McGinn, told him that "the client was wealthy and it was the custom of the agency to allow their operatives to overcharge, so as to make extra money, thereby swelling the regular weekly salary paid by the agency." Siringo was not comfortable with this shady practice, but he conceded "this added extra greenbacks for the lining of my own pockets."

In Denver, his direct boss was Charles Eams. When they first arrived, Siringo and his family lived with the office superintendent and his family. While Mamie searched for their own place, Charlie got to work on cases that ranged from divorces to crooked streetcar conductors. Finally, in the spring of 1887, he was sent out into the field, to Archuleta County in southwest Colorado. His role was to become an insurgent—posing as the enemy of the fellows paying the agency's bills.

Archuleta County was near the New Mexico border and was ruled by wealthy Hispanic sheepherders.[56] They controlled the voting, and in the next election, all five county commissioners were the consortium's selections. That the majority of "voters" were nonregistered sheep tenders angered the real voters in Archuleta County, all seventy-five of them, most of them Anglos. They grabbed their guns and escorted the five commissioners across the border into New Mexico where, they were told, they should remain or each of them would be voted out of office with a bullet.

The sheepherders hired the Pinkerton Agency to infiltrate and disrupt the Anglo insurgents enough that the county commissioners could be restored. The window for this operation was a small one because if the commissioners did not hold a meeting in Pagosa Springs, the county seat, within sixty days, they lost their positions. After Siringo was assigned to be the undercover op, he rode a newly purchased horse from Durango to Pagosa Springs and presented himself as Charles Anderson, an outlaw wanted in Texas for killing three Mexicans. This would, presumably, endear him to the Anglo "revolutionaries," as they wanted to be called, in Archuleta County.

The window began to close even faster. Impatient, the wealthy backers of the commissioners hired some sixty men, and this sudden militia headed to Colorado, stopping at the bridge over the San Juan River. On the other side of the bridge were the insurgent Anglos, also brandishing rifles and six-shooters. Truce talks were not successful. Siringo learned of a plot to be carried out that night for several insurgents to sneak across the river and set fire to a building where the commissioners were staying. It was the Pinkerton op who snuck out first, warning those on the other side of the San Juan River and the plot was foiled. During the standoff, Siringo did a delicate dance of sneaking back and forth between the two opposing forces and having to defend himself when accused of being a spy.

---

56 A reason why Siringo was chosen for this assignment was that during his cowboy days he learned how to speak fluent Spanish.

Eventually, before the deadline, a truce was reached. The five commissioners were allowed back into Pagosa Springs to have their meeting, but from then on, only registered voters would cast ballots. It was back to Denver for a relieved Siringo, who had been running out of reasons for his absences from the insurgent camp.

There were new risky missions to Wyoming and elsewhere in Colorado, and one even took him to Mexico City. In between, he was back with Mamie and Viola in Denver. But that turned out not to be the safest place either. Eams ran a corrupt office, with overbilling clients and even billing for work not done having become routine. Siringo refused to participate in these and similar schemes. Worse for his safety, he stopped a violent interrogation of a suspect accused of committing a robbery that was actually perpetrated by the two detective interrogators.

"Siringo's fast action on behalf of an innocent man, and his exposure of two dishonest detectives, incurred both the wrath of superintendent Eams and his determination for revenge," writes Ben E. Pingenot. "Eams told Siringo that just as soon as he could get in touch with W. A. Pinkerton in Chicago, he was going to order him to be discharged in disgrace."

This ploy backfired badly. Pinkerton had been hearing rumors of corruption in the Denver office, and when Eams overplayed his hand, he and the rest of the staff there were fired. The only detective left in Denver was Charlie Siringo. The new superintendent was James McParland—and that was when Siringo's best years as a cowboy detective began.[57]

---

57 In 1867, McParland had emigrated to New York from County Armagh, Ireland. He worked various jobs, eventually owning a liquor store in Chicago. After it was destroyed by the Great Fire in 1871, he applied to the Pinkerton Agency for a job.

17

DIED IN HIS ARMS

One of Charlie Siringo's more intriguing cases was conducted on behalf of the governor of New Mexico, Charles Leon. It began in February 1891—by then, sadly, the detective was a widower.

Though barely into her twenties, Mamie's health was fragile. Visits to doctors finally produced the conclusion that she had contracted pleurisy. It was probably more than that, but such was the state of medicine at the time. Mamie grew worse, and finally, in August 1889, it was decided that she should undergo surgery. At the insistence of her father, Clay Lloyd, Mamie, accompanied by Viola, was sent east, to Springfield, Missouri, where his personal physician could perform the operation.

Siringo went in the opposite direction, to pursue a Pinkerton case in California. Mamie survived the operation, but it was nine months before the family was back together in Denver. Her health continued to decline, though, and by the fall of 1890, it was clear her lungs were too damaged to last much longer.

As Charlie later recorded, "Poor Mamie died in my arms early in the winter as I was holding her at the window to get fresh air. Her suffering had been something awful." Both he and the physician attending her "shed tears when the end came. This was a surprise to me for I didn't think a doctor could shed tears, as they become so accustomed to great suffering."

After Mamie's funeral, Siringo agreed to turn the five-year-old Viola over to his late wife's aunt and uncle, who were childless and could provide a stable home back in Illinois.

For the next few months, Siringo, who had considered being away from his family a routine part of his detective occupation, keenly felt the absence of his daughter as well as his wife. He performed low-level, local jobs for the Pinkerton Agency. But finally he was ready to get back on the road.

His next case began on the night of February 5 in Santa Fe. Three members of the judiciary committee of the New Mexico legislature— Elias Stover, T. B. Mills, and Joseph Ancheta—were having a meeting in the law office of Thomas Catron.[58] Two men rode quietly through the snow, stopping in front of the Catron building. One had a shotgun, the other a rifle. When they opened fire, pellets and bullets poured into the office. Three of the men inside were frightened but unharmed while Ancheta was hit in the neck and left shoulder. He would barely survive the wounds.

The assassins galloped away. The Santa Fe marshal, John Gray, hastily pulled a posse together, and they gave chase. But other than noticing from an impression in the snow that one horse had only half a shoe, the posse let the gunmen ride on into the dark night.

The brazenness of the attack and the easy escape put the legislature into more of a lather than the posse's horses. It authorized Governor L. Bradford Prince to spend up to $20,000 to apprehend and punish the perpetrators. He immediately contacted William Pinkerton in Chicago,

---

58 Catron, a Missouri native and Confederate army veteran, used his knowledge of Spanish and Mexican land grants to acquire title to more than three million acres, making the lawyer the largest landholder in the state. He would later serve as mayor of Santa Fe and a U.S. senator from New Mexico.

who in turn contacted James McParland in Denver, who in turn told Charlie Siringo to pack his travel kit and head to Santa Fe.

The immediate suspects were the Knights of Labor, who were opponents of the mostly Republican territorial government, and especially a Hispanic organization known as the White Caps because of the white hoods they wore during public events. Out of public view, their activities included cutting the fences of ranches and even murdering ranch owners. Attempting to assassinate elected officials was an ominous escalation of tensions.

Siringo's plan was to infiltrate the White Caps. The first step was befriending Francisco Chavez, the sheriff of San Miguel County, which harbored White Caps members and supporters. The detective put his expense account to the test by buying the suddenly lucky lawman drinks and lavish dinners. During one such outing, Siringo was introduced to Pablo Herrera, who had recently left a New Mexico prison in time to be elected to the territorial legislature. Siringo was invited to visit Las Vegas—the New Mexico version, not the Nevada one—where Herrera introduced him to White Cap members.

Charlie and Pablo became good pals. Not only did the undercover op have a good gift of gab—in Spanish as well as English—but he also enjoyed having a swell time and could pay for it. Some of the best dinners enjoyed by his White Cap friends were at the Montezuma Hotel, a resort in Hot Springs near Las Vegas.[59] Two months later, Siringo snuck back to Santa Fe to give a report to Governor Prince.

The detective's surprising conclusion based on his undercover work was that the White Caps were not really affiliated with the Knights of

---

59 The Montezuma Hotel was a compound of ninety thousand square feet and four hundred rooms constructed in the Queen Anne style in 1886 as a luxury destination by the Atchison, Topeka & Santa Fe Railroad. The hotel Siringo dined at was the third edition. The first and second hotels, constructed in 1881 and 1885 by the railroad, were the first buildings in New Mexico to have electric lighting and both burned down. The natural hot springs on the site were widely thought to ease the suffering of people with tuberculosis, chronic rheumatism, gout, biliary, and what was called "renal calculi." Over the years, guests included Theodore Roosevelt, Rutherford B. Hayes, Ulysses Grant, William Tecumseh Sherman, John C. Frémont, and even Jesse James, who had stayed at the first version of the hotel.

Labor. Also, while the group was guilty of a range of crimes, its members had nothing to do with the Santa Fe assassination attempt—well, not completely. According to Siringo, Sheriff Chavez despised Thomas Catron, who was the real target, and the lawman had hired his own shooters, who, of course, were still on the loose.

For that reason, Siringo was back in the saddle. Based on his own inquiries—which, presumably, did not involve wining and dining at the Pinkerton Agency expense—Marshal John Gray had learned of two brothers, Felipe and Victoriana Garcia, who lived in Cow Springs, a village southeast of Santa Fe, and were known to have a horse with a peculiar footprint. Siringo headed there. It looked like he was closing in on the shooters until, while in Cow Springs, he contracted small-pox. He managed to return to Santa Fe, where he was laid up for six weeks. It was a miracle he survived at all.

At one point, the physician who cautiously visited him in his bed-room at a now otherwise empty boardinghouse "sat down by the head of my bed and taking hold of my hand, told me that I couldn't live till morning, as my temperature had been up to the highest pitch for four or five days, which was the limit; that my vital energy would be burnt out before morning. He advised that if I had any word or will to leave, that I attend to it then."

After the doctor left, "I began to think of dying and wondered what kind of a reception I would receive on the other shore from whence no cowboy detective has ever returned."

Siringo did not find out, at least until many years later. In the morning when the doctor returned, he "was as tickled as a little boy with his first pair of pants, when he saw I was alive." The patient's temperature had fallen to 101 degrees, and from that day on, he continued to recover.

By the time the weakened op was ready to do some detecting again, Governor Prince had lost interest in the case—that, plus being annoyed by the high expenses the Pinkerton Agency was billing him, even covering supposed activities during the weeks that Siringo was sick in bed.

The detective was ordered back to Denver, and the case was closed. However, the experience had a silver lining. Though Siringo had suffered a life-threatening illness there, he had fallen in love with Santa Fe and its surroundings. He purchased 365 acres outside the city, where he would establish the Sunny Slope Ranch. It included a two-room adobe house that offered a stimulating view of the Sangre de Cristo Mountains.

He was not idle in Denver for long. In fact, he was not in Denver long at all. McParland sent Siringo to Coeur d'Alene in the Idaho Panhandle where there was a lot of silver and lead mining activity. The assignment was to operate on behalf of the Mine Owners Protective Association (MOPA), which was worried that a militant faction of the Coeur d'Alene Miners' Union was going to foment labor trouble. Charlie was at first reluctant to go because he sort of sympathized with workers rather than the big companies and their brutal ways, but he was persuaded by McParland that there were members of this Idaho union who were no better and might be worse than the murderous Molly Maguires in West Virginia. Siringo said he would go and find out.

Once more, his mission involved a dangerous infiltration. He was hired as a mine worker and quickly ingratiated himself with his fellow laborers, so much so that after only two weeks he was invited to join the union. Two months later, he became the recording secretary. With this position and from talking to other miners, Siringo discerned that the leadership of the union was in the hands of anarchists such as George Pettibone, a miner who had risen through the nascent union's ranks and was virulently antiowner.

Siringo was right in the thick of things when the Coeur d'Alene strike of 1892 took place. By that time, the mine owners were raking it in—the year before, the Coeur d'Alene district had shipped ore containing $4.9 million in lead, silver, and gold. But cutting into their profits were the railroads, which had raised rates for hauling ore. Viewed as a way to reduce costs was the introduction of hole-boring machines into the mines. They displaced single-jack and double-jack miners, forcing the men into new, lower-paid jobs as trammers or muckers, or out of work altogether.

Mostly, though, the owners found a reduction in wages the easiest way to mitigate increased costs. After the machines were installed, the mine owners were going to reduce the mine workers' pay to $3.50 per day, depending on their specific jobs. On top of that, a day's work was extended from nine to ten hours. The workweek would be seven days long, with an occasional Sunday off. Also imposed were high payments for room and board in company lodging and check-cashing fees at company saloons.

Feeling that their backs were to the sooty walls, the union members walked off their jobs.

Soon, all of the mines in Coeur d'Alene were shut down. Hoping to halt the expanding conflict, the mine owners and the union agreed to a meeting to try to get each side to understand the other's grievances. However, when the meeting left too many matters unresolved, Pettibone confided to the recording secretary that the union's central committee was ready to escalate. Men very capable of violence had been chosen to not just intimidate scab workers but, if necessary, kill them. It was time for war against the mine owners, and it would include explosives.

Thus it was that a tip from Siringo probably saved many lives. After the failure of the meeting and facing the gloomy prospect of mines being idle, the Mine Owners Protective Association determined to bring in laborers culled from other states. They would include recent immigrants desperate for work who, with poor or no English skills, did not comprehend that they were strikebreakers. Hundreds of them were to be loaded on trains with Coeur d'Alene as the destination. Learning that the first train was to disgorge the scabs in Wallace, union members armed themselves and headed there.

But Siringo secretly let the mine owners know of the union's plans. So, the train bypassed Wallace and stopped at Burke, where the passengers, probably not aware of the deep danger they were in, disembarked and were guided up to a reopened mine. Subsequent trains were met by MOPA guards as well as injunctions issued by federal courts preventing the union members from interfering. Still, some uncomprehending scabs were separated from the pack and beaten. During these incidents, Siringo "learned some new lessons in human nature as he observed the fights and cruel acts by the union strikers on scabs for the next few months," writes Ben E. Pingenot.

Once again, the undercover cop barely escaped with his life after being accused of being a spy—in this case, accurately—by the union. "Soon I could hear the yelling of more than 1,000 throats as they came to get me," Siringo recalled. "It wasn't long before the street was jammed with angry men."

Clutching his Winchester and six-shooter, Siringo had to crawl under and through buildings, run through ravines, hide out in the back of shops, and in other ways try to get out of town, dodging the occasional bullet along the way.[60] With the striking miners relentlessly searching for him, he finally made his way into the mountains, where he could watch the fighting between the two sides taking place below.

Finally, on July 13, Idaho governor Norman Willey declared martial law. To back it up, President Benjamin Harrison had soldiers from Fort Sherman march into Coeur d'Alene and restore order. The military commander, Colonel William Carlin, appointed W. S. Sims, a physician working for MOPA, as sheriff, and, coming out of hiding, Charlie Siringo was appointed a deputy.

Howard R. Lamar writes, "Siringo was now engaged in a more familiar task: he was rounding up stray union members as if they were Texas cattle."

George Pettibone and other union leaders who had advocated and participated in the violence—which had seen at least six men killed—were arrested and kept in a stockade. After trials held in Boise City

---

60 A big help was provided by a boardinghouse owner, Mrs. Kate Shipley, with whom Siringo had been having an affair while her husband was farming in the Dakota Territory.

and Coeur d'Alene, which included testimony by Siringo, Pettibone and seventeen others were convicted of an array of crimes. Pettibone was shipped out of the area to be incarcerated in Detroit.[61]

The successful outcome of the Coeur d'Alene case did not earn Siringo much idle time. As he put it in *The Cowboy Detective,* "From now on I shall merely skim over the surface of some of my experiences, as I find that one medium size volume will not contain it all if given in full."

These experiences included being a cellmate of two suspected murderers in Pueblo to elicit their confessions, posing as a hobo on one case and as a wealthy mine owner in another, investigating a gold mill robbery in Alaska, in Cripple Creek presenting himself once more as an outlaw, and in other ways, as he put it, "There are times when a detective earns his salary deep down where the public can't see."

Though all his adventures had him on the road a lot, he decided to give married life another try. It did not last, but not because he became a widower again. In 1893, Charlie had married Lillie Thomas, who was twenty-one to his thirty-eight. Three years later, she gave birth to a son, William Lee Roy Siringo. But in addition to Siringo's absences, writes Pingenot, "Unsavory characters coming to their home and asking for Siringo by name or by one of his aliases caused Lillie to worry about her safety as well as that of her son."

When her parents moved from Denver to the West Coast, she and her son tagged along. "Lillie and I agreed to disagree because she wanted to live in Los Angeles, California, while I insisted on making the Rocky Mountains my home."

---

61 More than a decade later, George Pettibone would be back in a courtroom as a defendant. He was implicated in the 1905 assassination of Frank Steunenberg, a former governor of Idaho. Also implicated were Bill Haywood and Charles Moyer, general secretary and president, respectively, of the Western Federation of Miners. Haywood was represented by the renowned attorney Clarence Darrow, who obtained an acquittal. Pettibone was tried after Haywood and was defended by Orrin Hilton of Denver. Pettibone was also acquitted, and charges against Moyer were dropped. During the trial, an ill Pettibone learned he had stomach cancer. After his acquittal he underwent surgery in Denver. Surgeons pronounced Pettibone terminal following the operation, and he died two days later at age forty-six.

Home is where the heart is, and for Charlie Siringo, his heart was in being a detective. The Wilcox train robbery would give his heart a full feeling.

As Lamar observes, "It is an extraordinary coincidence that Charlie Siringo met and befriended Billy the Kid, the best known and most written-about of the nineteenth-century Western 'bad men,' with the exception of the James brothers and the Youngers. Then nearly two decades later Siringo spent four years chasing Butch Cassidy and the Sundance Kid and other members of their gang called the Wild Bunch."

But Siringo would not be the only lawman seeking what would become the most notorious outlaw gang in the country.

18

"KILLING MEN IS MY SPECIALTY"

Especially after the Wilcox train heist, any number of lawmen intersected with the Outlaw Trail. Catching Butch Cassidy and the members of his gang was the priority, of course, not just for the fame that would engender but also for the reward money, which was higher than that for any other fugitive from the law. Something had to go, the railroads or the bandits, and the railroads were certainly not going to disappear. Hence, Charlie Siringo was far from being the only peace officer or detective in pursuit of any Bandit Heaven veterans during the last few years of the nineteenth century.

One of them was Joseph Shelby Lefors. He had been born in Paris, Texas, in February 1865. His parents, Mahala West and James J. Lefors, must have had law enforcement in their DNA because Joe would be joined by four brothers—Sam, Ike, Rufe, and Newton—as peace officers in some capacity. Newton was killed in the line of duty serving as a deputy U.S. marshal in Indian Territory (Oklahoma), but it was another brother, Perry, a prominent rancher in Gray County, for whom the town of Lefors, Texas, was named.

Joe Lefors first came to Wyoming in 1885 as a cowpuncher, and when the cattle drive ended, he chose to remain rather than return to Texas. He began working for the larger ranchers and was credited with recovering a large herd that had been rustled. This made him an easy choice to be taken on as a livestock inspector, with thwarting rustlers and maybe capturing a few in the process being among his responsibilities. In August 1896, Lefors became a married man, wedding the sixteen-year-old Bessie Hannum in Newcastle, Wyoming.

His claim to fame as a Western lawman rests on three events. The first was heading a posse to track down the perpetrators of the Wilcox robbery, though Cassidy and the others eluded him. The second was in 1969 when the movie *Butch Cassidy and the Sundance Kid* was released. Though Lefors was not an outstanding lawman and did not have nearly the experience and results that Siringo did, according to the movie's screenwriter William Goldman, his posse was the one Cassidy most feared. With the straw-hatted Lefors leading it, the posse pursued the bandit duo relentlessly, leading to one of the movie's most quoted lines, when Paul Newman wonders, "Who are those guys?" and most memorable scenes—when Butch and Sundance, the latter confessing he can't swim, leap off a cliff into a lake; the only way to leave Lefors behind.[62]

The third event that Lefors was credited—or, rather, discredited— was for making sure that Tom Horn was convicted of murder and sentenced to die. The deputy marshal claimed to have gotten from Horn a confession that he had killed a fourteen-year-old sheepherder, Willie Nickel. The veracity of the confession was in doubt, but by then Horn had done enough bad things to deserve his fate.

In any case, Joe Lefors was a deputy U.S. marshal, appointed in October 1899, and he did his job well enough before sinking into obscurity.

Another noted lawman of the time was John T. Pope. He was a

---

62 Joe Lefors "appears" one more time in the movie, near the end, seen from a distance and wearing a straw hat. And he is portrayed by the actor Peter Weller in the 1979 sequel that was a prequel, *Butch and Sundance: The Early Days.*

Utah native, born in Farmington in Davis County in 1860. As a young man, being a rancher was his most likely career path, but one day, life took a turn. He happened to be standing on the street in Vernal, Utah, when one of the local merchants was shot and killed during a robbery. A posse took off after the killer. Pope leaped onto his horse and also gave chase, but instead of following the posse's path, he chose one that he figured to be faster. He caught up to the killer in a canyon and held him at gunpoint until the posse arrived.

Citizens in the county remembered this combination of smarts and courage. In the fall of 1890, Pope's name was placed on the ballot for Uintah County sheriff, without his permission. That he was elected unanimously would be impressive except there was no other candidate on the ballot. Shortly after his election, he became the first sheriff ever brave, or dumb, enough to venture into the badlands of Brown's Hole to make an arrest. His first effort in the area was to shackle a notoriously bad guy by the name of Ed Carouthers, who was known as "Buckskin" because of the stiff trousers he wore.

The arrest was almost the last time that Sheriff Pope put the cuffs on anyone. After he tracked Carouthers down, part of the return trip to Vernal involved crossing the Green River by rowboat. About halfway across, Carouthers pulled a knife from his pocket and stabbed Pope in the throat from behind. The sheriff was able to draw his revolver and fire over his shoulder. The bullet struck Buckskin in the face and knocked him overboard. Pope wrapped his neckerchief around his wound and continued on to Vernal. Sometime later, a local man found Carouthers's body stuck in a pile of driftwood.

Buckskin's demise did not endear Pope to the local outlaws, especially given that he had invaded their favorite hideout to do the deed. Then, the lawman had the nerve to start a ranch in the area. In what must have seemed like an odd friendship, Butch Cassidy and Elzy Lay often visited Pope at his ranch, and they developed a mutual respect. However, this by itself did not protect Pope. There were other outlaws who offered rewards up to several thousand dollars for the murder of the sheriff.

One bushwhacker took a shot at Pope and thought he'd hit pay dirt when the horse fell over. The sheriff was not hit, and he had managed to pull out his rifle as the horse fell. He played dead until the attacker approached, and when he was within can't-miss range, Pope killed him. There were many other attempts to collect the reward, but Pope, always on guard, escaped each of them, and the results to the outlaws were usually the same.

Alas, one incident put an end to the friendship with Butch and Elzy, and that was the aftermath of Matt Warner and his friend, Bill Wall, being attacked by three shooters (as described earlier). Warner and Wall were able to kill all three of the attackers, but warrants were issued for their arrest and Sheriff Pope had to do his job. When he had them in jail he met with Butch Cassidy and Elzy Lay about the situation. They agreed that as long as the pair of inmates received fair treatment, they would take no action.

But they had not counted on the sheriff having to leave town for several hours on business. Once it was dark enough, a lynch mob attempted to take the law into their own hands. The quick-thinking Matt Warner popped a paper bag, making the mob think the two men were armed and they backed off. Before they could refuel on courage, Butch, Elzy, and several others arrived. They stood guard at the jail until the Pope returned later that evening and the mob dispersed.

Even so, Cassidy told the sheriff that if the two prisoners were not moved to a safer place he would take them, even if it meant going through the lawman to do it. Early the next morning, Warner and Wall were transferred under heavy guard to Ogden. Needing some money for the prisoners' defense fund, Cassidy and Lay robbed the bank in Idaho.

Pope mounted a posse and came very close to catching them—not just once, but twice. The second time was the closest call. As the sheriff went in the front door of the Antler Saloon, Cassidy and Lay ducked out the back door. Three weeks later, Sheriff Pope received a postcard mailed from St. John's, Arizona, that read, "Pope, gawd damn you, lay off me. I don't want to kill you! Butch."

John Pope served a total of five years as the Uintah County sheriff and was awarded a gold badge by the governor. But he did not retire as a lawman. He continued as a deputy marshal; then in 1904, he was elected county attorney, though he'd had no formal schooling and did not pass the bar until two years later.[63]

And then there was Tom Horn. Lawman? It may be hard to believe that a man who was hanged for murdering a teenager could have worn a badge with any distinction, but Horn did have a varied and colorful career that included being a peace officer, stock detective, and, like Charlie Siringo, a Pinkerton op.[64]

Thomas Horn Jr. was born on the family farm near Memphis—the one in Missouri, not Tennessee—in November 1860. Though he was the fifth of twelve children, he was mostly a loner, partly to avoid his father's violent outbursts and partly because he enjoyed going off on hunts. Such outings on Sundays got young Tom into trouble. He would get a scolding from his mother and "a regular thumping" from his father for not attending church with the rest of the family. "I had nothing particular against going, if it had not been for the 'coon, tur-key, quail, rabbits, prairie chickens, 'possums, skunks and other game of that kind, and they were all neglected to an extent by the rest of the family, that it kept me busy most every Sunday, and many nights through the week," he later wrote in an autobiography published in 1904, *Life of Tom Horn: Government Scout and Interpreter, Written by Himself.*

---

63 Supposedly, another of Pope's achievements was digging the first oil well in Utah. One more was being one of the first men to become interested in rock asphalt and he perfected formulas using the product for roofing hundreds of area homes and businesses.

64 It would be also hard to believe Horn as a lawman of any kind after viewing *Tom Horn*, a 1980 feature starring Steve McQueen in his second-to-last film, which focuses on Horn's final escapades as a vigilante killer.

Butch Cassidy, age 28, when he was still Robert LeRoy Parker, as he appeared when an inmate in the Wyoming State Penitentiary. *(Courtesy of the Library of Congress)*

Harry Longabaugh, who became known as the Sundance Kid, could dress well when he was not wrangling horses or robbing banks. *(Courtesy of the Library of Congress)*

Quick-triggered Harvey Logan, also known as Kid Curry, with his most steady girlfriend, Annie Rogers. *(Courtesy of the Library of Congress)*

William Ellsworth "Elzy" Lay was Butch Cassidy's main sidekick until he decided to end his bandit ways. *(Courtesy of the Utah Historical Society)*

The Parker family was part of a large migration of Mormons led west to Utah by Brigham Young (above). *(Courtesy of the Library of Congress)*

Matt Warner (left, with Jim Peterson), born Willard Erastus Christiansen, was another of Cassidy's fast friends who gave up the outlaw life. *(Courtesy of the Utah Historical Society)*

One of the remote areas of Brown's Hole that made it an appealing hideout for rustlers and other thieves. *(Courtesy of the Library of Congress)*

BELOW: Robbers Roost was another remote location that was "heaven" for fleeing bank and train robbers. *(Courtesy of the Utah Historical Society)*

Bandits built cabins and enjoyed other lawless comforts of the infamous
Hole-in-the-Wall Ranch. *(Courtesy of the Wyoming State Archives)*

"Queen Ann" Bassett was one of two sisters
who were romanced by members of the Wild
Bunch. *(Courtesy of the Denver Public Library Special Collections)*

Laura Bullion was another of the Wild Bunch
women who found the outlaw life exciting . . .
until it wasn't. *(Courtesy of the Library of Congress)*

All that remains of the bandit George Parrott are most of his skull and the shoes made from his skin. *(Courtesy of the Wyoming State Archives)*

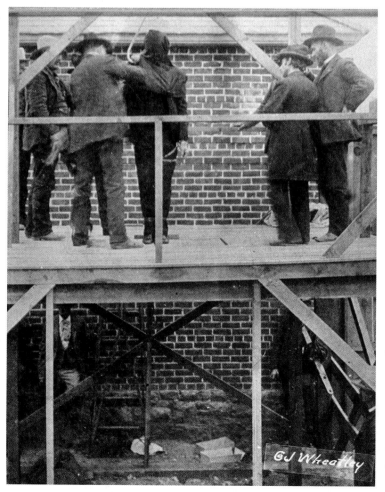

When Tom "Black Jack" Ketchum was being prepared for hanging, no one expected he would literally lose his head. *(Courtesy of the New Mexico History Museum)*

Charlie Siringo would make good use of any mode of transportation available when pursuing fleeing bandits. *(Courtesy of the Haley Memorial Library and History Center)*

This elegant portrait indicates why Charlie Siringo was a favorite among the ladies. *(Courtesy of the Haley Memorial Library and History Center)*

The Scotsman Allan Pinkerton founded the agency that employed detectives like Charlie Siringo to track down the most elusive outlaws. *(Courtesy of the Library of Congress)*

William Pinkerton, one of Allan's two sons, seen here in his Chicago office, over-saw the detective agency's western operations. *(Courtesy of the Library of Congress)*

James McParland was head of the Denver office of the Pinkerton Agency and was Charlie Siringo's direct boss. *(Courtesy of the Library of Congress)*

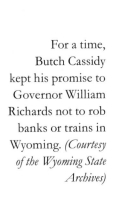

For a time, Butch Cassidy kept his promise to Governor William Richards not to rob banks or trains in Wyoming. *(Courtesy of the Wyoming State Archives)*

All that was left of the train car blown up by the Wild Bunch during the Wilcox train robbery. *(Courtesy of the Denver Public Library Special Collections)*

Blowing up the car was not enough— the safe had to be opened too. *(Courtesy of the American Heritage Center, University of Wyoming)*

The rapacious railroad baron E. H. Harriman, depicted here in 1907, funded several efforts to track down and capture Butch Cassidy and his gang. *(Courtesy of the Library of Congress)*

A posse prepared to pursue train robbers, led by Sheriff Joe Lefors (center in the white hat). *(Courtesy of the Wyoming State Archives)*

The infamous "Fort Worth Five" photograph features (left to right) the Sundance Kid, Will Carver, Ben Kilpatrick, Kid Curry, and Butch Cassidy. *(Courtesy of the Denver Public Library Special Collections)*

Tom Horn standing outside the jail cell that was his home until his hanging in 1903. *(Courtesy of the Wyoming State Archives)*

Ora Haley was a powerful ranch owner in Wyoming who backed the murders carried out by Tom Horn. *(Courtesy of the American Heritage Center, University of Wyoming)*

The rustler and rancher Isom Dart was one of Tom Horn's Brown's Hole victims. *(Courtesy of the Denver Public Library Special Collections)*

The Sundance Kid and Ethel Place had this portrait taken during a New York City sojourn in 1901. *(Courtesy of the Library of Congress)*

Rather than go back to jail,
Kid Curry eluded lawmen by
shooting himself. *(Courtesy of
the Library of Congress)*

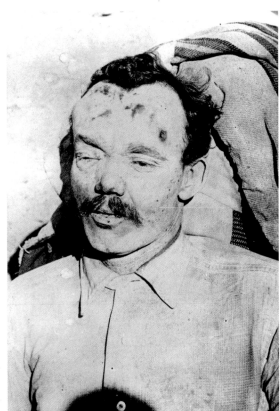

George "Flatnose"
Currie after being shot
to death in April 1900.
*(Courtesy of the Wyoming
State Archives)*

As he aged, Charlie Siringo was employed more as a bodyguard. Here, during the 1907 trial of labor leader Bill Haywood, he poses (with cane on right) with four other Pinkerton ops surrounding the suspected bomber Harry Orchard (in derby). *(Courtesy of the Idaho Historical Society)*

One of the last members of the Wild Bunch to die was "Tall Texan" Ben Kilpatrick (left), who, with Ole Beck, was killed in Sanderson, Texas, in 1912. *(Courtesy of the Library of Congress)*

His mother persisted in "trying to break me of my Indian ways, though I had never seen an Indian, and did not know what their ways were." His attitude was the same for school as church: "I could see far more advantage in having a good string of pelts than in learning to read, write and cipher."

Instead of a sibling or two, Tom's steady companion was Shedrick, his dog. The two went on long hunts together, and Tom had more affection for the devoted animal than any family member. On one of their journeys, Tom encountered two teenagers who were part of an immigrant train that was passing through. The older of the two carried a shotgun, and Tom boasted that real marksmen (like himself) wouldn't bother with a weapon as unreliable as a shotgun. Taking offense, both boys got off the horses they were on, and a fistfight began. Predictably, given the odds, Tom got the worst of it. But even when the dust settled, the fight was not over.

As the older Horn recalled, "Then the big one picked up the gun and helped the small boy on the mare, and he raised the gun and shot poor, old 'Shed.' He whined and I could scarcely believe such a thing had been done. The big boy then got on the mare with the other one and they went off at a gallop. I carried 'Shed' home, and he died that night."

He added: "I believe that was the first and only real sorrow of my life."

There was no sorrow in leaving home, which he did at age thirteen. He could not do so fast enough. In addition to being a violent man, Tom Horn Sr. was a crook, in and out of trouble with the law for swindling and similar crimes. Tom Jr. feared being tarred with the same brush.

The day came when the teenager simply set off: "I started on foot. I headed west, and walked and walked day after day, stopping at farm houses to get my grub. Many a good woman would give me a lunch to take with me. I never went hungry, and as it was in July and August, I could sleep anywhere. One woman made me stay all day at her house, and wear some of her son's clothes while she washed mine and started me out in the world again as clean as a new dollar."

Next to nothing is known about his early travels, but by the time he was fifteen, Tom Horn was an army scout and became involved in many Indian campaigns, including Geronimo's surrender in 1886. During these years, he learned Spanish. Horn would later write that he had played a significant role in the surrender of Geronimo. It is true that as a scout he was involved in various meetings with Apache warriors because of his fluency in Spanish, but chances are good that Geronimo would have surrendered without Horn's intervention.

A frequent scout companion was the man known as Mickey Free. His is one of the more legendary lives in the American West. In January 1861, the twelve-year-old Felix Ward was abducted by a Pinal Apache raiding party. He was later traded to the Coyotero Apache, who are also known as White Mountain Apaches. The kidnapping had lasting implications for relations between the Apache and the United States.

When his stepfather, John Ward, returned from a business trip to his home on Sonoita Creek in Arizona, he learned from neighbors that his cattle and stepson had been taken by Apaches. He went immediately to Lieutenant Colonel Pitcairn Morrison at Fort Buchanan, reporting inaccurately that the kidnappers were Chiricahua Apaches. Lieutenant George Bascom and his Company C, Seventh Infantry, were assigned to rescue the boy. What happened next became known as the Bascom Affair, which triggered the Chiricahua Wars.

With orders to retrieve Felix Ward at all costs, Bascom led his troopers to Apache Pass to seek out Cochise, the head man of the Chiricahuas. Cochise insisted that he did not have the boy, but he thought he knew who did, and if given ten days, he would bring him in. Bascom had the Apaches surrounded, informing Cochise they would be held as hostages until the child was returned. Cochise escaped and captured his own white hostages to offer in exchange, but Bascom refused. A series of violent retaliatory actions by each side followed before the Chiricahua Apaches eventually declared war.

During this time, Felix was adopted and raised by Nayundiie, a White Mountain Apache. When old enough, in December 1872, he joined the U.S. Army's Apache Scouts, and within two years, he was promoted to the rank of sergeant. He was posted to Camp Verde to serve as an interpreter, where he met Al Sieber. The Civil War veteran, who had been severely wounded at Gettysburg, was chief of scouts for the army and was the man who had hired Tom Horn as an interpreter.[65]

Because the soldiers could not pronounce many of the scouts' Apache names, they gave them nicknames. With his prominent red hair and other features, the soldiers claimed the scout named Felix bore a resemblance to a character named "Mickey Free" in Charles Lever's 1840 novel, *Charles O'Malley: The Irish Dragoon.*[66]

According to Horn, as scouts and interpreters he and Micky Free had numerous adventures. "He spoke both Mexican and Apache like a professor, and was the wildest daredevil in the world at this time," he wrote of Free. "He had long, fiery red hair and one blue eye, the other one having been hooked out by a wounded deer when he was twelve years old. He had a small, red mustache and a 'mug' that looked like the original map of Ireland."

Horn claimed that because Geronimo took a shine to him, Horn was often selected to interpret for the Chiricahua leader during negotiations, which often included him having "more grievances than a railroad switchman."

Horn continued: "At last Geronimo stopped talking, for he had asked for everything he could think of, and he was a natural born genius at thinking of things."

---

65 In 1887, Sieber would be shot and wounded again. This time it was not a Confederate soldier but the Apache Kid. He and his followers escaped their reservation to prevent being jailed again. During his various battles and fights over the course of his life, Sieber received twenty-eight wounds. Still, he lived to be sixty-three, when it was the twenty-ninth wound that finally got him for good. In February 1907, while leading an Apache work crew building a road to the new Roosevelt Dam, Sieber was killed when a large boulder rolled over him. He was buried with military honors in Globe, Arizona.

66 After leaving the army in 1893, Free moved to the Fort Apache Indian Reservation and lived out the rest of his life as a farmer until his death in 1914. He married four times and had two sons and two daughters.

After helping to thwart Geronimo's final attempt at freedom, Horn was discharged as a scout. For a short time he was a miner in Aravaipa, Arizona, then there was his reported role in the Pleasant Valley War, also known, a bit more colorfully, as the Tonto Basin Feud. To be sure, there was nothing "pleasant" about a conflict that lasted over ten years and had the highest number of deaths of any range war in U.S. history. It began in 1882 and the combatants were the Graham family, who were cattle ranchers, and the Tewksburys, who were part-Native American and also ranchers but expanded their operations to sheep, a primary cause of the conflict.

Pleasant Valley is in Gila County but bloody events spilled over into Apache and Navaho Counties, all in Arizona. The original feud between the families soon involved entire cattlemen associations, sheepherders, hired guns, cowboys, and Arizona lawmen. The last known killing took place in 1892, and by then, it is believed that as many as fifty people had died, resulting in the near-annihilation of the men of the two feuding families. A political consequence was the chronic violence gave Arizona Territory a reputation for not being ready for statehood, and it did not become a state until 1912.

Two of the lowlights of the war: In February 1887, a Navaho employee of the Tewksburys was herding sheep in an area called the Mogollon Rim. Until that point, the rim had been tacitly accepted as the line across which sheep were not permitted. The Navaho was shot and killed by Tom Graham, who beheaded the corpse and left it as a warning or taunt after burying the body. In August, another member of the Graham family, William, was rounding up horses when he was shot in the gut. The young man managed to ride back to his home, but his wound was so severe that when he arrived his intestines were hanging out. He was able to divulge Ed Tewksbury as his murderer before, mercifully, he expired.

It was in between these gruesome events that Tom Horn arrived. In his autobiography, he writes, "Early in April of 1887, some of the boys came down from the Pleasant Valley, where there was a big rustler war going on and the rustlers were getting the best of the game." Horn says he was tired of working his mining claim, "so away we went." He contends that he "became the mediator" of the conflict, even serving as a deputy sheriff. However, it is much more likely that he was hired by one of the feuding families. Horn worked on a ranch owned by Robert Bowen, where he became one of the prime suspects in the disappearance of Mart Blevins.

One morning in August 1887, a number of horses were discovered to be missing from the nearby Canyon Creek Ranch and presumed to be stolen. "Old Man" Blevins went out, well-armed, in search of the horses and against the advice of his sons. Like the horses, he disappeared and was never to be seen again. After about a week of Mart being missing, his son Hampton "Hamp" Blevins and a group of other cowboys went out searching for him.

Finally, Mart Blevins was presumed dead, yet a body was never found. Stories about his fate circulated for many years. Three years after his disappearance, in 1890, a skeleton with a spike driven through the skull was found not far from the ranch, and many believe that this was Mart Blevins. But in 1894, a foreman for another cattle ranch on Cherry Creek found a human skull in a hollow tree on one side of the upper tributaries of that stream. Leaning against another tree was a rusty rifle that was identified as the property of Mart Blevins, with no other bones found in the area. Still, the murder of Mart Blevins was never solved.[67]

Tom Horn's closest brush with being a lawman may have come when he assisted Sheriff Glenn Reynolds in the hanging of three suspected rustlers of the Graham faction in August 1888. It seems that this grisly event prompted Horn to become more interested in law enforcement. He was hired by Pinkerton National Detective Agency. The idea was he

---

67 Though there had been dozens of deaths during the Pleasant Valley War, it ended with not a bang but a whimper. Ultimately, Edwin Tewksbury was the only adult male member left of the rival clans. After the second trial for the murder of Tom Graham resulted in his release, Tewksbury moved to Globe, married, sired four children, and died in 1904 at only age forty-six.

would emerge as a second "cowboy detective," following in the long-legged footsteps of Charlie Siringo. And in fact the two men crossed paths—in saloons, at least, more so than on cases.

Horn kept getting into legal scrapes, which persuaded James McParland at the Denver office to assign Horn as more of a roving gunman. Horn took this to mean assassin because he reportedly gunned down as many as seventeen men. He was pressured to resign by the Pinkerton Agency—he was respected as a tracker, but he was generating too much bad publicity.

Horn himself did not seem to have any regrets. He had a practical view of his abilities, saying, "Killing men is my specialty. I look at it as a business proposition, and I think I have a corner on the market." He saw that the next corner for him was in Wyoming, where in 1894 he went to work for the beef barons as a stock detective, receiving a bounty for every rustler he captured or killed. Horn probably had no idea that this was fine preparation for the profound impact he would have on Bandit Heaven.

19

A RED-LETTER DAY

Hoping to emulate Butch and the other big boys, what was dubbed the Junior Wild Bunch was formed in the fall of 1896. This was in the wake of the successful Montpelier bank job and before Cassidy and Elzy Lay relocated to Robbers Roost for the winter. During that interval, stories of the robbery, some told by Butch and Elzy themselves, circulated in Brown's Hole. Whether intended or not, they seeded a sort of hero worship among some listeners for the bandits who had pulled one over on the law.

The stories "told with great gusto around campfires and firesides, aroused the imaginations of the younger boys," Charles Kelly writes. With their own gang "they could see no reason why they should not be equally successful. After proving their mettle they would be eligible to join the older organization," meaning the Wild Bunch, led by Butch and Elzy.

The Junior Wild Bunch began with four members, the eldest being only twenty years old: George Harris, George Bain, Joe Rolls, and a companion identified just as "Shirley." Their outlaw experience thus far was, to be generous, limited. "Joe Rolls already had a reputation as the poorest horse thief in Brown's Hole," writes Kelly. "According to Sheriff Pope, Rolls used to wear out his stolen animals moving them from one place to another."

What happened to three of these Wild Bunch wannabes was less an homage to their elders than a gruesome glimpse of the fate that would befall many of the residents of Bandit Heaven during the next few years.

On a Tuesday afternoon in October 1896, four armed young men rode into Meeker, Colorado, seventy-five miles east of Brown's Hole. Stopping outside the Bank of Meeker on Main Street, they tied their horses to a freight wagon, and three of them entered the building. After two warning shots were fired, the eight store patrons and employees were disarmed and corralled in the center of the room. An estimated $1,600 was then placed in a sack. Everything seemed to be going smoothly, and the gunmen readied for a quick getaway.

But the warning shots, albeit dramatic, were a foolish gesture. They were heard by W. H. Clark, who was a deputy game warden. He immediately put out the call to help cover the exits of the Hugus store next to the Bank of Meeker as well as the bank itself. Meanwhile, inside the building, the young robbers were instructing their captives to walk single file out the door where their horses and the fourth man awaited.

The gunshots, calls for help, and Clark's shouting "attracted the attention of Tom Shervin of the Meeker Hotel, who ran down to the Hugus corner and seeing what was up gave the alarm," reported the *Meeker Herald*. "C. J. Duffy, who was passing at the time, 'caught on' and running up street, spread the alarm. Phil Barnhart also gave the alarm down street, and in less than three minutes' time every avenue of escape was guarded and a dozen unerring marksmen were awaiting the appearance of the robbers while the others were hastening to the scene of action."

Once the trio exited the bank behind the hostages, they found themselves staring down the barrels of rifles, shotguns, and pistols in nearly every direction. The next foolish gesture was to rule out the option of surrender. Instead, they chose to try to shoot their way out of a nearly impossible situation.

The head bandit took the first shot and struck Deputy Clark in the chest. Then, as soon as the two other bandits left the protection of their human shields to mount their horses, all hell broke loose. Volleys of shots seemingly came from every tree, wagon, and window in sight. When the smoke cleared, two of the bank robbers and one of their horses lay dead on the ground. Two unfortunate hostages had also been hit. A third bandit, though struck several times, limped down a side street while continuing to shoot until he finally fell to the ground. He lived for another hour or so until, according to the *Meeker Herald,* he proclaimed "Oh, mother!" and took his final breath.

The man who died after the shooting stopped was George Harris. George Bain and "Shirley" had been the two young bandits who had died earlier. Joe Rolls might have been a poor horse thief, but he was smart enough to jump on his horse and ride off when the first alarm was sounded.

The bandits had learned something from the Butch Cassidy method, though they never got to use it. A camp consisting of rifles, ammunition, and a relay of horses was discovered about six miles northwest of Meeker. Seventeen days after the shoot-out the horses were found tied-up without food or water, and one had already died. However, the other, sturdier horses were nursed back to health.

Despite such a serious wound, Deputy Clark made a full recovery, as did the two wounded hostages.

In its subsequent coverage of the violent event, the *Meeker Herald* intoned, "Tuesday, October 13, will stand as a red-letter day in Meeker's history. On that day three bank robbers and would-be murderers were sent to their final account. The work of the holdup showed evidence of amateurishness in many particulars but the lightning-like promptness by which they were disposed of showed that the citizens of this town know how to act and shoot."

The bodies of the three dead thieves were put on exhibit in Meeker and photographs were taken. They were finally buried two days later.

The *Herald* concluded, "Thus was justice meted out to three bold bandits who struck the wrong town in which to ply their villainous calling."

Joe Rolls had ridden hard to Brown's Hole, where he delivered the bad news, which was soon confirmed by other reports. No more bank robberies for him—Rolls returned to being a simple horse thief.

Supposedly joining Butch Cassidy and Elzy Lay in Robbers Roost that winter of 1896–97 was the Sundance Kid. And he did not travel alone. Charles Leerhsen writes, "According to some witnesses," when the gang headed to Robbers Roost, "the beautiful Ethel [Place] was one of the women who traveled with them and played a role in a winterlong idyll that set the tone for a stretch of excitement—the stuff of which outlaws dream."

What would become that "stretch of excitement" was gestating during the winter and would bloom in the spring. With the bank robbery in Montpelier having turned out so well, why not do another one? The location chosen was Castle Gate in Utah because all five hundred or so residents of the town worked for the Pleasant Valley Coal Company and every two weeks the payroll of as much as $8,000 arrived via the Denver and Rio Grande Railroad.

And there was not heightened security or much of any security at all. A wagon simply collected the bags of money at the train station, hauled them to the company's office, and when the time came to pay the workers, someone in the building let loose with a loud steam whistle. And so it was that on April 21, 1897, Butch Cassidy and Elzy Lay were in position to pick up the payroll before the whistle alerted the workers to do so.

The day after the event, the *Salt Lake Herald* informed readers of what had transpired in Castle Gate. The reporting relied on what was relayed by an eyewitness, E. L. Carpenter, a cashier for the Pleasant

Valley Coal Company who the newspaper described as "as plucky a little man as walks."

That day, Butch Cassidy and Elzy Lay waited outside of the company's main building, beneath the stairs that led up into a higher entrance. The outlaws soon confronted Carpenter and another employee, ordering the workers, "Drop them sacks and hold up your hands." Once the money had been handed over, one of the outlaws, Carpenter said, began "whirling a sixshooter in his hand and firing shots promiscuously to create consternation."

When a sufficient level of consternation was achieved, Butch and Elzy hurried toward the Halfway House and began to cut telegraph wires. They did not act fast enough, however, because a message did get through to Gus Donant, the sheriff of Carbon County. He hastily gathered three other men, and the quartet set off. They, in turn, were not fast enough. As the *Herald* declared, "The robbers were lucky to escape that day, but the effects of this crime would shock all of Utah and the West." Indeed, newspapers as far away as Sacramento covered the robbery.

Another, less prominent, or plucky, eyewitness and thus not named, claimed that during their escape, Elzy and Butch "gave an impromptu demonstration of horsemanship rodeo style for the 100 or so open-mouthed witnesses" as well as a shoot-out straight from a movie that involved a man "being robbed and chasing outlaws around in his bedroom slippers, and continued with Butch Cassidy, loot in hand, chasing his horse around Castle Gate."

Even less believable was a claim by another supposed witness that Carpenter chased the robbers "in a locomotive detached from the rest of its train." However, there was some truth to this, as we'll see.

The *Herald*'s account left out a mishap that almost landed Butch back in jail. Elzy had reached their horses first and mounted his. When Butch hastily approached, he tossed the two bags containing the stolen gold coins, silver, and cash. (The entire take would total $7,000.)

While catching them, Elzy let the reins to Butch's horse loose and the animal, distressed by the sudden commotion, took off. Elzy chased it while a crowd of miners, realizing their pay had just been purloined, took off after Butch. He suddenly turned and aimed his pistol at them. They stopped in their tracks. Sullenly, they watched as Elzy returned with Butch's horse and then the two bandits exited Meeker, leaving clouds of dust in their wake.

Chagrined Pleasant Valley Coal Company executives discovered they could not telegraph other lawmen, thanks to the thieves' sabotage. All they could do was order a train locomotive to fire up and steam down the tracks to Price, where the next sheriff's office was. By the time the call for posse volunteers went out, Butch and Elzy were long gone.

20

GO DIRECTLY TO JAIL

While Butch Cassidy and Elzy Lay were busy, where were their comrades Kid Curry and the Sundance Kid? Occupied with their own gang.

Sundance and Curry had formed a Wild Bunch offshoot outfit and with it planned to rob the bank in Belle Fourche, South Dakota. George "Flatnose" Curry and Harvey Logan's brother Lonie were to be part of this enterprise along with minor players Tom O'Day and Walt Punteney.

The gestation of this plan took longer than anticipated, so it was not until June 28 that the six men rode into Belle Fourche. The previous weekend the town had enjoyed a reunion of the region's Civil War veterans, which was good for business owners, who had subsequently deposited their surge in earnings in the Butte County Bank. It was estimated that the institution held assets of around $30,000, the equivalent of over $1 million in today's money.

A competent group of criminals—especially one led by Butch Cassidy—would have figured out the best way to relieve the bank of such a bounty. But that was not what rode into Belle Fourche that

Monday morning. Tom O'Day, an affable man but not the brightest of the bunch, was unwisely chosen to remain outside the building as the lookout as the other five thieves entered.

Inside the bank at the time were the cashier, Arthur Marble, his assistant, Harry Ticknor, a shopkeeper, Sam Arnold, and three customers. As the bandits burst in demanding the money, Marble and Ticknor complied, offering everything they had. That was when the Sundance Kid and Kid Curry and their colleagues realized this job would not turn out well—all the cash on hand totaled just ninety-seven dollars, or a haul of sixteen dollars and change per gang member.

As the take was being dropped into an embarrassingly large sack, a hardware store worker across the street spotted what was going on and shouted an alarm. O'Day's response was to fire off a warning shot, which spooked his horse, causing it to run off. The robbers ran out of the bank, mounted the remaining five horses, and rode away.

Literally left in the dust, O'Day ran to a nearby outhouse. He tolerated its odors for only a few moments; then he exited to be greeted with handcuffs in addition to fresh air. Adding insult to injury, the local jail had recently burned down, so authorities had no recourse but to hold O'Day in the vault of the very bank he and his associates had just robbed.

Perhaps feeling a tad guilty, when the thieves reached the top of a hill they paused to look down to see if they could spot O'Day. Instead, they saw gaining on them a Belle Fourche blacksmith who had ridden out from the town to confront them. Alas, the bold blacksmith's horse was shot out from under him by another citizen perched on the second floor of a flower mill who had been aiming at the outlaws. O'Day would be on his own: the bandits then turned and rode away.[68]

_____

68 The dimwitted O'Day, sardonically saddled with the nickname "Peep," was not reformed from his Belle Fourche experience and he continued as a minor criminal. That checkered career ended in November 1903 near Casper, Wyoming, when he was arrested while in possession of a herd of stolen horses. Convicted and sent to prison, O'Day was released in June 1908 whereupon he settled down, got married, and served as a celebrity of sorts at a saloon in Deadwood, South Dakota. He died sometime in 1930, around sixty-eight years old.

Sundance's ad hoc gang made their way to Hole-in-the-Wall in Wyoming, along the way evading a posse led by George Fuller, the Butte County sheriff. One would think that after such a futile escapade this group would stay there. They did, until September, when, with the ninety-seven dollars long gone, they decided that a bank in Red Lodge offered a more promising opportunity.

It did, but not for this particular gang, which had been whittled down to Sundance, Kid Curry, and Punteney. When the three men arrived in Red Lodge, the strategy was to bribe the marshal, Byron St. Clair, to ignore the robbery about to take place—or better yet, to leave town. However, the lawman, being either honest or underbribed, alerted the county sheriff, John Dunn. He pulled together a posse that included the stock detective W. D. "Lame Billy" Smith, who just happened to have participated in the arrest of Harry Longabaugh at the N Bar Ranch in June 1887.

Sheriff Dunn and his posse caught up with the unprepared trio on September 22 as they were setting up camp on the Musselshell River, twenty miles north of Lavinia, Montana. Gunshots were exchanged, and Kid Curry's horse was shot. Worse, Curry himself was shot in the wrist. He was chased down and arrested as were Punteney and the Sundance Kid, who had obviously shown himself not to be the equal of Butch Cassidy in planning and executing robberies.

While in a calaboose in Deadwood—a fellow inmate turned out to be the former lookout Tom O'Day—Sundance and Curry waited for their opportunity. It came on the evening of October 31. When Deputy Sheriff John Mansfield and his wife stopped by after attending late Sunday church services, the inmates tricked the lawman into opening the cell doors. The couple were roughed up a bit as O'Day, Sundance, Kid Curry, and a fourth inmate, William Moore, busted out. Lonie Logan had tethered four horses behind the jail, and within a minute, the escapees were hurtling out of Deadwood. The posse that went after them contained as many as sixty men.

Two days later, O'Day, not much better as a fugitive than as a bank robber, was recaptured, as was Moore, not far from Spearfish. The more skilled Kids—Sundance and Curry—outfoxed and outrode their pursuers and disappeared somewhere along the Outlaw Trail.

While the Sundance Kid had been having his rather feeble fling as a gang leader, Butch Cassidy was solidifying his hold on leadership of the Wild Bunch. During the years after he had been released from the Wyoming penitentiary "notorious desperadoes from across the West made their way to Robbers Roost, or Brown's Park, or Hole in the Wall," observes Thom Hatch in *The Last Outlaws*. "Most of these wanted men soon made the acquaintance of Butch. Many had heard about the mastermind Butch Cassidy and wanted to throw in with him and his partners for adventure and profit."

Somewhere along the way, as the size of Butch's operation ebbed and flowed with various bandits coming and going, it acquired the Hole-in-the-Wall Gang moniker. Apparently, the Hole-in-the-Wall in Wyoming was the one Bandit Heaven location most associated with Cassidy, and newspapers, bank officials, and even the Pinkerton National Detective Agency referred to his gang that way. It did have more of a ring to it than Brown's Park Bandits or Robbers Roost Ruffians.

As flattering as it was to be seen as a bold and cunning leader of the outlaw pack, the increasing attention put a bigger bull's-eye on Butch. As the activities of the inept gang led by Sundance and Kid Curry and the doomed Junior Wild Bunch had shown, there were offshoots of the larger organization committing crimes. Editors eager for large-type headlines often attributed almost every bank and train robbery to Butch. He seemed to be everywhere in Montana, Utah, Colorado, and Wyoming at the same time. Every man who marched into a bank with a pistol demanding money was Butch Cassidy. From time to time, he was. But much more often, he was not.

If the Federal Bureau of Investigation had existed then, Cassidy would have been Public Enemy No. 1.[69] As it was, thanks to his growing

---

69 Certainly, no threat was posed by J. Edgar Hoover, who in 1897 was just two years old.

notoriety as well as genuine success in committing crimes and eluding capture, Butch had become the poster boy for what remained of the Wild West outlaw. It was time to do something with Butch Cassidy as the primary target. Governors were being pressured by bank officials and railroad barons to get Butch behind bars. Or whatever had to be done: One governor, Alva Adams of Colorado, boasted that he had hired James Catron, a bounty hunter, specifically to track Cassidy and bring him or his body in.[70]

With the fire being turned up under his feet, Butch decided to have them take him elsewhere. Soon after 1898 dawned, he lit out for New Mexico. The ever-loyal Elzy Lay went along. Maybe this was a ripe time as any for the good friends to go straight and settle down far away from Bandit Heaven. If this had actually happened, then neither would the Wilcox job—which changed everything.

---

70 Catron spent more time in saloons forecasting how he was going to find and capture Cassidy than actually doing so, and Governor Adams rescinded his assignment.

21

OFF TO WAR?

The holdup of a train near the town of Wilcox in Albany County, Wyoming, took place on June 2, 1899. It was, as some historical events are wont to be, both a high point for what had become the most famous outlaw gang in America and the beginning of its end. This pivotal heist might not have happened if Butch Cassidy and a few of his colleagues had followed through and joined the U.S. Army to fight in a war.

As ludicrous as this seems, it almost happened.

It is not known exactly where Cassidy, the Sundance Kid, and other members of the Wild Bunch holed up in the winter of 1897–98. Butch may well have been working as a ranch hand in the less-frigid climes of New Mexico. In his biography of Butch, Charles Leerhsen tells us that in his 1928 memoir, William French, an Irishman and former British army officer who owned the WS Ranch, recalled Cassidy and Elzy Lay accompanying Perry Tucker, the ranch's new foreman, when he showed up to work. French willingly accepted the names the two ranch hands gave him—Butch was Jim Lowe, and Elzy reached back into his past to come up with William McGuinness.

They turned out to be good and reliable workers during the first few months of 1898. French relished "Jim's" cowpuncher skills, observing that the way "he handled those poor cattle over the long and dusty trail of over two hundred miles was a revelation. . . . Truly, the way these two men handled stock was a marvel."

The WS Ranch owner was equally pleased with the reduction in rustling. Like many operations, French's had suffered losses of cattle and especially horses, and the year before, he had been the victim of an especially brazen act. Not only had a prized saddle horse been stolen but a buggy team as well. The rustler responsible was believed to be Tom Ketchum, one of the more ruthless robbers who met one of the more macabre ends.

As young men, Tom, who would acquire the nickname "Black Jack," and his older brother, Sam, left their home in Texas to become cowboys in the Pecos River Valley in New Mexico. They soon found that this occupation paled in comparison to being bandits. The Ketchum Gang was formed and its first known act was relieving an Atchison, Topeka, and Santa Fe train of a large payroll in 1892.

With such an auspicious start, the Ketchum brothers kept traveling the Outlaw Trail. When in Brown's Hole, a regular stop was to visit Herb and Elizabeth Bassett and their daughters. Over the years, men joined and dropped out of the gang, including, in 1895, another set of brothers, Harvey and Lonie Logan. After only a few months, though, they were former members. The two duos had a falling out, probably over money, and Kid Curry and Lonie left. The Ketchums continued their robbing and rustling ways, which would include pilfering the precious horses from the WS Ranch.

A pivotal series of events for the Ketchum crew began when, without Tom present, Sam led the gang on a robbery of a train agent at Twin Mountain, in New Mexico.[71] With the loot, the bandits steered their horses to the supposed safety of the mountains southwest of Raton. But the next day, a posse led by Sheriff Ed Farr of Huerfano

---

71 It has been reported that during this raid, one of the participants was Elzy Lay.

County in Colorado and W. H. Reno, a special agent with the Colorado & Southern Railroad, with five deputies, found the bandits' trail
and tracked them to a camp near Cimarron. During the exchange of
shots, Sam Ketchum and two deputies were badly wounded. Ketchum
was taken into custody.

The rest of the gang escaped but not for long. The posse, minus
the two wounded deputies, found the outlaws the next day in Turkey
Creek Canyon. There was another shoot-out, and this time, Henry
Love, a deputy, was mortally wounded while Sheriff Farr was killed.[72]
While the lawmen were occupied, Sam Ketchum jumped on a horse
and fled. But he was found a few days later by Special Agent Reno at
the home of a rancher, and Ketchum was captured again.

He would never stand trial. Sam Ketchum was taken to the Santa
Fe Territorial Prison, where he died from the gunshot wounds suffered
in the first confrontation.

Somehow, Sam Ketchum had apparently been unaware—obviously,
to his detriment—that just a few weeks earlier his brother had tried
to rob a train nearing the Twin Mountain stop. Tom was also unsuc-
cessful. The conductor, Frank Harrington, recognized the notorious
Black Jack approaching the moving train. He grabbed a shotgun and
shot Tom Ketchum in the arm, knocking him off his horse. The train
continued, and the next day a posse came out and found the badly
wounded bandit still lying beside the tracks. He was taken to Trinidad,
Colorado, where his right arm had to be amputated.

Unlike his older brother, Tom Ketchum recovered from his wound.
Once healthy enough, the thief's next stop was back to New Mexico,
where he was tried and convicted in Clayton. The judge sentenced him
to death.

Ketchum then accumulated a few unhappy distinctions. One was

---

72 The death of Henry Love, of the Colfax County Sheriff's Department in New Mexico, proved
that when your time was up, your time was up. During the shoot-out a bullet struck a knife that was
in his pocket, causing the knife to cut him. He had used the knife to treat sick cattle with a form of
anthrax and was thus infected with the disease. He succumbed to it four days later.

that after he was found guilty and sentenced to death, he would become the only person ever hanged in Union County. He was the only person condemned to die in New Mexico for being convicted of "felonious assault upon a railway train"—a law later found to be unconstitutional. And he literally lost his head.

This occurred because of an unlucky combination. During his time in jail, the cuisine must have been better than most calaboose fare because Black Jack gained quite a bit of weight. Apparently, he could shovel it in with one arm as well as two. And in Clayton, no one had any experience in conducting hangings, and the ad hoc executioner used a rope that was too long. On the day of the hanging, April 26, 1901, Ketchum's last words were, "Goodbye. Please dig my grave very deep. All right, hurry up." Moments after he dropped through the trap door, the added weight and accelerating speed combined to rip Black Jack's head off.

Three years earlier, Ketchum and other rustlers in the area had been persuaded by Cassidy (possibly helped along, also, due to their being friends with Elzy Lay) to keep their stealing to a minimum, so the two hands had a happy employer in Mr. French. And so far, the governor of New Mexico had not teamed up with the other governors along the Outlaw Trail in schemes to rid the region of its most notorious outlaws. However unlikely, it was possible that Cassidy, perhaps enjoying his sojourn and being at peace with the peace officers there, thought about extending his stay indefinitely.

But in the spring of 1898, Butch began considering if his skills would translate to a military setting. In April, a declaration of war was made by the United States against Spain. Like many Western outlaws, Butch had probably paid little attention two months earlier when an American ship—especially one named the *Maine*, after a state more than two thousand miles away—had exploded in a harbor in Havana, Cuba. While it was certainly a tragedy that 266 people died, to Cassidy and others on the Outlaw Trail, an event in Cuba might as well have taken place in China.

On the other hand, a war could mean two things to a wavering bandit—action and amnesty. Newspapers in the West exhorted young men to volunteer and punish the Cubans and their former Spanish overlords for their perfidy. Among those who gave it serious thought were a group of cowboys and outlaws who convened at Steamboat Springs in Colorado. They included Butch Cassidy, Sundance, Kid Curry, Lonie Curry, and Elzy Lay.

One might wonder why the U.S. Army would accept bandits—was it really that desperate for soldiers? It was true that when 1898 began, the army was understrength, totaling a mere 26,000 men. On April 22, gearing up for the war declaration two days later, Congress passed the Mobilization Act that allowed for an army of at first 125,000 volunteers (later increased to 200,000) and a regular army of 65,000. So, conceivably, almost anyone could be swept along in this flood of new soldiers. Unless a man declared himself to be a criminal, enlistment offices simply accepted a signed application.

And suddenly, there was a precedent. Cassidy and company may have known by the Steamboat Springs meeting that one member of their loosely affiliated gang, Dave Lant, had already signed up. He'd had a more urgent motivation—thanks to Harry Tracy, who in any era would have been labeled a cop killer. The *Seattle Daily Times* once wrote about him, "In all the criminal lore of the country there is no record equal to that of Harry Tracy for cold-blooded nerve, desperation, and thirst for crime. Jesse James, compared with Tracy, is a Sunday school teacher."

He was born in Wisconsin in about 1874 as Harry Severns. At a young age, he ran away from home, landing in Chicago, where he worked in the stockyards. Later, he migrated to Colorado, where he labored in the goldfields before moving to Billings, Montana, where he learned the cowboy trade—and cattle rustling. Unlike Butch Cassidy, he could not avoid killing: After murdering a deputy sheriff named Arly Grimes, he fled back to Colorado, where he reportedly gunned down two more men.

After the death of a lawman named Hoy (an event soon to be detailed), Tracy made his way to Portland, Oregon, where he teamed up with an outlaw named Dave Merrill. After a new crime spree, they were arrested in February 1899 and given long sentences to serve in the Salem prison. However, on June 9, 1902, with the help of a female accomplice, Tracy and Merrill escaped the facility, killing three men and wounding another in the process. While the two were on the run, Tracy felt Merrill was becoming weak and so he killed him near Chehalis, Washington. Tracy went on to the Seattle area, where during a shoot-out he killed Detective Charles Raymond and a deputy named John Williams.

He was pursued to a ranch southeast of Creston, Washington, where a gunfight occurred on August 6. In the melee, Tracy killed posse members Cornelious Rowley and Enoch Breece. However, the cornered outlaw took a shot in the leg. Surrounded by authorities and unable to escape this time, Tracy committed suicide rather than be captured.

Back in early 1898, after another prison breakout, Tracy and Dave Lant had the misfortune to encounter a man named Swede Johnson and be with him in March when he murdered William Stang, still only a teenager. They were now a trio on the run, and things got worse. They were on their way to Douglas Mountain in Colorado when their trail was picked up by a posse. Leading it was a lawman named Valentine Hoy.

The posse caught up to the three outlaws in Lodore Canyon. Hoy made the mistake of riding too far out front and was an easy target for Tracy, who shot him in the heart, killing him instantly. The rest of the posse turned tail and rode off.

But immediately a new and bigger posse formed, including volunteers from hundreds of miles away. The outlaws were finally located and surrounded near Lookout Mountain in Colorado. At the height where they were cornered, the air was very cold and getting colder as night approached. The falling temperature, more than threats from the posse, persuaded Tracy, Lant, and Johnson to give up.

The jail in Hahn's Peak, Colorado, like other jails, was no match for Tracy and his companions and they soon vacated it. They were captured once more, though, and moved to a calaboose in Aspen. They escaped from this one too, with Tracy nearly killing a guard with a lead pipe.

Lant wanted out of a life on the lam and the war mobilization gave him that opportunity. He ambled into a recruiting office and enlisted, using a fake name. He endured the rigors of basic training and was shipped off to the Philippines, where, according to Thom Hatch, "Lant served with distinction and was highly decorated for bravery in action."

Maybe Cassidy and his colleagues could also follow the path to war against foreigners instead of the Outlaw Trail. But on further thought, the idea was rejected. The most patriotism the gang showed was a note sent to Governor Richards of Wyoming vowing not to rob any trains. This was actually a worthy gesture because the railroads were carrying troops and goods and were more vulnerable because of all the peace officers who were now on duty elsewhere in the country or fighting overseas.

Cassidy kept his promise. And before the end of the year, the Spanish-American War was over, with the U.S. celebrating a victory. For bandits, it was time to begin robbing banks and trains again.

22

─•─✦─•─

A MILE WEST OF WILCOX

It was almost dawn on that first Friday in June 1899 when the Union Pacific Overland Flyer No. 1 pulled into the Medicine Bow, Wyoming, station. The engineer W. R. "Grindstone" Jones, still rattled by the experience of being robbed—and with dynamite, no less—had a telegram sent to his superiors in Omaha: "First Section No. 1 held up a mile west of Wilcox. Express car blown open, mail car damaged. Safe blown open; contents gone."

Within minutes of when Jones's terse report was received, a dispatch was sent from the Union Pacific Railroad offices offering a staggering $1,000 reward for each and every one of the train robbers "dead or alive." Later, the Pacific Express Company, whose safe was robbed, made the same offer, as did the U.S. government. It was believed that six bandits had been in on the job, so at $3,000 a head, the total reward was $18,000. A bounty like that could buy a lawman a less risky career or even retirement.

The railroad company quickly had the No. 4, a specially outfitted train kept ready in Laramie, deployed. It contained cars for horses, equipment, food, and men. This posse train arrived at Wilcox Station about 9:00 A.M., seven hours after the holdup began. Although the Union Pacific had its own detective force, it also brought the Burlington Railroad and the Pinkerton National Detective Agency into the chase. These professionals joined with the local posses, one of which even employed bloodhounds. Wyoming's Governor DeForest Richards also dispatched Company C of the state militia. Within twenty-four hours, nearly one hundred peace officers, detectives, soldiers, and bounty hunters were out chasing the train robbers.

The explosive Wilcox heist would become one of the American West's most famous train robberies. Some historians point to it as the peak of Cassidy's criminal career, while others claim he was not there at all in the early morning hours of June 2.

While Butch Cassidy has often been credited as the mastermind, there have been doubts expressed over the decades that he took part in the Wilcox heist. It has been pointed out that in January 1896 when he had been pardoned by Governor Richards, Cassidy had pledged to never again participate in any crimes within the borders of Wyoming—or at least serious ones like robbing a train. And it has been reported that shortly after the Wilcox job, Butch ran into William Simpson, his onetime friend who had put him behind bars. The attorney accused Butch of going back on his word, but Butch assured him that he had nothing whatever to do with the Wilcox robbery.

How then to explain that Butch received an equal share of the stolen loot—for just planning the job? There was no report of Cassidy being anywhere else at the time of the Wilcox heist. The *New York Herald* needed no convincing—it published a photo of Butch, obtained from the Wyoming State Penitentiary, along with an article that recounted the daring robbery and the subsequent death of a lawman in somewhat breathless prose. No doubt this made E. H. Harriman, owner of the Union Pacific Railroad, fit to be tied when he read the newspaper in his Fifth Avenue apartment.

And it is worth noting that Charles Leerhsen, author of the most recent authoritative biography of Cassidy, puts Butch on the scene.

He writes, "It was his first train robbery, and it played out like a rough draft of what you see in the movies." He later adds, "Some scholars still insist Butch never went to Wilcox. Really, for a master of misdirection like Butch, there could be no finer compliment."

It was a formidable vehicle that Cassidy had chosen to rob. The Union Pacific Overland Flyer No. 1 had two sections, each pulled by its own locomotive. The first section was flagged down by two men, Butch and Kid Curry, with red lanterns at milepost No. 609 at 2:18 that rainy morning. Thinking that a small wooden bridge ahead might have washed out overnight, Jones brought this first section to a screeching stop. It was the prudent thing to do, but it would cost his company a lot of money.

The two men, wearing masks, boarded the locomotive and ordered Jones and the fireman, named Dietrick, to pull forward to the bridge and then stop again. Dynamite had already been fastened under the trestle. It was ignited and Jones was again ordered to pull ahead and "be quick about it." When he moved too slowly for the outlaws, that was when an aggravated Kid Curry clubbed him with a gun butt.

The train had barely cleared it when the bridge erupted, with flames and debris clawing the air toward the dark clouds. The structure was not destroyed but the bandits had prevented the train's second section, whose headlight they had seen, from following. They then told Jones to stop the first section so that the passenger cars could be uncoupled. Probably with some relief, the conductor, a man named Storey, walked through the car, telling passengers that, yes, a robbery was underway but the passengers would be safe if they remained in their seats. The mail and express cars were what interested the thieves. Following the bandits' orders, Jones and Dietrick pulled ahead another two miles.

They stopped when told to, and out of the darkness four more thieves appeared—the Sundance Kid, Lonie Curry, George "Flatnose" Currie, and a Logan cousin, Bob Lee. Three of the masked men herded Jones and Dietrick over to the mail car and ordered the clerks inside, Robert Lawson and Burt Bruce, to open up. When the clerks did not immediately comply, the door disappeared in another blast of dynamite.

If the mail car had contained plenty of loot, Charles Woodcock might have been spared his ordeal. But it was slim pickings in the first car, so the bandits moved on to the express car. The messenger Woodcock was ordered to open up, and he too refused. Try, try again: the thieves put a match to a couple of sticks of dynamite and easily blew the express car open. Whoever had measured out the amount of explosive had overestimated, and the car's roof and one side were turned into toothpicks.

Fortunately, the defiant messenger was only dazed in the explosion. Woodcock was unable to supply the bandits with the combinations to the two Pacific Express Co. safes (or this was one more act of defiance). With no hesitation, more dynamite was used to blow open the safes. This charge proved to be the right amount, saving the bandits from harm too.

By 4:15 A.M., the six bandits had gathered unsigned bank notes, cash, nineteen scarf pins, twenty-nine gold-plated cuff button pairs, and four Elgin watches. The initial estimate claimed a total of $30,000 was taken.[73] Butch, Sundance, and the others hopped on their horses and took off to the north. They knew where they would be safe.

Once the bandits had left the scene, the crew gingerly moved the train forward. The explosion, thankfully, had not derailed the train. In Medicine Bow, Jones, who had suffered a painful scalp wound, sent the telegram and a few minutes later sent another. It reported that "the bent of the bridge was shattered." The damage turned out not to be so severe and soon the bridge was in sound enough condition for trains to rumble across it.

Oddly, a few Wyoming newspapers carried the story that the gang

---

73 Five years later, in 1904, the Union Pacific superintendent W. L. Park wrote that the railroad had actually lost more than $50,000, some of it in gold.

leader was the hapless Tom O'Day, and two of the men accompanying him on the job were local toughs Bob Taylor and Manuel Manetta. Then another area man named Cavanaugh was accused. However, the professional detectives focused their full attention on members of the Wild Bunch. They were pretty much convinced once the train crew provided them with telling physical descriptions, even though the men had been masked.

One of those descriptions was recorded as, "One man about 31 or 32 years of age . . . 5'9" . . . 185 . . . blue eyes . . . peculiar nose, flattened at bridge." This was a pretty close match for George "Flat-nose" Currie. Another description recorded was, "Two men looked like brothers . . . 5'7" and 5'5" . . . about 28 and 30 . . . very dark complexion . . . 1/4 Cherokee . . . dark hair & eyes." This indicated the Logan boys, now known more as Kid and Lonie Curry. Given the three identified, it was assumed, only half-correct, that the other train robbers were the Sundance Kid, Ben Kilpatrick (who was sometimes referred to as the "Tall Texan"), and another Wild Bunch regular, Will Carver.

While the authorities were gathering information, Cassidy and his cohorts were getting farther away. Predictably, the bandits, to outrun the posse, had set up horse relays along their escape route. Feeling safe enough when they reached Lost Cabin, southwest of Hole-in-the-Wall, the gang stopped and divided up their plunder.

Then, to further enhance their chances of evading the law, they split up. One group consisted of Butch, Sundance, and Bob Lee. The other group was "Flatnose" Currie and the Curry brothers. They turned out to be the unlucky ones.

When the trio had stopped off to water and rest their horses at a ranch near Horse Ranch, Wyoming, the owner, Al Hudspeth, had figured out who they were, though he pretended not to. As soon as the outlaws left, Hudspeth alerted lawmen. A ten-man posse led by Sheriff Josiah Hazen of Converse County set off at full speed. Born in Illinois, the forty-four-year-old Hazen had worked in Wyoming as a cattleman, operator of a livery stable, and had part interest in a local copper mine before becoming the county sheriff in 1897. Along the way, he had married a waitress, Nettie Burlingham, and the couple had two sons.

On June 6, the posse caught up to the bandits at Castle Creek, a deep ravine surrounded by rocks and crevices some seventy-five miles from the holdup site and six miles northwest of Casper.[74] Obviously not expecting the law to be so hard behind them, Currie and Kid and Lonie Curry were occupying an abandoned cabin.

However, the outlaws saw the lawmen approach and were well hidden. After dismounting, the posse men unknowingly walked right in on them. Joe Hazen, as the leader, was out in front, and Kid Curry shot him. The wound would prove to be fatal.

The remaining lawmen were so shocked by the sheriff's sudden demise that they concentrated on hiding, giving the Currys and Currie the opportunity to sneak away. However, to do so, they had to leave their horses behind and carry what stolen loot they could.

When the posse realized the trio was gone and the danger had passed, they put Hazen's body across his horse and made their way to the town of Douglas. There, somewhat red-faced, they claimed that the outlaws had managed to ambush them in part because of a relatively new invention, smokeless gunpowder.

What was indisputable was that a gang of bandits, led by arguably the most famous outlaw left in the not-as–Wild West, had a spectacular success robbing a Union Pacific train and it had resulted in the death of a brave (if unwise) sheriff. This could not stand. The *Cheyenne Tribune* declared it "one of the most daring holdups in the western country."

The railroad signed a contract with the Pinkerton National Detective Agency to track the bandits down. In turn, William Pinkerton assigned who he considered his best field man to the case. Charlie

---

74 In later years, this area was renamed Teapot Dome because it was involved the scandal involving its fraudulent leasing by Secretary of the Interior Albert S. Fall during Warren Harding's administration.

Siringo would be accompanied by another veteran detective, W. O. Sayles. And a direct line could be drawn from the Wilcox job to another man hired—Tom Horn. However, he would not be acting in the capacity of detective or lawman. His assignment was to be an assassin, and his targets would be those who called Bandit Heaven home.

ACT IV

FALL FROM HEAVEN

23

RED FLAGS

To William Pinkerton, the Wilcox job was also a tipping point for his detective agency. And by extension, he pondered, for the future of law enforcement in the American West.

Public enemy number one was a "train robbers syndicate," the term he used for Butch Cassidy and his mix-and-match companions who comprised the Wild Bunch gangs. If no one was punished for the Wilcox crime, how would that look to outlaws everywhere west of the Missouri River? Worse, getting away with it could encourage a new crop of bandits, yet another generation of crooks. They could begin popping up like prairie dogs, raiding and evading and disappearing into the Bandit Heaven hideouts instead of being captured and tried in court for their depredations.

Such ruminations may have kept Pinkerton awake during nights at his Chicago home. It could have been while thrashing about in twisted sheets when he composed (and later dictated) the message he would send to James McParland in Denver, warning that this "syndicate" was "composed of outlaws and thieves headed by a cowboy gambler and rustler [Cassidy], and is composed of members of the Curry and Logan gangs [and] they intend to make railroads and express companies their victims."

This feverish scenario of escalating lawlessness just when a new century offered a more civilized society may have already haunted the sleep of the Denver branch manager. According to Nathan Ward in his Siringo biography, *Son of the Old West*, McParland had in his office a map of the western United States adorned with tiny flags where robberies had taken place. White flags denoted resolved robberies, with the bandits either in jail or dead. Red flags symbolized the irritation of unsolved crimes and the crooks laughing at the law, jeopardizing the credibility of the Pinkerton National Detective Agency along with it. "As the century closed out," Ward writes, "the pattern of robberies still flagged in red on his map troubled him enough to summon the best detectives he knew to Denver for a conference."

With Pinkerton's blessing, those detectives were invited. One was W. O. Sayles, who was called "Billy." The other was Charlie Siringo, whose thousands of miles traveled in pursuit of criminals had earned him an elevated status, certainly in McParland's eyes.

Not much is known about the life of Billy Sayles—unlike Siringo, he did not write autobiographies. The former Montana cowboy was well-regarded by his Pinkerton higher-ups, and he and Siringo had collaborated four years earlier on a stolen-gold case in Juneau, Alaska. Sayles had just concluded an investigation that had taken him even farther away—this time, to South Africa—and had reported to William Pinkerton in Chicago for his next assignment. Teaming him with another successful and seasoned operative made for a formidable detecting duo.

Between the time of Charlie Siringo and his wife, Lillie, going their separate ways in 1897 and the Wilcox train robbery two years later, the Pinkerton man had remained busy. A cattle-swindling case had taken him back to the LX Ranch in the Texas Panhandle, which revived memories of meals and conversations with Billy the Kid. When this investigation was complete, there was barely time to visit his ranch home and animals in New Mexico before being assigned to the next challenge.

Even with the twentieth century hard approaching, there seemed no end to malfeasance and even murder. As Ben E. Pingenot observes, "Just when the Wild West seemed ready to bow to the inevitability of law and order, a large band of outlaws began a crime spree that ranged across several western states. The outburst was the last gasp of the cowboy-criminal-badman to ply his trade before civilization had him completely hemmed in."

Even with a bevy of bandits to pursue, not all of Siringo's time had been spent, depending on the time of year, ramming through snow drifts while buffeted by howling winds or raising dust on a scorched stretch of desert on the back of his tongue-swollen horse. Though his second wife had not cared for the isolated life, Charlie was devoted to Sunny Slope Ranch and was already thinking of it as his forever home. North of the Arroyo Chamiso, he had built a two-room adobe house. It had to have been difficult to leave his new home, even though it was now without wife and child, but even for such a bare existence there were bills to pay. Right after his boss, McParland, contacted him, Siringo set off for Denver.

The urgency of the summons indicated the Pinkerton Agency's belief that the Wilcox job had hardly been just a "last gasp." McParland stressed to his two detectives that, instead, it may have been a new and powerful setback in the effort to create a law-abiding American West. They must not hesitate to get on the trail of the Hole-in-the-Wall Gang or the Wild Bunch or whatever the newspapers were calling the miscreants.

Having loaded up packhorses with supplies and ammunition, Siringo and Sayles set off for Carbon County in Utah. Outlaws were known to travel through there on their way to or from Robbers Roost. And the sheriff, C. W. Allred, based in the town of Price, was a well-known law-enforcer. One notch on his belt was the killing of the notorious outlaw

Joe Walker, who certainly contradicted the belief that the West was becoming a safer place to live.

Born about 1850 in Texas, Walker was still a baby when his father died. His mother turned management of the family's cattle herd over to her brother, a man referred to as Dr. Whitmore. About 1870, the Whitmores moved their stock and the stock belonging to the Walkers to northern Arizona. The new home was not a welcoming one as Dr. Whitmore was soon killed during an Indian raid. Understandably, his widow and children moved on, to Utah. They built a thriving cattle ranch and became successful bankers, based partly on the Walker stock they had entwined with their own.

After Joe Walker became an adult and had spent some years drifting from job to job, it finally occurred to him that he was entitled to a share of the Whitmore operation. He returned to Carbon County and approached his relatives, who were busy breeding fine horses in Nine Mile Canyon. However, they refused to even acknowledge the family relationship, let alone listen to any of his demands.

An angry Joe Walker returned to the drifting and working life. A gasket burst in 1895 when during a drinking spree in Price, he yanked out his gun and began shooting up the town. Thanks to the considerable property damage, he rode out of town a wanted man. He fell in with Wild Bunch affiliates, who took him along on some of their outlaw escapades. For two years, Walker did his part, primarily rustling other people's animals. There was a special joy in stealing stock belonging to the Whitmore family. He gained a reputation as an expert rustler, and lawmen could not touch him, especially when he was hiding out in Robbers Roost or the Hole-in-the-Wall ranch.

Maybe a $500 bounty on his head would help. It did generate more interest in Walker's capture. In 1896, he narrowly escaped a posse of five riders. Walker watched them approach, and when they refused to be waved off, he opened fire. A running gunfight followed, with Walker, apparently on a stronger horse, able to inch ahead, and he galloped to safety into the Robbers Roost hideout.

The next year, Walker's luck began to run out. He once again raided the Whitmore ranch, with his partner in crime being James Otis Bliss, a Boston native who by then was known as "Gunplay" Maxwell. They hid the stolen stock in a secluded area known as Mexican Bend on the San Rafael River. But the two had a falling out, and Maxwell got word to the Whitmores where they could find their hidden horses.

Enter Sheriff Allred. He and his deputy, Azariah Tuttle, took off for the San Rafael and surprised Walker near the river, cutting him off from a nearby house. Clambering halfway up the steep bank, the outlaw drew his pistol and started firing. While Allred and Tuttle were in hot pursuit, the latter took a bullet in the leg. The two lawmen found shelter behind some large boulders.

When Walker steadfastly refused to surrender, Allred left the wounded deputy and went back to town for help, herding the stolen horses ahead of him. Walker and Tuttle continued to exchange sporadic shots, but by sunrise, weak from blood loss, the wounded man asked for a truce. Walker agreed to get him a bucket of water if he would toss his guns aside. Each did as agreed; then Walker staggered out of the canyon and, finding a stray horse, took off.

But later that same year, the outlaw was camped near the town of Thompson with Johnny Herring, a passing cowboy who had shared Walker's supper. The two bedded down for the night unaware that a nine-man posse had encircled their camp. At dawn, when the sleeping men were emerging from their slumber, the relentless Sheriff Allred and Joe Bush, another member of the posse, called to them to surrender. Instead, Walker and a confused Herring rolled out of their bedding with guns blazing. The posse returned fire. Walker and the unfortunately misidentified cowboy—of course, the posse had believed him to be Butch Cassidy—lay dead near their riddled bedrolls.

Allred had gotten his man but was pretty steamed for missing out on the $500 reward for the capture or death of the real Butch Cassidy.

Because we may not encounter him again, we can't leave Gunplay Maxwell in the dust just yet. Few, if any, bandits had such intriguing postoutlaw lives. His bandit career ended in May 1898. He and an accomplice robbed the Springville, Utah, bank of some $3,000. They fled toward Hobble Creek Canyon with a posse hot on their trail. Nearly one hundred horsemen had caught up with the thieves, who attempted to hide in the brush. Six-shooters spit bullets and the second bandit was killed. Doing the arithmetic, Maxwell surrendered, so instead of being filled with holes, he was taken to the Provo, Utah, jail. In short order, Maxwell was soon convicted of bank robbery and sent to the Utah State Prison. He was back out in only five years because his sentence was commuted when he helped stop a prison break.

In an odd turn of events, the man formerly known as Gunplay found the straight life could be more profitable than the outlaw life, and with less chance of prison. In the fall of 1904, Maxwell, trying his hand at prospecting near Colton, Utah, found ozokerite, an odoriferous mineral wax. He soon formed the Utah Ozokerite Company with his lawyer, and the pair hired a superintendent to manage the operations. The mine soon became the largest known ozokerite mine in the world and did so well that it went public.

Making easy money was not terribly interesting, though, so Maxwell next turned up using the name Thomas Bliss in Goldfield, Nevada, working as a spy for mine owners. While keeping an eye on the union's striking workers, he was involved in the death of a man named Joseph Smith but was not prosecuted. He soon drifted back to Utah, where in July 1907, taking up his nickname again, Gunplay Maxwell was involved in a shooting with a railroad foreman named L. C. Reigle. When the smoke cleared, both were wounded. Maxwell was initially arrested but, once again, was not prosecuted.

He next popped up in San Francisco, as William Seaman and claiming to be descended from one of the oldest titled families in Italy. This assertion impressed Bessie Hume enough that the wealthy widow married him. Even after "Seaman"—how Italian was that?—pawned most of his wife's jewelry, she stayed with him, and the two soon moved to Ogden, Utah. At first, the alleged Italian blueblood shaved his mustache, donned fashionable clothing, and lived the part of an upstanding husband. But, bored again, he strapped on his guns once more. Arrivederci, Bessie.

In June 1908, he and another man, William Walters, held up a Wells Fargo stage at Rawhide, Nevada, and were captured. Maxwell was released on bail and—yes, you got it—never prosecuted. It was, finally, not the law but a bullet that, fittingly, got Gunplay.

In August 1909, Maxwell confronted Deputy Sheriff Edward Black Johnstone in a local saloon in Price, where Allred had once patrolled. Johnstone suspected that Maxwell planned to rob a large payroll. Maxwell already held a grudge against Johnstone because he had earlier identified him to a local sheriff in Goldfield as a badman and ex-convict. That this was true did not deter Maxwell from challenging Johnstone in the saloon. Outside on the street, Gunplay told Johnstone he intended to kill him, drew his gun, and fired on the deputy. However, his shot missed, going through his opponent's shirt and scratching his arm.

Not depending on luck to save him, Johnstone fired back, hitting Maxwell first in the elbow and then in his heart. Though this may have been the hardest part of his body, Maxwell kicked up dust as he collapsed into the street. He tried to shoot again but Johnstone was faster, hitting the seasoned bandit in the chest. Confirming the obvious, Maxwell exhaled, "Don't shoot again, Johnstone, you have killed me."

There was one last twist to Gunplay Maxwell's life: when his body was being prepared for burial, it showed that his arms were covered in track marks, and opium was found concealed in a pocket. Now viewed as a drug addict in addition to outlaw, he was buried in the pauper's section of the Salt Lake City Cemetery—under the name William Seaman.

One would think that Sheriff Allred would welcome two veteran Pinkerton operatives to Price to share the law enforcement burden. But the lawman did not recognize them and in fact thought they might be suspects in the Wilcox heist. "Allred had more recently made notable purchases of rifles and ammunition in Salt Lake City and was armed for war when the strangers caught his eye riding into Price," writes Nathan Ward.

The sheriff was suspicious enough that he thought to arrest them first and ask questions later. But Siringo and Sayles checked into and then out of a hotel before Allred could act. However, that night, they were back at the hotel. The tip they had received proved worthless, and all they had gotten was wet from riding through a rainstorm. They were soon visited by the editor of the *News-Advocate* newspaper, who asked for an exclusive interview with two of the Wilcox train robbers before they—one of whom he knew was Kid Curry—were arrested. If they did not believe him, look out the window. When the Pinkerton ops did, they saw the sheriff and several other men brandishing Winchesters.

However, Siringo and Sayles convinced the editor that they were indeed prospectors who had nothing to do with the train heist. The newsman conveyed this to Allred, who was disappointed at not having made good use of the town's new arsenal of firearms. The next day, the detectives literally headed for the hills.

Their search did not become any more fruitful. The two sleuths pursued clue after clue, riding hundreds of miles from Utah to New Mexico. After coming up empty again in the latter territory, Siringo and Sayles decided they should continue separately, with Sayles heading to Colorado where, supposedly, some of the stolen money had turned up. Siringo turned east and made his way to Tennessee.

He did not see any bandits but his vision got a workout anyway. "In Nashville I saw more pretty girls to the square inch than I had ever seen before or expected to see again," he would report in *A Cowboy Detective*. "I sat at a dinner table with about a dozen college girls and each one was a beauty of the first water, and on the streets my neck was almost disjointed looking around at the pretty young women. I was glad to get away so as to give my eyes and neck a rest."

Siringo worked his way back west, and during the ensuing months, he endured all kinds of weather and a series of mishaps. After a dunking in a river, he wryly commented, "Undressing in the cold wind to wring the water out of my clothes gave me a taste of old-time cowboy life."

He figured that gaining more information about Kid Curry would help his efforts, so he traveled to Landusky. There he "quickly gained the confidence of the outlaw community," reports Pingenot. "He was a man of slight build, almost grizzled in appearance, with a sun-weathered face and pointed handle-bar mustache. Siringo rode under the name Charles Carter and confided that he was on the run from a murder charge."

The residents of Landusky were mildly curious about the stranger, but he soon fit in well enough. For the next several weeks he "made himself increasingly useful in his new town, roping and branding when it was roundup time, breaking broncos with the younger men, charming Lonie Logan's longtime girlfriend Elfie into sharing her 'secrets' from Lonie's letters."

His cowboying almost killed him. One June day, "I came within an ace of losing my breath, which would have put me out of business for all time." He had been loaned a bronco team to make the twenty-five-mile trip to Rocky Point on the Missouri River in Montana. The horses were not truly broken in to doing this kind of domestic labor and were resisting Siringo's efforts to keep them under control. He tried to turn them away from a gulley and got thrown off the buckboard.

When he woke up, "I was lying flat on my back with the hot June sun shining in my face. I couldn't move or open my eyes. Finally, by making a strong effort, I got my right hand up to my eyes; the left arm couldn't be raised." His face was covered with crusted blood. He managed to turn over and "discovered that I was throwing up blood." Everything hurt, "My back pained the worst, and it was like pulling a tooth to try to get to my feet. Therefore I started to crawl back to the Jim T. ranch about five miles."

After a few hundred yards, "I managed to gain my feet. Several times en route I was on the eve of giving up and lying down to rest, but the fear was I wouldn't be able to get to my feet again kept me pushing ahead." He did make it back to the ranch, barely. He arrived "reeling from one side to the other like a drunken bum."

He recovered and returned to the trail, which included a trip with the lawman Joe Lefors to El Paso. But Texas did not yield any Wild Bunch bandits either, so Siringo took a train into Mexico, where word had been received that "Flatnose" Currie was hiding out, at the foot of the Sierra Madre Mountains. However, after securing a horse and saddle and roaming about for two weeks, the Pinkerton op came up empty. He wired Lefors in El Paso "that we were on the wrong trail hence he could return home to Cheyenne."

Charlie Siringo had run out of leads. To his enormous frustration, it did seem that Butch Cassidy and his bandit colleagues had gotten away with it. He made his way back to Denver to report to James McParland and, he hoped, be given permission to rest and fully recuperate at his sanctuary in New Mexico.

Then came the Tipton train robbery—which included another explosive encounter with the unfortunate messenger Charles Woodcock. This resulted in not only Siringo being back on the trail of the Wild Bunch but also his closest brush with the man-killer Kid Curry, who was still bristling over the violent death of his brother.

24

DEATH AT THE FARMHOUSE

When Butch Cassidy and his gang had committed the Wilcox train heist, conspicuously absent had been Elzy Lay. One would think that with him being so tight with Butch and the daring robbery viewed as a big score, Elzy belonged there as much if not more so than the Sundance Kid, Kid Curry, or "Flatnose" Currie. But he had been elsewhere, and then he fell in with the Ketchum brothers. The events of the Folsom job would lead—it would turn out to be fortuitously—to the end of Lay's criminal career.

Displaying much cheekiness, Butch Cassidy and now best buddy Sundance Kid returned to New Mexico, specifically to the WS Ranch, where one morning they came out of the bunkhouse yawning and stretching like any other hand preparing to begin the workday. Whatever reason they gave William French for their absence, he bought it. The bandits' aim was to stay on there until the commotion about the Wilcox job began to wane.[75] This also may have been when Butch, at

75 Though some time passed and there were other robberies, the Wilcox job stuck in the craw of those who had gotten robbed. In October 1900, the Union Pacific Railroad rerouted its track to the Southwest, bypassing the Wilcox station. And even that was not enough: The railroad blew up the

least, had first thoughts about leaving the United States because of the appearance of a Pinkerton detective.

His name was Frank Murray, and he was one of the agency's ops following up on any leads they could stumble on. Somehow, Murray had heard of a man named Jim Lowe who had reappeared in the Alma area after the Wilcox robbery and could be Butch Cassidy. When Murray arrived, he visited French at the WS Ranch and showed him several photographs. The owner recognized one man as Jim Lowe. Murray said the "Lowe" was actually Butch Cassidy, the leader of the men who had committed the Wilcox crime.

By now, French had to have his own suspicions about his trail boss who disappeared from time to time. However, he was not about to share them with a stranger, especially a Pinkerton detective. What did French care about a train heist in Wyoming when he had in his employ in New Mexico an especially good hand? He confirmed to Murray that Jim Lowe worked for him and offered a glowing appraisal of the foreman. If Murray thought Jim Lowe was really an outlaw, what was he going to do about it?

Nothing, Murray admitted. He had no backup here, and the op was certainly not going up against the near-legendary outlaw alone. He would send a report to the Denver office and see what the powers-that-be there wanted to do. Murray soon made himself scarce in Alma.

French did not have to vouch for another employee who traveled with Lowe because by then the Sundance Kid had left the area. There was a girl in Galveston he wanted to see. Or this could be, like almost everything about Ethel Place, subject to speculation. "Sundance headed for Texas," offers Donna Ernst. "Presumably, that was when and where he met her. Except for her half-dozen years with Sundance,

---

bridge over Rock Creek that Cassidy's crew had damaged. The debris was gathered into a dam to create a watering hole for the stock of surrounding ranchers.

very little about her is certain." Whether or not they had previously known each other, Sundance and Ethel were content to stay south for the winter.

Though Butch mourned the loss—to the prison system—of his close friend Elzy Lay, and the absence of the Sundance Kid, the remainder of 1899 was a tranquil time for him. With one exception: when he was arrested for horse rustling.

Though Frank Murray had left Alma, Cassidy could not be certain he would not return with a gaggle of lawmen accompanying the Pinkerton detective. So, it was time to leave Alma once more. But Butch, being Butch, on the way partnered with a man calling himself Red Weaver; the two rounded up a remuda of horses belonging to a nearby ranch owner and led them into Arizona, looking for a willing and gullible buyer. However, while buying supplies, Cassidy and Weaver were arrested by a sheriff in Apache country.

This lawman must not have known who he had in custody because if he had, he would have immediately become the most famous sheriff in the U.S. He would be spoken about in the same way as Pat Garrett was for having gunned down Billy the Kid. But nothing came of it. The duo was either let go—perhaps Cassidy charming his way out of the situation—or released on bail, and with or without the stolen horses they kept going until shut of Arizona.

Next stop? Charles Leerhsen informs, "As the page turned on the new century, in the first few months of 1900, Butch headed to Salt Lake City, the capital of his birth state, with a plan for a truly fresh start."

Not so fortunate was Lonie Curry. As Gary Wilson writes, "Cassidy was now in limbo. Harvey [Logan] was hiding in Texas, and Lonie Logan and cousin Bob Lee were left to meet their own fates."

After the killing of Sheriff Josiah Hazen in June 1899, Kid Curry and his brother and their cousin managed to escape several posses and make it into Montana. Despite the heat of summer, their trail grew cold. Kid Curry went off to Texas while Lonie and Lee remained north to operate a saloon in a town called Harlem in Chouteau County.[76] To anyone who would listen, Lonie had an array of alibis to support his claim that he and Bob Lee had nothing to do with the Wilcox train heist, including that he had been visiting family and friends in Landusky. Certainly, no one in that Logan stronghold would contradict him.

Maybe Lonie was leaving the outlaw life for good. He had paid for a half-interest in what was now the Bowle and Curry Club Saloon. It did a brisk business and Lonie moved Elfie Landusky and their two children to a house in Harlem. Bob Lee had not stayed, preferring the life (and anonymity) of a prospector off in the hills. Maybe a person could leave the past behind.

"Lonie had matured since the days when he'd shot up Landusky with his brothers," explains Thom Hatch. "He made friends with the merchants and town's citizens, especially J. D. B. Griegg, the newspaper editor. In fact, Lonie was photographed helping to ink Griegg's first edition. Lonie also played fiddle and banjo for local dances. A holiday turkey shoot was also planned to take place in their saloon, with thirty turkeys to be awarded."

And then Lonie got careless. Between buying his share of the saloon and social activities, his ready cash was depleted, and he was forced to carve out some of the Wilcox take. Five hundred-dollar notes were removed from the safe at the Cecil Hotel and brought to the post office to be exchanged for smaller bills. When the postmaster was unable to do that, he forwarded them to the Stockman's National Bank, located at Fort Benton. Suspicious officials there sent the bills on to the Pinkerton Agency, who confirmed that they had been part of the Wilcox haul. With Charlie Siringo off somewhere on the trail trying

---

76 The name has nothing to do with the African American community in New York City. As they had done with some other towns along what was called the "Hi-Line," Great Northern Railway officials chose the name of a European city—in this case, it was Haarlem, in the Netherlands.

to find "Flatnose" Currie and Kid Curry, McParland got hold of Billy
Sayles and had him hurry to Helena.

The op arrived in December 1899. Stockman's Bank officials had
been holding off on sending smaller bills to Harlem, which was frus-
trating for Lonie and his cousin Bob, who needed cash too as prospecting had not proved profitable. Suspicions that they were being set
up soared when a stranger came to Harlem asking questions about the
cousins. Perhaps Sayles could have been more subtle, but he probably
stood no chance anyway in the small town. That the stranger did not
leave implied he was waiting for others, such as men with badges.

Lonie Curry and Bob Lee did not hesitate. The half-interest in the
saloon was sold practically overnight to a Great Falls businessman for
$300—less than Lonie had paid, but better than paying a lawyer from
behind bars. Perhaps to make up for this, or they were simply not very
nice guys, the cousins stole the money raised from a raffle to assist
an ailing elderly woman. Whatever good will they had earned during
their time in Harlem was left in the dust of their horses' hooves as they
hightailed it out of town.

They sold their horses after the sixteen-mile trip to the Zurich Great
Northern depot and boarded the next train out. After stops that included Great Falls and Helena they entered Colorado, eventually step-
ping off in Cripple Creek. Bob Lee tried to blend in right away, taking a
job as a poker dealer at the Antler Club. Lonie was anxious to move on.
Though calling himself Frank Miller and having shaved his mustache,
he felt exposed in the town just west of Colorado Springs. The anxiety
cost him. He stopped by the post office so often asking for a letter from
Jim Thornhill (which presumably contained more getaway money) that
the postmaster was at first curious and then suspicious. He telegraphed
the Pinkerton Agency to inquire if it was looking for a Frank Miller.

That was good enough for Billy Sayles, when he was informed. By
this time, "Charles Carter"—Charlie Siringo—had joined the other
op in Helena. It was decided that Sayles would go directly to Cripple
Creek while Siringo made his journey to Landusky.

Bob Lee was found and arrested. He would go on trial for the Wilcox train robbery. He insisted to the jury that he had not participated in the heist and denied knowing anyone who had participated. He was not believed and was found guilty and sentenced to prison.[77]

Not waiting around to be caught had been a jumpy Lonie, who had left Cripple Creek well before Sayles got there. He stopped for a while in Dodson, ten miles south of Kansas City, where he wrote and posted a letter to Elfie. It may not necessarily have been legal, but one of the routine practices of the Pinkerton Agency was to intercept mail to and from suspects and family members, and that is what happened to this one. It was believed that Lonie was hiding out at the farm belonging to the Lee family that was a mile outside Dodson.

A posse was formed that consisted of Kansas City lawmen and Pinkerton operatives, and February 27 was the date chosen to descend on the Lee farmhouse. Instead, they had to wait out a snowstorm. The next morning, a clear one, after thrashing through almost a dozen miles of fallen snow in horse-drawn carriages, the posse members took up positions around the farmhouse.

Lonie was indeed inside. He and his aunt were in the kitchen having breakfast. When two approaching detectives were spotted, Lonie jumped up and faced two choices. One was to hold out against any assault. But there were several other people in the house, including his young cousin Lizzie Lee. Better to make a run for it. Maybe there were not enough lawmen to adequately surround the farm. There was a third option: surrender. It was not considering that option seriously enough that got Lonie killed.

Only seconds after he ran out the kitchen door, at least two officers were in pursuit. There were woods nearby, and Lonie aimed for them. In one hand was a Colt .45 pistol. The posse men called to him to toss it aside and stop running. Struggling in the heavy snow, the outlaw did

---

77 Bob Lee survived his incarceration but did not have a long life to reflect on that experience. He was a construction worker and married to a woman named Minnie when he died at his home in Kansas City in December 1912, just forty-three years old.

not see the trees getting any closer. There were now four men chasing him. They paused to open fire, pulling the triggers repeatedly. Lonie stumbled, tried to plunge ahead, but then fell face-first into the snow. He had been hit several times, but the bullet that mattered most was the one that struck the back of his head and passed into his brain.

On his last birthday, Lonie Logan had turned thirty. He was buried in the Lee family plot in a Kansas City cemetery.

Unlike Bob Lee and Lonie Logan, Butch Cassidy still had a chance for a new life. His trip to Salt Lake City was a departure from the Outlaw Trail—perhaps a permanent one. He met with Orlando Powers, the attorney who had served as an associate justice of the Utah Territory Supreme Court. Butch told him about some of his criminal exploits and that he was still a wanted man. Was it possible, the soon-to-be-reformed robber wanted to know, that he would be pardoned if he turned himself in?

No, Powers told him bluntly. His criminal résumé was too long not to spend some time in jail, and that was just in Utah. Who knew what Wyoming and Colorado and even New Mexico might have in store for him. Butch was not deterred. He figured he would have to go to a higher power than Powers.

Thanks to a respected former sheriff, Parley Christensen, who knew Butch's parents, a meeting was arranged with Heber Wells. It says something about Cassidy's charisma or the desire to end his criminal career that the governor of Utah would agree to such a get-together. And it actually went well. Butch believed a pardon was on its way. But he believed wrong. Though he had not committed the deed, he was wanted for murder in Wyoming, and that was too hot a potato for the Utah governor to touch.

There was one more attempt. This time, though, it seemed like Mother Nature herself was against Butch Cassidy going straight.

Earning credit for creative thinking, Orlando Powers pointed out that Butch had a brighter future working for the railroad companies than robbing them. If Butch and his Wild Bunch gang acted as roving guards, that would reduce the raids on railroads. What at first blush had appeared to be a farcical scenario—Butch Cassidy as a sort of railroad marshal, maybe the Sundance Kid as his deputy—was actually embraced by Union Pacific officials.

They and Cassidy agreed to meet at Little Soldier Pass. This rugged location close to the Utah-Wyoming border offered some protection for Butch in that if he saw it was a setup, he could easily take off for the hills. Extra protection was offered by his friend Douglas Preston, his former attorney, who would escort the railroad representatives.

The day came, and so did a violent thunderstorm. Even when it ended, the railroad party's buckboards kept getting stuck in mud. By the time they arrived at Little Soldier Pass, Cassidy had gone. They instead found a message left under a rock: "Damn you Preston, you have double-crossed me. I waited all day but you didn't show up. Tell the U.P. to go to hell. And you can go with them."

After cooling off, Cassidy might have given the unusual scheme another try. And the Union Pacific may have been anxious to make up for a missed opportunity. But then came the Tipton train robbery. It mirrored the Wilcox job in several ways, including the outrage that followed it. Any hope of a pardon was history.

It took place in the early morning hours of August 29, 1900. Tipton was a stop on the Wyoming line of the Union Pacific Railroad. To this day, Western scholars and writers are divided over whether Butch was the leader of the bandit gang, though the similarities in execution of the heist could persuade one that he was. Kid Curry was present for sure, and among the other thieves in the gang were two Texans, Bill Cruzan and Ben Kilpatrick. For Cruzan, this was an escalation of his crime career, having previously concentrated on cattle rustling and doing time in prison for it.

A masked man who the train crew later pointed to as the leader descended into the engineer's cabin from the coal tender. The engineer was assured that he would not be hurt—a Cassidy hallmark—but the gun in the bandit's hand made a strong impression, nonetheless. The train eased along and stopped where there was a small campfire at the side of the tracks. There, several more masked men boarded.

The conductor, E. J. Kerrigan, was ordered to disconnect the engine, baggage, and express cars from the passenger cars. He did so after first instructing the nervous passengers to stay in their seats and, certainly, no sticking of heads out windows. The engine car eased forward once more, then it stopped. The thieves, with rifles on the train crew, walked back to the express car, where shouts ordered the messenger to open up.

He refused. When Kerrigan saw sticks of dynamite being prepared for use, he informed the messenger and assured him there would soon be an explosion. A few fraught seconds later, the doors opened. The messenger turned out to be the truly unfortunate Charles Woodcock.

His surrender did not save the express car, however. As at the Wilcox job, the dynamite to blow the safe was excessive and the roof and sides were blown out too. Once the debris settled, the safe yielded cash, jewelry, and watches. And as with the Wilcox heist, sometime later the Union Pacific Railroad admitted the true haul was as much as $55,000—which would be close to two million dollars today. Hence, the renewed outrage.

Maybe lawmen would be luckier this time. They weren't. The bandits galloped to the southeast. That their hideouts were the ranches owned by Charles Tucker and Jim Ferguson implies that the Sundance Kid was in on the job, as both were friends of his. Various posses never found the gang there or anywhere.

They tried, though. Railroad officials offered rewards beginning at $1,000 for the capture of gang members. As many as five posses were formed, though mostly they wound up with tired horses for their trouble.

Poor Charles Woodcock had survived two sensational and explosive events. No doubt, a lesser—or more sensible—man would have found another occupation. But the stubborn messenger stayed on, working for the Union Pacific Railroad, including traveling the same route on which he had been robbed, for a total of thirty years. As late as 1934, he posed for photographs outside of railroad cars near his home in Ogden, Utah, where, unscathed, he had retired.

25

THE FUTURE IS NOW

Two of the more remarkable what-ifs about the Tipton job are that it thwarted one last attempt to convince Butch Cassidy to go straight and almost resulted in a confrontation with Joe Lefors.

Orlando Powers had not given up on Butch leaving the Outlaw Trail. He correctly assumed that the Union Pacific officials felt that a good opportunity had been lost in Little Soldier Canyon and were receptive to the attorney's new plan. It involved Butch's old buddy Matt Warner.

Powers knew that Warner had just been released from the penitentiary, and presumably he wanted a good start on a law-abiding life. He readily agreed to Powers's plan, which was in return for a $175 fee, he was to ride the rails to Rock Springs. It was assumed—this time, incorrectly—that Cassidy was concealing himself in Brown's Park and would welcome his newly freed friend. Warner would explain the weather-related snafu that had prevented Preston and Union Pacific representatives from showing up at the canyon. Could they try again?

Matt Warner was game. It would certainly enhance his postprison prospects if he helped end the career—peacefully—of the man who had become the country's most notorious outlaw. He took the train but only so far as Bridger Station. There, a telegram from no less than Governor Wells tersely ended his mission: "All agreements off. Cassidy just held up a train at Tipton."[78]

Then there was the pursuit by Deputy Marshal Joe Lefors. He led one of the at least five posses to go after the Tipton bandits that had formed and gone out of Rock Springs and Rawlins. Some accounts say that all they found was discarded money wrappers on one bank of the Little Snake River outside Baggs, Wyoming. But his search was a tad more complicated than that.

Lefors and his eleven men had departed from Rawlins with alacrity, pushing their horses hard enough that they had covered 120 miles to reach the border with Colorado. They paused at the Little Snake River, and though it was near sunset, Lefors spotted three riders leading a packhorse up a hill across the river. But both the posse men and their mounts were too tuckered out to ford the river and ride any farther. They slid the saddles off their horses, watered them, and made camp for the night.

A new day offered a fresh opportunity to nab the bandits. On the other side of the Little Snake River, Lefors saw hoofprints. His posse followed them. Thirty-five miles later, they halted. Just up ahead was a grove of willow trees and some branches appeared to be moving without a breeze to cause it. The setting practically screamed, "Ambush!"

First, the posse spread out and approached with caution. Then Lefors had the full group stop, and he and two men advanced on foot. Every man had his six-shooter held tight and ready to fire. The deputy marshal next noticed the legs of several horses within the willow grove. Maybe the posse would be doing the ambushing instead of the other

---

[78] Word of the event went out faster than usual. The new century's progress included wiring parts of Wyoming for telephone service, and the Union Pacific officials in Omaha were informed of the heist in a long-distance call placed by the train's conductor at a pay phone. It was not recorded if he called collect or had enough loose change on him.

way around. Lefors signaled his men to surround the grove. When they were in position, they charged into the trees.

Again, Cassidy had the last laugh. The horses indeed had been accomplices in the Tipton train robbery as members of the relay teams Butch had spread out across the region. If there was a reward for capturing tired, hard-ridden horses, Lefors and his posse would be rich.

The Tipton heist slammed the door on any possibility of the members of the Wild Bunch going straight. And then what happened at Winnemucca put an exclamation point on that.

On September 19, the target of the Wild Bunch was in Nevada—the First National Bank of Winnemucca. It was at the northwest corner of Fourth Street and Bridge Street. The Sundance Kid was already familiar with the building and its surroundings, having visited Winnemucca, cased it, and then traveled to Twin Falls, Idaho, where he made a presentation to Butch and Will Carver.

A surviving member of the Black Jack Ketchum Gang, Carver, a thirty-two-year-old from Coryell County, Texas, was known for his nickname and romantic entanglements. He was dubbed "News" because he enjoyed reading newspapers that carried accounts of the Wild Bunch's exploits. While working as a cowboy in Utah, Carver met and married Viana Byler, whose aunt was Laura Bullion, who would soon ride the Outlaw Trail as an accessory of the Wild Bunch.

Here is where Carver got busier as a lover than as a bandit. His wife died only six months after the wedding, and not long afterward, he took up with one of Herb and Elizabeth Bassett's daughters, Josie. When that affair cooled off, he and Bullion became smitten with each other. By early 1900, Carver was involved with a prostitute named Lille Davis, whom he had met at Fannie Porter's brothel in San Antonio (which we will soon visit). This put Carver at odds with Laura Bullion, who expressed her resentment by taking up with Carver's good friend, the Tall Texan Ben Kilpatrick. However, by the time of the Winnemucca escapade, Carver and Bullion were back together again.

After buying enough horses for the ride into Nevada and to be members of the relay teams, Cassidy, Sundance, and Carver left Twin Falls. They apparently spent enough on the purchase of horses that their pockets felt empty because when still in Idaho they committed a robbery while on their way to commit a robbery. In Three Creek, they took supplies without paying for them from an old man and his wife, Jim and Lizzie Duncan, who owned a general store. In a peculiar twist, the old man gave the outlaws new hats.

On that glaring, already hot Wednesday morning Cassidy, Sundance, and Carver arrived in Winnemucca and treated themselves to breakfast. Near noon, they entered the bank building. They were without masks, but no one recognized them anyway.

There is, as usual, some debate as to who the robbers actually were. It is at least 600 miles from Tipton in Wyoming to Winnemucca. It would have been a tall order, some skeptics insist, to have ridden horses that distance in two weeks. According to Charles Leerhsen, however, the three men managed the trip "covering the distance by train and then scrambling to acquire horses and set up their relay system."

Butch Cassidy approached George Nixon, a cashier who was also an owner of the bank, and pointed a gun at him. "Open the safe," the robber ordered, "and give me them gold coins." It was later reported that when Nixon refused, the robber displayed his other hand, which held a large knife. "This is to cut your throat with," he said. But this smacks of at least an embellishment, as it was uncharacteristic of a Cassidy operation and especially of Butch himself.

During this parley, Carver, who was wearing a long coat even in the heat, raised from it a rifle. He aimed it at the quaking bystanders, who consisted of three other employees and a customer with bad timing.

The gleaming weapons impressed Nixon sufficiently that he complied with the demands of the bandit leader. He opened the safe and hauled out of it what was later estimated to be $32,640 in gold coins.

The third thief made his presence felt by depositing the coins into a canvas bag.

This task accomplished, the bandits forced all four employees and the customer out the back door into a fenced enclosure so no one from the front street could see what was happening. They then escaped over the fence and into the alley where they had horses waiting. As the bandits rode off, the plucky George Nixon went back into the bank and came out with a revolver, as did one of his fellow employees, the bank stenographer. Shots were exchanged, but there were no injuries on either side.

Bystanders at the Reception Saloon heard the shooting and dashed outside to let off a few shots but missed the fleeing horsemen. The only bullet to hit something found and smashed one of the saloon's windows. A daredevil deputy marshal, George Rose, clambered up the town windmill and got off a few shots, to no avail.

The escape plan called for circling around toward the east. It did not call for dropping the sack of gold coins when they crossed White's Creek Bridge, but that was what happened and they lost valuable time retrieving it. The bandits then pushed on, making their way toward Golconda where they had fresh horses waiting—a Butch Cassidy trademark.

Furious citizens in Winnemucca quickly organized a posse and even fired up a yard locomotive to follow along in an attempt to capture the group. But the outlaws were able to stay ahead of the posse thanks to having stashed fresh horses about every ten miles. Also, the road they traveled veered away from the railroad track, so the locomotive proved useless as a pursuer. The trio was followed as far as Clover Valley, where they had another set of fresh mounts, then on to Tuscarora. By that time, the citizen posse had given up the chase.

Once back in Idaho, the bandits paid another visit to the Three Creek general store. It was nighttime, and it appeared the elderly proprietor and his wife had gone to bed. Quietly, after toting up the cost of the supplies they had taken and the hats they had been given, and doubling that number, they left the money for the Duncans on the front porch. They could afford to be generous—Butch later indicated in a letter to a friend that the trio's take was $30,000.[79]

George Nixon and his partners could certainly not expect a middle-of-the-night reimbursement. Gritting his teeth, the cashier could do nothing more than contact the Pinkerton Agency.[80]

It does seem that Butch was making up for time lost when he had dallied with the desire to go straight. If he was going to be an outlaw, he might as well be recognized as the best. "The Winnemucca bank robbery could be counted on as another remarkable achievement by Butch and the boys," observes Thom Hatch. "Considering the enormous risks in robbing a bank, they had once again defied all odds with this bold act. It was as if Butch had the desire to flaunt his abilities by successfully robbing both a train and a bank within a span of three weeks, showing the railroad and the Pinkertons that he could not be deterred."

But it was not just defying Charlie Siringo and other lawmen—plus, inevitably, more bounty hunters as the rewards multiplied—that had them looking for fast cash. As Leerhsen explains it, Butch Cassidy, probably more so than Sundance, realized that he was "no longer merely in the business of outrunning posses, but in a race with the end of the outlaw era; there was no future in riding around on horses like medieval highwaymen, robbing enterprises made vulnerable by their remoteness, not in an age when remoteness itself was under assault. Yet if they hurried, they might squeeze in another score or two before retiring."

---

79 According to Pearl Baker, during one of the stops to change horses, Butch told a farmhand to give his horse to a ten-year-old boy named Vic Button, the son of the owner of a ranch where the gang had camped on the way to Winnemucca. Button related this story to Baker seventy years after the robbery.

80 George Nixon's courage almost under fire was bad financially as a part owner of the First National Bank of Winnemucca, but it turned out to be good politically. He was later elected to the Nevada state legislature and then to the U.S. Senate.

Could it happen before Butch ran out of banks, trains, and especially time? There was good reason for haste in the aftermath of the Winnemucca raid: New rewards being offered brought the total up to at least $10,000, and Charlie Siringo was back on the trail.

26

———◆◆◆◆———

"GODFORSAKEN DESERT COUNTRY"

It is not known how aware Butch Cassidy was of world and national events in the first year of the new century. Probably, the more he knew, the more he was convinced that the Wild West outlaw—even a successful and resilient one like him—would soon be extinct. When authorities could be alerted so quickly about a train robbery, as had happened with the Tipton heist, the world was becoming too modern for thieves and rustlers, even those who felt safe in Bandit Heaven.

In 1900, there were fewer wide, open spaces in the country. A decade earlier, the U.S. Census Bureau had declared the frontier was closed—there were no new regions to explore in the lower forty-eight. At the turn of the century, there were seventy-five million people living in the United States, more of them in the West than ever.

In New York City, the first electric bus was rolled out and work had begun on an underground "rapid transit railroad." A professor at Johns Hopkins University discovered the cause of the Earth's magnetism. In sports, eight baseball clubs joined together to form the American League and in tennis the Davis Cup was founded. At Kitty Hawk in North Carolina, the Wright brothers began their experiments with manned glider flights. In food, Milton Hershey introduced a bar of chocolate and in New Haven, Connecticut, a diner, Louis's Lunch, was credited with serving the first hamburger.

Outlaws were not keeping track of the many advances in the sciences being made when the new century began, but they were happening, nevertheless. Thomas Edison invented the alkaline storage battery. German scientists invented the seismograph to detect and measure the intensity of earthquakes. Also in Germany, the first Zeppelin dirigible was launched. The psychiatrist Sigmund Freud published his landmark tome *On the Interpretation of Dreams*. The physicist Max Planck announced the basis for quantum physics. Closer to home, in Wyoming, Barnum Brown discovered the first partial skeleton of a *Tyrannosaurus rex,* launching a new frenzy of archaeological research.

Clearly, the world and America were changing, creating a shrinking environment for a Western bandit. What chance did cowboys turned bank and train robbers have against quantum physics?

Charlie Siringo was determined that the future home for Cassidy and his rotating company of thieves was a prison. His odyssey had not ended—thanks to the Tipton job, it had only paused.

Early in this next phase of his dogged pursuit, he was atop a mountain ridge in Monticello, Utah. As Nathan Ward describes what he observed: "From there Charlie could see at least a hundred clear miles, the landmarks of what would be his longest case spread before him like an outlaw's map: north toward the Wild Bunch stations at Brown's Park and Rock Springs; west to the Colorado River, lined with cliffs the gang traveled; and beyond the difficult plateau of Robbers Roost, the uninviting desert and the Henry Mountains into which the gang often scattered."

While there, Siringo had temporarily teamed up with a grizzled character he identified only as "Peg-leg," who claimed to have information about the Tipton bandits. He did seem knowledgeable enough but if any of the robbers were in the area, they did not accommodate Peg-leg by revealing themselves to the Pinkerton operative.

Still, Siringo roamed the region, hoping for a stroke of luck, which did not arrive.

While in Hanksville, a message was received from McParland in Denver telling the detective to give Circleville a try. Perhaps the Parker family and their prodigal son kept in touch. Siringo's stay of a week there was pleasant enough thanks to enjoying the charms of a Parker woman, one of Butch's younger sisters, who was the deputy postmaster of Circleville. "I had hard work to keep from falling in love with Miss Parker," he conceded.

Another romantic entanglement would turn out to be the only enjoyable outcome of his visit to Parker territory. Siringo only learned that there was nothing to be learned. In the area, and even among some family members, the boy who had been Robert LeRoy Parker was a fading memory.

The Pinkerton man may have received one useful tip, though, because his next destination was New Mexico. He might have thought twice if he had known how arduous this journey was. It was "a horseback ride of over 1000 miles through the most Godforsaken desert country in the United States." Included in those thousand miles were detours to lands occupied by the Navaho, Moqui, and Zuni tribes to inquire about unfamiliar white faces. It turned out, however, that the only one belonged to Charlie Siringo.

At first, when he arrived in Alma, it seemed that he had struck gold in what was otherwise an unimpressive town: It "supported one store and one saloon, both being well-patronized by the wild and wooly population thinly scattered over the surrounding country."

He made the acquaintance of Jesse Black, a man who counted among his friends Jim Lowe—who was, he confided, Butch Cassidy. He further revealed that "Jim" and a friend, Red Weaver, were passing time in a mining camp near the Arizona border. Siringo was amused to hear that Frank Murray, who was technically his superior in the Pinkerton Agency, had been in Alma conversing with Jim Lowe without any idea (until later) that the bartender was the bandit he sought.

Rubbing his face in it a bit, Siringo telegraphed Murray at the Denver office to remind him of Lowe's real identity.

It was less amusing when Murray's response was to order the op not to head to the mining camp to make an arrest but instead sell his horse and ride the rails to Denver for further instructions. This seemed dumb to Siringo, but either Murray was covering up how easily he had been hornswoggled by Cassidy or he simply did not believe the new information. Gritting his teeth, Siringo did as he was told. He consoled himself by making a boozy stagecoach ride part of the trip.

On the stage, another passenger was Blake Graham "a warm friend of Jim Lowe." It would get even warmer for the two new acquaintances.

There was plenty of liquor aboard, and Graham's stories about Lowe/Cassidy were accompanied by the singing of Bill Kelly, the stagecoach driver. "Before reaching Silver City about night, the liquor began to work. Then Graham and I pulled our pistols and emptied them through the canvas-covered top of the stagecoach. This set fire to the canvas top and the wind carried the fire to my roll of bedding in the rear; then we all became fire-fighters. We drove into Silver City without a buggy-top and all the liquor gone."

What Siringo did not know was that Murray's face-saving order would almost get him shot by Kid Curry.

First, though, he discovered that Butch Cassidy had been a sort of Ben Franklin of the American West by establishing a postal system. All along the Outlaw Trail were "blind post offices," meaning establishments, usually saloons but also some general stores, where the managers or proprietors were inclined toward protecting Cassidy and his Wild Bunch comrades. Members could stay in touch with each other—which included informing what lawman was on what bandit's trail—through cipher messages left at these underground post offices. It was Charlie Siringo who busted the ad hoc system.

In Grand Junction, Colorado, his next stop after being given new instructions in Denver, the op met Jim Foss, a known cattle rustler. To reduce the risk of arrest, Foss lived twenty miles outside of town and on a mountain. He came to trust the newcomer Lee Roy Davis (Siringo) enough that he sent him into Grand Junction to get his mail. The nascent postal carrier did and noted that one letter—apparently not in code—advised Foss that detectives were closing in. Of course, this letter did not survive the trip back up the mountain.

Eventually, Foss trusted Siringo with the cipher code and gave him a letter of introduction to other gang members he might encounter. There was also a letter that was to be delivered to Elzy Lay in the New Mexico territorial prison. Siringo traveled there and met briefly with Cassidy's close friend (still going by the name Bill McGinnis), then he turned over the code to authorities.

With a companion he identified only as "Bert C.," supposedly another Wild Bunch hanger-on, the Pinkerton man pushed on to Rawlins, Wyoming, chasing a rumor that one of the Tipton thieves was there. Or as Siringo put it, "We hobnobbed with his tough cowboy friends." The rumor was true—Kid Curry was there. What could have saved Siringo's life was that he did not see Curry, but the man-killer saw him.

In a saloon one night, Siringo was chatting up the bartender, hoping to glean some useful information, when Curry glanced out of the back room and spotted the unfamiliar face. The Pinkerton op later learned: "He singled me out as a suspect, saying that I looked too bright and wide-awake for a common rounder. I considered it quite a compliment to be called bright by such a wide-awake judge."

Curry decided that night to keep his distance, and he moved on from Rawlins. As it turned out, during his long odyssey, this was the closest Charlie Siringo would get to any of the outlaws involved in the Wilcox and Tipton train robberies. It was not for lack of trying, but his desire to put handcuffs on Butch Cassidy, Sundance Kid, or other prominent members of the Wild Bunch went unfulfilled.

It might seem like Charlie Siringo's inability to track down and arrest or kill Butch Cassidy or any other prominent member of the Wild Bunch constituted a failure that could have further emboldened bandits. However, the Pinkerton op's travels were an important part of the larger picture of gradually wearing the Wild Bunch down. Siringo can be credited with being a relentless lawman. He "continued to pursue various gang members, dogging their trails over mountains, across deserts and frozen rivers, through blizzards, from Wyoming to Arkansas and back again," reports Ben E. Pingenot. "In all, he spent four years in the saddle chasing the Wild Bunch and covered an estimated twenty-five thousand miles. The relentless pursuit by Siringo and other Pinkerton detectives, as well as by civil authorities, gradually diminished and ultimately closed the outlaws' avenue of escape."

Siringo himself put a positive spin on his exhausting but rarely dull adventures: "During these four years of strenuous life along the West-Pacific Railroad lines, I secured much valuable information for the Dickinson agency.[81] That is, information not connected with train holdups, the agency having a system wherein matters of importance are put on record, for immediate or future reference."

This is where Tom Horn comes back into the Outlaw Trail. He had concluded that gleaning information and the grind of bureaucracy that was being a Pinkerton detective were not for him. Horn's pursuit of bandits was much more simple and direct—get a rifle and shoot them.

---

81 Because of Siringo's protracted legal tussle with the Pinkerton brothers after his retirement, he could not use the agency's actual name in *A Cowboy Detective*.

27

"A COOL DEVIL"

There are some differing accounts about who Tom Horn may have killed, when, and why leading up to the summer of 1900. What is certain is that at that time, he was ordered to clear out Brown's Hole of bandits. And that is just what he did.

For reasons that become obvious, Tom Horn's own—and somewhat sanitized—account of his life ends when he quit working for the Pinkerton National Detective Agency and took up with the Wyoming Stock Growers Association. Why he signed on as a Pinkerton op in the first place was a mystery—maybe he was curious and it was a regular wage. "I came to Denver," he recalled, "and was initiated into the mysteries of the Pinkerton institution." He would eventually conclude that "my work for them was not the kind that exactly suited my disposition; too tame for me. There were a good many instructions and a good deal of talk given to the operative regarding things to do and the things that had to be done."

In other words, too much talk and not enough action. One of his cases illustrated Horn's ambivalence about the agency. James McParland had asked Horn what he would do if put on a train robbery case. "I told him if I had a good man with me I could catch up to them." After a Denver & Rio Grande Railway train was held up between Cotopaxi and Texas Creek in Colorado, this confident statement was put to the test.

Horn was sent to the site of the heist. While waiting for a second operative, Cyrus "Doc" Shores, Horn began to try to get a bead on the thieves. He had picked up a trail but did not make much headway because "there were so many men scouring the country that I, myself, was being held up all the time; that I had been arrested twice in two days and taken in to Salida to be identified!"

Once the various frustrated lawmen posses gave up, Horn and the just-arrived Shores had the investigation to themselves. They resumed following the trail Horn had detected across the Sangre de Cristo range. Pushing on, they found that the bandits had come down by the Villa Grove iron mines, crossed back to the east side of the Sangre de Cristos, and then went through Huerfano Canon east of Trinidad before dropping into Clayton, New Mexico. After a shooting incident at a saloon the thieves moved on, from New Mexico into Texas and across the Panhandle into the Indian Territory portion of Oklahoma.

This pursuit had to have seemed endless: Below Canadian City, "They then swung in on the head of the Washita River in the Territory, and kept down this river for a long distance." Finally, however, after displaying Siringo-like persistence, Horn and Shores realized that "we were getting close to them, as we got in the neighborhood of Paul's Valley."

In a house owned by a man named Wolfe, they found and cuffed Bert Curtis, who they believed was one of the train robbers. With him in custody, Shores began the long trek back to Denver.[82] The second bandit was left to Tom Horn to find—or to wait for, as it turned out. He staked out the Wolfe residence, and his patience was rewarded a few

---

82 The inscription on the tombstone of Doc Shores, who died in October 1934 at age eighty-nine, reads, "Western Colorado's Most Noted Frontiersman, Pioneer, and Lawman." One of his more notorious cases was tracking down and capturing Alfred Packer, known as the Colorado Cannibal for hatcheting to death and eating five companions during a gold-hunting expedition.

days later when a man named "Peg Leg" Watson rode up. Horn confronted him. Watson—not the same Peg-leg who had befriended Charlie Siringo—was "considered by every one in Colorado as a very desperate character." However, "I had no trouble with him." While he was at it, Horn tracked down and arrested an accomplice, Joe McCoy. McParland was quite pleased to receive the telegram informing that his op was bringing in both men. Peg Leg Watson and Bert Curtis were tried in federal court and found guilty. They received life sentences because the theft had included breaking into the railroad car carrying U.S. mail.

Though Horn had other successful outcomes, "I never did like the work," he declared. He moved on from the Pinkerton Agency to work for the Wyoming land barons, have his Spanish-American War adventures, and then head back to Wyoming. He wrote his autobiography while in jail waiting to be hanged. It ended with, "And I think that since my coming here the yellow journal reporters are better equipped to write my history than I am, myself!"

But the reporters had plenty of help. As the biographer Larry D. Ball observes, "Since his return from Cuba in September 1898, Tom Horn's tendency to boast about his misdeeds had become more pronounced, especially when in his cups, and had the effect of reinforcing public doubts about him." It would get worse: "As more and more newspapers covered Tom Horn's man-hunting activities, more and more misinformation about him circulated."

The idea of ridding Brown's Hole of undesirables with a rifle had apparently been on Tom Horn's mind for some time. In 1895, the year after he left the Pinkerton Agency, Horn was summoned to meet with Governor William Richards of Wyoming.[83] Being cautious about being seen with someone known mostly as a gunman, the governor held the meeting not at his office but at the nearby office of Dr. Charles Penrose, who had ridden with the ill-fated Johnson County invaders.

---

83 To prevent any confusion: William Richards was the fourth governor of Wyoming. DeForest Richards, who took office in January 1899, was the fifth governor of Wyoming and the first to die while still in office, in 1903, four months into his second term.

When Horn arrived, Governor Richards expressed his frustration with the rampant rustling in Big Horn County and the harboring of other thieves there. The former Pinkerton op offered to get rid of the rustlers in return for $5,000. "When everything else fails," Horn boasted, "I have a system which never does."

This was more than the governor bargained for—not so much the money, but the blatant threat of violence. Richards abruptly ended the meeting. After the rugged visitor left, the governor said to Dr. Penrose, "So that is Tom Horn! A very different man from what I expected to meet. A cool devil, ain't he?"[84]

But by the summer of 1900, more was at stake in Big Horn County. The larger cattle owners were feeling squeezed by an increasing number of small farmers and ranchers. A major reason "for the changes in the range business was an influx of homesteaders," explains another Horn biographer, Chip Carlson. "The 'nesters' or 'grangers' as they were referred to disdainfully, proved up on claims to some of the best bottomlands. By doing so they decreased the availability of water for the herds of the dominant, larger ranchers who depended on the availability of open range."

More than before, Brown's Hole was seen as the epicenter of the barons' troubles. It had been occupied by "nesters" for years and was a safe haven for rustlers who preyed upon the large herds. One of the most irritated owners was Ora Haley, who owned large swaths of land in northwest Colorado and southeast Wyoming. He and other aggrieved owners had formed yet another organization, the Little Snake River Valley Cattleman's Association.

Haley had come far geographically as well as financially. He was born in December 1845 in East Corinth, Maine, and while still a teenager he had served in the Civil War as a member of the Maine Militia State Guards. Like many young men after the war, he struck out on his

---

84 There is also an account that Horn met with several cattle barons at the Cheyenne Club, and he said, "Gentlemen, I have a system that never fails. Yours has."

own, heading generally west, getting as far as Iowa. He signed on with a wagon train going to Denver, learning how to be a bullwhacker. After some time spent in Denver, Haley moved on to Wyoming.

Over the years, he worked for various ranches. He must have saved his money as well as made some good connections because in 1880, he founded the Two Bar Ranch. It prospered, and over time he acquired more and more land.[85] Hiram Bernard, a Texas trail driver who became the Two Bar foreman, later wrote that Haley "was a smart and lucky financier. He started in the cow business at Laramie with three old dairy cows. He was smart enough to see opportunities and capitalize on them, lucky to find a sucker to handle a range cattle business better than he could, and he was wise enough to keep from meddling with the range end."

Where Haley did meddle was in politics, becoming a prominent player in Wyoming. This included serving in the legislature of the territorial government and then in the first Wyoming State Senate as an ardent Republican.

And then there was the meddling that put a killing rifle in Tom Horn's hands. Early in 1900, Hiram Bernard was ordered to attend a meeting at his boss's office in Denver. When he arrived, three other men were with Haley: Charles Ayer, Wilfred Wilson, and John Coble. All had extensive ranch holdings in Wyoming and were fed up with the rustling and other encroachments by the nesters—and, conveniently, at the time Tom Horn was working for Coble, who thought highly of him.[86]

After collectively grousing about Brown's Hole and its unsavory residents, Coble suggested to the three other ranchers a course of

---

85 Haley had an ongoing rivalry with the "cattle queen" Ann Bassett. Never letting bygones be bygones, Haley had her arrested and tried for rustling in 1913.

86 To his detriment, Coble remained loyal to Tom Horn. In 1901, when Horn was charged with the murder of young Willie Nickell, Coble paid Horn's legal bills, which eventually totaled tens of thousands of dollars. This proved to be too much of a burden even for a rich rancher. Coble's operations struggled to survive and his wealth dwindled. Eventually, he shot himself in the lobby of a hotel in Elko, Nevada.

action—pay a man to kill cattle thieves, with $500 for every one sent to the afterlife. Horn was the name of the man he had in mind. There was not much hand-wringing over this proposal. Ora Haley not only assented but ordered his foreman to give Horn whatever horses and supplies he needed from the Two Bar barns and larder.

Horn was helped by the fact that despite all his roaming around as a detective and cattle baron enforcer, he was not known in Brown's Hole. He arrived in early April, introducing himself as Thomas Hicks, a horse buyer who could use a job. He was given one by Matt Rash, who by this time was the head of the Brown's Park Cattlemen's Association, a big name for a loose coalition of small ranches.

Rash was also still rustling. Initially, Horn served as a spy for Haley, Coble, and the others. He reported on Rash's illicit activities and supplied evidence, including parts of two butchered cowhides that bore the brand "VD," belonging to Ora Haley. A herd of twenty-eight cattle had recently disappeared and were presumed stolen. One of the cowhides had been found at the summer camp of Matt Rash, the other at the camp of Jim McKnight, the husband of Josie Bassett.

After examining the cowhides handed over by "Hicks," Hi Bernard recalled, "that looked like the boldest, most outrageous cattle-rustling job I had ever seen or heard of. Acting for the general welfare of all range users adjacent to Brown's Park, the appointed committee gave Horn the go-ahead signal."[87]

Oddly, Horn took to letter-writing—perhaps he still believed in fair play. He had created a list of the men in Brown's Hole who he believed, based on what he had seen and heard, were the guiltiest of rustlers. He sent or posted on their properties letters warning them that if they were still in the area after thirty days they would "suffer the consequences."

---

87 Ann Bassett, McKnight's sister-in-law, later claimed that Tom Horn, doing a little rustling on the side, had driven the small herd himself. While he was in Rock Springs looking for a buyer, a man named Charley Ward stole the stolen cattle. Discovering this, Horn told his bosses that Rash was the rustler.

The scheme was almost exposed. During the first week in May, a clandestine meeting was held in a livery stable corral in Craig, Colorado. It was for "Hicks" to give Hi Bernard an update, but another participant was someone known only as "Mexican Pete." Bernard told Hicks that he had permission from the Coble and company committee to kill Matt Rash and Isom Dart and "Longhorn" Thompson, the rustlers at the top of Hicks's list. In addition, Ann Bassett and her brother, Elbert, and another man, Joe Davenport, who aided rustlers, were to leave the area, the farther away the better. A local man, George Banks, revealed only years later that Bernard told Hicks that if he followed these instructions "you can get your pay anytime you want it." Because Banks said nothing at the time, the intended victims were not warned.

Hicks did not help keep his illicit intentions hidden. The following month, again in Craig, he encountered an acquaintance, Cyrus Shores, the Pinkerton operative, who knew that it was Horn posing as Hicks. The latter confided, "I'm doing a little rat cleaning in Brown's Hole" and that it was "kind of a touchy situation."

As if saying that to a detective was not indiscreet enough, Horn discussed his new 94 Winchester, a .30–30-caliber rifle. After marveling at the smokeless powder it used, he said, "You can shoot a long way off and that don't make no smoke" and noted that this was helpful "to men in our line of work."

During the first week in July, Matt Rash went to Rock Springs to attend Independence Day celebrations. On his return trip, he visited Ann Bassett. Many locals believed that they were engaged. Then he went on to his cabin on Cold Spring Mountain. There would be no wedding.

The next morning, Tom Horn appeared in the doorway and shot Rash twice, in the arm and back. Rash staggered to his bunk, where he bled out.[88] As if this was not message enough to rustlers, before he left Horn shot Rash's horse in the head.

---

88 Rash tried to write the name of his assailant on an envelope using his own blood, but life left him too soon.

Rash's body was found two days later. He was buried next to his cabin. A coroner's inquest was held, which determined nothing more than Rash had been murdered. When Rash's father and brother arrived at the cabin, Horn met them and blamed Isom Dart for the killing. There was not much they could do about that so they exhumed the body and brought Matt Rash home to Acton, Texas, for reburial.

A few days later, the killer almost joined his victim in the great beyond. Horn was on his way to John Coble's ranch when, because it was closing in on 3:00 A.M., he stopped in Baggs, Wyoming. The Bull Dog Saloon was still open and serving patrons who remained from the Saturday night crowd. Horn ordered a whiskey, then another, and midway through the third one he was becoming ornery. When he refused the offer of a man to drink with him, a fight began.

Horn was outnumbered immediately because the man, Newton Kelly, had a brother, Edward, with him. Horn was beaten up pretty good in the brawl. Worse, Edward Kelly had a knife, and he used it. Horn fell to the dirty floor with blood oozing out of slashes in his chest and neck. A doctor was summoned and managed to stitch Horn up before he bled out like Rash had. The *Rocky Mountain News* would report that on the previous Sunday a man named John Hicks had been in a fight with the Kelly brothers and "his condition is serious; but he will probably recover. No arrests have been made."

While recuperating, the assassin received his next assignment. John Coble was irate that sheep farmers were letting their animals loose to graze on pastureland he owned for only his cattle to enjoy. He wrote to a friend that he could have the sheep owners arrested, but they "are hiring all the six-shooters and badmen they can find. I want Horn back here; he will straighten them out by merely riding around."

Horn was about to do more than that. Back in Brown's Hole in August, still with the flimsy Tom Hicks alias, he circulated the story that it was Isom Dart who had murdered Matt Rash. Perhaps the motive was to reduce any sympathy and curiosity should Dart turn up dead. He might have sooner but for the appearance of Theodore Roosevelt.

In the late summer of 1900, his misfortune during the Great Die-Up not having deterred him from returning to the West, Roosevelt was still basking in the glow of his Spanish-American War service, which had helped propel him to becoming governor of New York. In June, at the Republican convention in Philadelphia, Roosevelt had been nominated to be the running mate of President William McKinley, who was seeking reelection.[89] Taking a break from campaigning, the soon-to-be vice president was in the area on a hunting expedition.

Tom Horn had known Colonel Roosevelt during his service in Cuba, but given what the gunman was engaged in, he avoided any contact with such a high-profile figure. Horn literally kept his smokeless powder dry, waiting until Roosevelt had returned East to resume campaigning before making his next move. And the first week of October, Isom Dart died.

It happened on the morning of the third. It is murky if Dart was the intended victim. It had become clear to Jim McKnight that if indeed there was a list of rustlers marked for death, he was on it, so he had moved out of his cabin in Summit Springs. Not wanting to see a useful structure go to waste, Dart and a business partner named John Dempshire had taken up residence there. Probably as far as Tom Horn was concerned, either one, Dart or McKnight, would do.

Early that morning, Dart and Dempshire exited the cabin because, of course, it did not have indoor plumbing. While they were about their business, there were two gunshots, originating from behind a tree near the corral. Both bullets found Dart, and he died. Horn backed away to his horse and rode off, stopping at a nearby ranch where he had arranged to have a fresh horse waiting for him.[90]

With two Brown's Hole rustlers dead and McKnight (and no doubt

---

89 The tally to nominate Teddy had been 925–0, with one abstention, cast by Roosevelt himself.

90 This arrangement was revealed by the rancher's young son to a friend, Tim McCoy, who was nine years old at the time. McCoy would go on to become a moderately popular actor in Hollywood westerns and served in the army in both World Wars I and II. In a you-can't-make-this-up coincidence, McCoy died in 1978 as production began on the feature film *Tom Horn*.

others) on the run, it appeared that Horn's strategy was successful. And it was. Rustling activity declined severely, and suffering fewer losses, the larger cattle operations prospered. Almost negating his own profits earned, Horn nearly put himself in jail.

Rashly, that November, he agreed to be interviewed by a reporter for the *Wyoming Tribune.* The purpose of the piece was for Horn to reminisce about his days as the Pinkerton Agency detective. This he did, but the assassin also used the interview as an opportunity to extol the advantages of the sharp reduction of rustlers in Brown's Hole. With such "undesirable residents" gone, he predicted, "respectable stockmen will go in there and settle."

What had once been a haven in Bandit Heaven began to settle down to earth. Certainly one indication of a quieter Brown's Hole was that Ann Bassett, the "Cattle Queen," married Hiram Bernard. Tom Horn went back to work as a range detective and as a hand for John Coble and his Two Bar Ranch.

28

THE FORT WORTH PHOTO

Happy with their haul from the Winnemucca heist, Butch Cassidy, the Sundance Kid, and Will Carver left many a frustrated posse man behind on their way to Texas. The plan was to rendezvous with Kid Curry and Ben Kilpatrick. After such a busy summer it was time for a vacation, and the sooner the better because they might not have too many similar celebrations left, if any.

"Sundance and Butch realized that the time had come for them to make a change," claims Donna Ernst. "All their friends and associates were either being killed or caught and jailed. As the new century began, the breakup of their gang seemed inevitable."

But first, they would have some fun in Fort Worth. Specifically, their destination was known as Hell's Half-Acre. During the decades following the Civil War many growing frontier towns had their red-light districts, but Fort Worth's was particularly notorious. It took root in the 1870s when the town—established in 1849 as an army outpost on a bluff overlooking the Trinity River—became a convenient stop for the dust-caked drovers on cattle drives between south Texas and

Kansas. It quickly became populated with saloons, brothels, and other dens of iniquity offering gambling, liquor, and prostitutes. The half-acre block was originally designated from Tenth Street to Fifteenth Street while intersecting with Houston Street, Main Street, and Rusk Street.

At its peak, Hell's Half-Acre was not only a cowboy playground but also a favorite hideout for thieves and violent criminals. The twenty-two-thousand-square-foot ward was visited by many Wild West luminaries, including Wyatt Earp, Bat Masterson, Luke Short, Doc Holliday, and Sam Bass. Every so often there were crackdowns by law enforcement, but because the red-light district was an important source of income, the Fort Worth fathers were reluctant to take serious action.

The most well-known of the city's peace officers was Jim Court-right. More than most, he represented the thin and often-crossed line between lawman and criminal.

James Courtright was born in 1848 in Sangamon County, Illinois. Lying convincingly enough about his age enabled him to enlist in the Union army and he was wounded during the war. Afterward, recovered, Courtright wandered until he stopped and stayed in Fort Worth, where he found a job as a jailer.

Along the way, he had acquired good shooting skills, being accurate as well as fast. This turned out to be an extra source of income because when he married a woman named Sarah Weeks and taught her how to shoot, the couple for a time put on shooting exhibitions. They did well enough that they were performers in an early edition of Buffalo Bill's Wild West show.

Courtright cut quite a figure. Fancying himself something of a Wild Bill Hickok, he wore his hair long and displayed two pistols with the butts facing forward. In 1876, the first election for a city marshal was held in Fort Worth, and Courtright won by three votes over four other candidates. For him, Hell's Half-Acre was both a responsibility and an opportunity.

A common occurrence was lawmen versus unruly drunken cowboys. During one such incident, in August 1877, a Fort Worth deputy, Columbus Fitzgerald, was shot and killed. Courtright did not wait for an arrest warrant—that same night, he tracked down the cowboy and killed him. He would be "credited" with at least four more such killings during his time as marshal.

It was also believed that there were several off-the-books killings. The deceased were stubborn business owners who would not pay into the protection racket Courtright had instigated. Most met his demand to avoid the risk of becoming the target of his anger and gun. Voted out of office in 1879, he no longer wore a badge, but his much more lucrative protection system remained. It was this that eventually led to Courtright's demise.

Luke Short was a gunfighter, gambler, and bar owner in Dodge City during its "wicked" heyday. Among his friends were Wyatt Earp and especially Bat Masterson. It was because of that friendship that Earp and Masterson returned to Dodge City War in 1883, after a coalition of competing saloon owners tried to toss Short out of town. The so-called Dodge City War doomed that effort. Previously, he had reunited with Earp and Masterson and another fast friend, Doc Holliday, in Tombstone where his contribution to Wild West history was gunning down Charlie Storms outside the Oriental Saloon. On Masterson's advice, he headed back to Kansas.

When Dodge City lost its allure, Short relocated to Fort Worth, where he ran the most well-known of Hell's Half-Acre saloons and gambling houses, the White Elephant. He was just as reluctant to be pushed around in Fort Worth as he had been in Dodge City—meaning, Short refused to participate in the former marshal's protection racket. For this, Jim Courtright realized, he had to make an example of Short or risk expensive defections.

One night in February 1887, a drunk Courtright called out Luke Short, challenging him to emerge from the White Elephant. A friend, Jake Johnson, managed to calm Courtright down and suggested instead that they should talk to resolve their differences. Short was persuaded, and he stepped out of the White Elephant.

Apparently, the conversation was not constructive because after both men had walked up the street and were in front of bar and brothel owner Ella Blackwell's Shooting Gallery, they turned and faced each other just a few feet apart. Some angry words were exchanged, and moments after Courtright blustered, "Don't you pull a gun on me," he drew one of his own pistols.

What happened was witnessed by visiting friend Bat Masterson, who years later wrote of the event: "No time was wasted in the exchange of words once the men faced each other. Both drew their pistols at the same time, but, as usual, Short's spoke first and a bullet from a Colt's 45-calibre pistol went crashing through Courtright's body. The shock caused him to reel backward; then he got another and still another, and by the time his lifeless form had reached the floor, Luke had succeeded in shooting him five times."[91]

Two years later, with Courtright's killing still fresh in their minds—even as much of a scoundrel as he was—and there being more recent serious bouts of violence in the city, Fort Worth officials shut down many of the activities that were deemed as the worst offenders. But by 1900, when Cassidy and company were on their way, much of Hell's Half-Acre was up and running once more—proving again that money talks louder than mayhem.

During their trip, Butch and Sundance had sold or gifted their horses and saddles and resorted to the railroad. When they emerged from the Union Depot, it may have been like a portal from the familiar recent past to a present that kept catching up to the future. As they walked to the Maddox Hotel on Main Street they observed the glow

91 Jim Courtright's funeral was attended by hundreds of Fort Worth residents. Luke Short was arrested for the shooting, and though he was almost lynched soon afterward, he was never brought to trial. Instead, all of the charges against him were dismissed with no explanation. He'd had his fill of Fort Worth, however, and he returned to Dodge City, where he got married and lived a quieter life.

of electric lights, dodged streetcars, and might have had to jump out of the way of honking automobiles.

Officially—as if such a reason other than pleasure was needed—the five members of the Wild Bunch were in Fort Worth for the marriage of one of them, Will Carver, to Callie May Hunt. The ceremony was to take place on December 1 and be held at one of Hell's Half-Acre brothels, probably Fannie Porter's, as that was a favorite one among the Wild Bunch members. Hunt, who also went under the name of Lille Davis, was a prostitute, but she plied her trade in San Antonio.

One member of the gang recalled seeing a sign for the Swartz View Company. It was a photography studio on Main Street, just a few blocks away. Given how dapper the men looked and as they rehearsed for the joyful event, why not have a picture taken? Likely, by that point in the party, alcohol had helped to chase away caution.

Cassidy, Sundance, Kid Curry, Kilpatrick, and the groom Carver walked to 705 Main Street, which had a ground-floor office and a second-floor studio. Greeting them was the coproprietor and photographer John Swartz. Then forty-two years old, he and two brothers, David and Charles, had grown up on a farm in Virginia but, after a few detours, were reunited in Fort Worth in the mid-1880s. For the next three decades, the three of them observed the city through a camera lens, snapping pictures of people, events, and architecture. They collectively produced thousands of photographs that were scattered to the four winds after their deaths. Hundreds of those images have survived, although the brothers themselves became largely forgotten.[92]

Two of the Wild Bunch gang members stood—Will Carver on the left and Kid Curry on the right. Seated left to right were Sundance Kid, Ben Kilpatrick, and Butch Cassidy. All wore brand-new derby hats, and they were dressed in three-piece suits. The only visi-

---

92 But not completely forgotten: the Swartz brothers' extensive photographic chronicle of early Fort Worth served as the inspiration for a major downtown revival and historical preservation development known as Sundance Square. Their cumulative work provided a visual chronicle of late nineteenth- and early twentieth-century Fort Worth as well as a window into American life during that era.

ble remnant of riding the Outlaw Trail was some dust on their shoes. Four men look to their left and only a cocky Butch Cassidy gazes directly at the camera.

"The well-dressed gentlemen in the photo might have been mistaken for a group of bankers or merchants," remarks Thom Hatch.

As befits the celebratory mood, they told Swartz to use the more expensive dry plate processing method. Each outlaw ordered a set of 6.5-by-8.5-inch prints, to be ready for pickup later in the week. Once Swartz saw how well the image turned out, he placed a copy in the first-floor front window of his shop.

According to Charles Kelly, "The change from overalls and Stetsons made them feel so proud they decided to have their pictures taken in a group—a bit of foofaraw which almost got them into serious trouble."

Cassidy did not have a date for the Will Carver and Callie Hunt nuptials ten days later. But three other men brought their significant others: Sundance Kid brought Ethel Place, Ben Kilpatrick brought Laura Bullion, and Kid Curry brought Annie Rogers—at least, that was the name she was using at the time.

Her real name was Della Moore. Next to nothing is known about her origins other than she was born near El Paso and was about twenty years old. Beginning five years earlier, Della had worked in brothels in Arkansas and San Antonio as well as Fort Worth. She had met Kid Curry in mid-1898, probably while employed at Fannie Porter's bordello. The Kid thought her trustworthy enough that he would sometimes hide stolen loot with her. By the time of the Carver-Hunt wedding, she had stopped working as a prostitute and was Curry's traveling companion.

The photograph on display at the gallery might have remained nothing more than a conversation piece except for Fred Dodge. The Wells Fargo detective, working undercover as a gambler, happened to stroll past the Swartz studio window and thought he recognized one of the men in the photograph on display. After examining it more closely, Dodge became convinced that the man was Will Carver. Given that he was a known outlaw, the others could well be outlaws too, perhaps with active warrants.[93]

As Donna Ernst gloomily commented on what would soon become a famous photograph: "With their faces recorded on film, their demise began."

Fred Dodge ordered a batch of copies of the photograph. He carried them up Main Street to his office and sent out queries as to the identities of the other men, including to the Pinkerton Detective Agency. Not only were the other four men identified, but immediately after a copy got into the hands of George Nixon at the bank in Winnemucca, he responded that Carver, Sundance, and Cassidy were the men who had made him poorer.

It was almost like sending up a flare to police agencies. "Before long, every core member of the Wild Bunch had been identified," reports Thom Hatch. "Wanted posters were updated with the photograph and distributed to seemingly every town and village in the West. Law enforcement's quest to put an end to the gang's career had been made much easier by one click of a camera's shutter."

As Charles Leerhsen poignantly notes, "It was a happy time, their last happy time together. In less than a year, Carver would be dead, and Kilpatrick and Logan would be in prison."

In her book on Robbers Roost, Pearl Baker contends that an imprudent Cassidy himself sent a copy of the photograph "to the bank in Winnemucca with a note thanking them for their contribution." Butch also mailed a copy to Vic Button, the young boy who had previously been the recipient of the outlaw's horse.

An impish sense of humor was surely not enough protection from the law. Just as Fred Dodge had recognized one of the gang members, Will Carver or another of his companions may have recognized the

---

93 Several of my previous books, beginning with *Dodge City*—named after a different man named Dodge—have provided background on Fred Dodge. Suffice to say that he was an especially durable detective whose journals of his experiences extended to twenty-seven volumes.

veteran railroad detective. Immediately after the wedding took place, the Wild Bunch was gone from Fort Worth.

Baker also points out, "The United States was getting pretty hot for the boys. Pinkerton's detectives were becoming better organized, and more efficient men were in the field. The dream of going to South America to retire looked better and better."

To underwrite such a venture—in the wake of blowing too much cash in Fort Worth—Butch and his buddies began to think about one more big job.

29

DEAD SERIOUS

Then they thought again. Butch Cassidy, at least, had to realize by now that there really was no more Wild West for wanted men to hide in. As Hatch points out, "Bandits were not up against random individuals any longer; they faced an organized system that connected various arms of the law that could throw a net over virtually the entire country. The sophistication of these innovative law enforcement practices, combined with the $10,000 bounties on their heads, had convinced Butch Cassidy that it would be only a matter of time before the Wild Bunch would be eliminated."

First for Butch and the Sundance Kid, with their fellow gang members gone or soon to be, was New York City. And from there, South America. This was not a new idea—it was likely that Cassidy had begun considering this far-off destination a few years earlier. But now he was dead serious. With whatever resources were available to him—popping into a public library in Wyoming or Utah or Texas was probably not an option—he researched the fertile features of the Patagonia region in Argentina.

It was soon settled. Sight unseen, Argentina would be their new home. Ethel Place would be part of this journey too, to cook and clean as well as being technically, if not officially, Mrs. Harry Longabaugh. It is believed that Butch furtively returned to Wyoming. This was a risky venture, but he and Al Hainer still owned the Horse Creek ranch, and he wanted to sell his share and add the proceeds to the pot of stolen money.

For Sundance, there would be a different and somewhat sentimental detour. After greeting the new year of 1901 in New Orleans, he and Ethel traveled to Phoenixville, Pennsylvania. Harry Longabaugh was making his return home after almost two decades as a cowboy, ranch hand, and outlaw.

With his parents having passed away, on hand to greet him were three siblings who still lived in the general area: his brother Harvey, his sister Emma, and his sister Samanna.[94] He introduced Ethel as Mrs. Longabaugh—which, ironically, was how the Pinkerton National Detective Agency was already referring to her in its files.

"They had a delightful time together," writes Donna Ernst, "one that remained in Samanna's memory for the rest of her life." Though Emma "still frowned upon her brother's reputation," Samanna "was especially pleased to know that Sundance was planning to go straight once he arrived in Argentina."

It was because that long trip loomed that Mr. and Mrs. Longabaugh did not stay in Phoenixville more than just two weeks after Christmas. There was a tearful farewell, and then the couple moved on but not yet to New York. Claiming that he needed treatment for catarrh, a serious sinus condition, Sundance and Ethel went north, to Buffalo. He checked into the Pierce Medical Institute. It is not known if the doctors there were of any help.

Finally in New York City at the beginning of February, Sundance

94 Harry's sister Samanna was unaware that there were U.S. Mail employees who, illegally bribed by the Pinkerton Agency, were monitoring letters sent to her, looking for ones from Harry that might tell of his whereabouts. It apparently did not occur to them he might actually return to his hometown.

and Ethel were reunited with Butch. They rented rooms at a boarding house on West Twelfth Street in Manhattan. The couple were H. A. and Ethel Place, with H. A. claiming to be a Wyoming cattleman. Butch was James Ryan, Ethel's brother.

The trio was far removed from their much more familiar surroundings of the West. Tall, snowcapped mountains had been replaced by tall, slender buildings and valleys with alleys and nights brightened by streetlights. There were motor cars and streetcars competing with horse-drawn wagons. There were restaurants and saloons catering to a much different crowd than cattlemen. And, of course, all the people: the population of New York City had recently surpassed four million, while, for example, the population of all of Wyoming in 1901 was ninety-two thousand.

The couple and her "brother" enjoyed being tourists. Hey, they had money in their pockets and felt untraceable in the big city, even though the Pinkerton Agency had an office there, presided over by the oblivious Robert Pinkerton.[95] For almost a month, the trio roamed the streets, the winter weather mild compared to what a February was like out west, probably marveling at storefront displays, wincing at restaurant prices, and sampling the recent invention of motion pictures.[96] If they were homesick for their former havens of Brown's Hole, Robbers Roost, and the Hole-in-the-Wall, there was nothing they could do about it. For Butch and Sundance, certainly, the only place left back home to lay their heads was a jail cell.

Fort Worth be damned, it was time for another photograph—at least, for Sundance and Ethel. The couple entered the Union Square studio of Joseph DeYoung and posed for a formal portrait. Sundance liked the result so much that he mailed one to a friend in Little Snake River Valley, noting that the lady was from Texas and he had recently married

---

95 When he later learned of the trio's excursion, William Pinkerton wrote a scathing letter to his brother about New York being so accommodating to the two most sought-after outlaws in the country.

96 Butch and Sundance went a step further than window shopping at Tiffany's. The former purchased a $40 gold watch that he then gifted to Ethel, and not to be outdone, Sundance bought a $150 gold lapel watch for Ethel as well as a diamond stickpin for himself.

her. Another copy was sent to Samanna in Pennsylvania, which is probably how, thanks to a Pinkerton payoff, it wound up on a wanted poster.

If the trio had any thoughts of staying in the relative safety of New York indefinitely, they ignored them. And as a practical matter, however much of their stolen money they had stashed and however frugal they were, New York was not indefinitely affordable. So, sticking to the plan they had agreed on, on February 20, 1901, Butch, Sundance, and Ethel were taken to Brooklyn. At Red Hook, they climbed the walkway and set foot on the *Herminius.* This was not a pleasant passenger liner but a Scottish freighter. In the depth of winter, there were very few options to sail to Buenos Aires, even for those willing to pay ninety dollars for a one-way ticket.

After such a pleasant stay in New York City, it is understandable if they had second thoughts about their lives being about to take such a significant turn. But they were clear-eyed enough to see that they really did not have any other choice. As Charles Leerhsen notes, "For Butch and Sundance, the time when they could holster their six-shooters, put away their bandanna masks, and blend seamlessly into the American cattle business had long since passed."

They were at sea for almost five weeks, arriving on March 23 in Buenos Aires, with a population topping one million. Butch must have done more research in advance—probably not all of his hours in New York had been idle ones—because the newcomers knew who to go to. George Newbery's day job was as a dentist, but the native New Yorker had lived in Argentina for over two decades and was the U.S. vice-consul. Though that was mostly a ceremonial title, he knew the country well along with many of its officials. When Newbery learned that his visitors wanted to buy and work a ranch that raised cattle and horses, he suggested Chubut because it was a good substitute for the American West.[97]

---

97 We have to assume that the outlaws used fake names, perhaps the same ones as in New York. As well informed as the American dentist was, he might have heard of Butch Cassidy and the Sundance Kid and would not have risked his Argentinian connections and vice-consul title by assisting wanted outlaws.

The province lies between the Atlantic Ocean to the east and a section of the Andes Mountains to the west that is the border between Argentina and Chile. There were already (mostly) English-speaking people there because in 1865 a boat full of Welsh farmers had put in, and they headed for the Chubut Valley, where many of their descendants still worked the land. It could be very cold in the winter and hot in the summer, not unlike the Dakotas. Newbery pointed out that there was plenty of land available at favorable prices.

Even better, the would-be ranchers enjoyed considerable buying power. With Ethel in tow, Cassidy and Sundance marched to a bank Newbery suggested a few blocks away. For once, they did not take money out but put money in—the equivalent of $250,000 today. Newbery had also suggested the Cholila region in western Chubut, so after enjoying a couple more days in Buenos Aires, the trio took a train there.

What they found would seem to serve their purposes fine; better than most, in fact. The land was fertile, and there was plenty of it. Water was for the taking. There were few people. And as Charles Leerhsen points out, "The remoteness might have been a negative for some—the region was also several hundred miles from the nearest telegraph line—but for fugitives who had the Pinkertons on their trail and wanted nothing more than to live peacefully, it added to the paradisiacal quality of the place."

They wasted little time in getting going on their new home and lifestyle. Cassidy and Sundance acquired 1,500 acres on the Rio Blanco River and to live and multiply there they purchased horses, cattle, and sheep. These friendly gringos—who said their names were James Santiago Ryan and Harry Enrique Place—could draw from a seemingly bottomless reservoir of funds at the Buenos Aires bank. Once the paperwork was approved and the operation was up and running, it was legally known as Place y Ryan.

What was needed was a physical home on the property. They could not be content in a canvas tent for long, especially once winter arrived, even though that would not be until the following June. In October, that began to take shape: Using fresh-cut logs culled from their surroundings, and with the help of local laborers, Cassidy and Sundance began to build a community of cabins and barns. As with Charlie Siringo on his ranch in New Mexico, the two men and Ethel were grateful to have a view of the mountains.

Butch Cassidy and the Sundance Kid were through with being bandits.

And that was the way it could have stayed. There could have been a peaceful end of the trail—far removed from what happened to their fellow gang members back home.

30

"LEGITIMATE WARFARE"

"The hunt was on," proclaims Charles Kelly in *The Outlaw Trail*, and as the days of the new centuries piled up, there were fewer bandits to track down.

The criminal career of George "Flatnose" Currie had come to an end—as well as his life—in April 1900. That month, as spring was making an appearance in Grand County, Utah, Currie was busy rustling. He was caught doing it by forty-three-year-old Sheriff Jesse Tyler. When Currie resisted arrest, guns were drawn. Tyler either fired first or at least more accurately because Currie fell dead.

An unfortunate footnote to this for Sheriff Tyler is that when word of his friend's death reached Kid Curry—who was still furious over his brother Lonie's death in Missouri—he vowed revenge. He rode from New Mexico to Utah where, twenty miles north of Thompson Springs in Grand County, he found Tyler and a deputy, Samuel Jenkins. Curry killed them both.

Butch Cassidy and the Sundance Kid and Ethel Place were just finding their way in Argentina in 1901 and probably did not hear about the death of another Wild Bunch member, Will Carver. He was in Sonora, Texas, and was recognized by Sheriff Ed Bryant. (More about this follows.)

For those bandits who remained, the summer taking hold up north meant that it was train-robbing season. Charles Kelly called it "the last exploit of the Wild Bunch in the United States." That was half-true. It was a sensational crime that was committed by a Wild Bunch that was much reduced in manpower.

The "last exploit" was the Great Northern railroad heist. It was set into motion about 2:00 P.M. on July 3, near Wagner, Montana. The robbers were Kid Curry, Ben Kilpatrick, and Orlando Camillo Hanks. That such a previously peripheral player in the Wild Bunch should now have such a prominent role in a high-profile heist is less a reflection of his abilities as a bandit than that by mid-1901 there were few outlaws left who Kid Curry could call on.

Hanks had been born in December 1860 in DeWitt County, Texas, which in the early 1870s had experienced a lot of bloody turmoil thanks to the Sutton-Taylor Feud, until a company of forty locked and loaded Texas Rangers led by Captain Leander McNelly had calmed things down.[98] One nickname for Hanks was "O.C." while another was the less delicate "Deaf Charley" because he could not hear in one ear and had to cock his head when listening.[99]

He was not yet three years old when his father was killed in the war and was buried, appropriately, on Confederate Hill in Baltimore. His mother remarried after the Civil War ended, but that husband did not last long either, murdered during an attempted robbery. Maybe the shooting of his stepfather did Hanks a favor because as soon as he could be on his own, he hit the Outlaw Trail. During the 1880s, robbing trains became his specialty—not that he was terribly good at it.

---

98 For more details on this turbulent series of bloody events, please see a previous book by yours truly, *Follow Me to Hell*.

99 It is believed that Orlando Hanks was a grandnephew of Nancy Hanks Lincoln, the mother of the sixteenth president. This would also make the outlaw a distant ancestor of Tom Hanks—probably something the actor does not include on his résumé, especially having voiced the lawman Woody in *Toy Story*.

In 1892, Hanks was arrested in Teton County, Montana, for the raid on a Northern Pacific train at Big Timber, Montana. Worse for his immediate future, authorities discovered that he was wanted in Las Vegas, New Mexico, for murder. Soon after being escorted there, Hanks was convicted and sentenced to hang. For some reason, his miserable life was spared by the governor and instead he was hauled back to Montana and given ten years in the state prison. Hanks served eight of them and was released on April 30, 1901. Two months later, perhaps pining to be back behind bars, he was ready to rob the railroad again, with the remnants of the Wild Bunch.

The Wagner job was supposedly the brainchild of Kid Curry who, in the absence of Cassidy and Sundance, was the de facto leader of the Wild Bunch. The idea "wasn't a bad one," writes Gary A. Wilson, "if only because the Great Northern wasn't on the outlook for Logan, and so there would be no special trains of rangers and trackers to deal with. In theory, it should have been much like the earlier days of outlawing—in other words, easy."

On that early July afternoon, as the Great Northern westbound train No. 3 pulled away from Malta, the conductor, Alex Smith, saw a tall, red-faced man board the baggage car. Thinking the man was a hobo, Smith ordered him off the train. Instead of obeying, the "hobo," Orlando Hanks, pulled a pistol and warned the conductor not to stop the train. Smith quickly retreated, and Hanks headed for the engine. When he climbed over the tender, he produced the pistol again, and told the engineer, Tom Jones, to "just keep on drilling." As if he had to make the situation more clear, he informed Jones and the fireman, Mike O'Neil, that he was going to rob the train.[100]

A few tense moments later, he ordered Jones to stop at a small bridge over Exeter Creek where two more holdup men—the short

---

100 In the small world department, earlier that day Kid Curry and his companions had hidden out in a barn on a ranch belonging to Mike O'Neil—the first cousin of the fireman. Years earlier, the two Mikes had traveled together across the Atlantic Ocean, emigrating from County Clare in Ireland.

Kid Curry and the tall Ben Kilpatrick—were waiting with rifles and dynamite.[101]

One of the passengers on the train was the Valley County sheriff, William Griffith. When the train stopped unexpectedly, Griffith got off to investigate but was forced to take cover back in the train when he was shot at. While Hanks and Kilpatrick fired their rifles to keep Griffith and the passengers inside, Curry marched Jones and O'Neil to the baggage car where the mail clerk, James Martin, and the express messenger, Clarence Smith, were hauled outside. Meanwhile, Hanks and Kilpatrick stood on each side of the train, their rifles discouraging any passengers from trying to leave, or even dumber, be a hero.

That would happen, but not to a passenger. Two men, a traveling agent named Douglas and the brakeman Woodside, had gotten off the train and were waving warning flags to alert any following train of the stopped train ahead. Both were wounded by gunfire, probably by Hanks and Kilpatrick. It was later reported that one of the railroad workers died but was not identified. Another casualty was Gertrude Smith. The eighteen-year-old passenger was struck by a wayward bullet. She would be treated and released from a hospital in Great Falls.

Curry and the messenger Smith went to the express car. The latter later told the *Great Falls Daily Tribune* that when they entered the express car the robber "commenced taking his dynamite from a sack and laid it on top of the safe. When it got to sputtering, I said, 'I would like to get out of here,' and he said, 'You wait a minute and I will get out of here with you,' and when it was ready we both went out."

On the second trip to the express car Curry took O'Neil along to carry the dynamite. The fireman waited outside while the robber entered the car and found the safe unopened. After placing another charge on the safe Curry hurriedly exited and another explosion rocked the car. As soon as the smoke cleared, he returned to find the safe still unopened. O'Neil

---

101 It makes sense that there was a fourth gang member whose role was to take care of the horses, but if so, he has never been identified. Some accounts have even included Butch Cassidy and/or the Sundance Kid, but as we know, they were a continent away from Montana.

again waited outside while another charge was placed on the safe. Finally, with Kid Curry losing his patience, after the third try, he found the door ripped from the safe. (The explosion also blew the windows out of the smoking car.)

Curry entered the smoldering car and ordered O'Neil to join him. O'Neil later told the *Tribune*, "He threw what stuff was in the sack out and told me to hold it. He started tearing the broken pieces of the safe off so he could get the stuff in there. He picked up one package and made a remark about it, something like $30,000 or $40,000, and dropped it into the sack."

Once the safe was emptied, the train crew was ordered to walk toward the rear of the train. Smith, the express messenger, pushing his luck, asked Kid Curry for a souvenir. The bandit obliged, empty-ing one of his pistols and presenting it. The robbers then disappeared around the front of the engine and were next seen by the passengers riding south toward the Little Rockies.

Less than an hour after the robbery, train No. 3 limped into Wagner, twelve miles west of Malta, where Sheriff Griffith began organizing a posse. Undersheriff Richard Kane was contacted at Glasgow, and he and seven deputies were soon on their way to Wagner aboard a light en-gine. Later a special car loaded with horses was brought from Glasgow to Malta where a second posse was being formed.

Meanwhile, Kid Curry, Ben Kilpatrick, and Orlando Hanks and possibly a fourth thief were putting distance between themselves and their pursuers. One man saw them south of Malta and said that they rode a wide circle around him and fired one shot in his direction when he tried to approach them. A rancher named William Ellis met the same men eighteen miles south of Malta about two hours after the robbery. He claimed he recognized two of the robbers and identified them as Harry Longabaugh and Kid Curry—probably mistaking Kilpatrick for the Sundance Kid.

Perhaps they had little to worry about. As one man opined to the *Tribune*, "If the robbers have a 10-mile start on the pursuers they are safe. They are in a country that has been a refuge for many criminals, and while posses have frequently gone there, they have never caught anyone."

Still, the first reports from the Griffith posse were encouraging. On July 5, the *Helena Independent* predicted that the robbers "will probably be captured by morning." They said that the posse had caught up with the robbers the previous afternoon at Buck Allen's ranch, forty miles south of Wagner. "The sheriff Griffith and 15 men had them completely surrounded and were expected to make an attack as soon as reinforcements arrived."

Alas for the lawmen, the report was, to say the least, premature. All that was captured were tired horses. Kid Curry, having learned from Butch Cassidy, had arranged for relay stations along the way. By this point in their careers, if there had been rewards for the arrest of Wild Bunch gang members' horses, there would be plenty of rich and retired posse men.

The next report was even less encouraging. A courier arrived in Malta with news that Sheriff Griffith's men were exhausted and their horses were too spent to continue the chase. The posse had lost the robbers' trail the previous afternoon near Rocky Canyon, and unless fresh horses could be obtained, there was little hope that the bold bandits would be captured.

Sheriff Griffith certainly did not show any loss of resolve when he arrived in Glasgow late on July 7. He told a *Tribune* reporter, "The men I want are in the Little Rocky mountains and cannot possibly get away, as I have a complete patrol of the Missouri river both day and night. I will need a least 50 more men, and as soon as I get them I will drive every point on the river. The fighting men from some of the outlying precincts can now report and I will lead them where they can tangle up in legitimate warfare."

Or not: the *Helena Independent* reported, "It is known definitely that the Great Northern train robbers crossed the Missouri river about seven miles above Fort Peck about 7:45 Monday evening [July 8] and that they are now on the south side. Sheriff Griffith and posse have been notified, but by the time . . . he reaches the point where the robbers crossed the river he would be 40 hours behind them." A Great Northern official at Glasgow confirmed the report, stating that he had received reliable information that the train robbers were already south of the Missouri and that any further pursuit from the north was hopeless.

Undaunted by the printed word, Griffith left Glasgow with twenty-eight men and ten days' rations on July 10. The next day he arrived at Jim Winters's ranch, six miles east of the Little Rockies, where he was joined by posses from Great Falls and Chinook. By the following day, the sheriff had sixty-five men combing the Little Rockies. Day after day, though, they came up empty.

A disgruntled *Independent* commented, "After a careful review of all the stories and all the real and manufactured information, the consensus of opinion among those who have participated in the man hunt, is that they have been chasing phantoms. According to a report here the bandits were last seen at a point south of the Little Rockies. They were also last seen at Rocky Point, and were also last seen at several other place, and the funny part of all of this seemingly childish man hunt is that men can be found who believe it."

But they would not believe for much longer. Even Sheriff Will Griffith called it quits.[102]

This was not true, however, of the Pinkerton National Detective Agency, which continued to hunt for the train robbers. William Pinkerton himself left the comforts of his office in Chicago for Denver to personally supervise the efforts of his operatives. As part of its inves-

102 Will Griffith was a hard-luck lawman. The previous year, as a deputy sheriff, he had been attacked and disarmed by Ab Allen, recently paroled after doing fifteen years in prison for murder. Bystanders had to intervene to save Griffith from further damage. In July 1904, Allen and Griffith encountered each other in front of the Star Saloon on Austin Street in Jefferson, Utah. Allen held a shotgun he had borrowed for the purpose of shooting his son, Ernest Allen. But he met Sheriff Griffith first and used the shotgun on him instead. The lawman managed to pull his pistol and fire off several shots, striking Allen in the groin. Allen staggered into the saloon and fell to the floor and died minutes later. Shot in the bowels, Griffith was taken to a doctor's office where he died that evening.

tigation, the agency distributed the serial numbers and a description of the stolen Bank of Montana bills to banks throughout the United States.

Their efforts paid off, almost three months later, enabling them to do what the posses could not—lead them to Orlando Hanks and Ben Kilpatrick, and, finally, the bigger prize of Kid Curry.

31

ONE AFTER ANOTHER

The Great Northern train robbery was indeed the last exploit for several members of the Wild Bunch, but one stalwart did not even make it that far. For Will Carver, the reason why the gang had gathered in Fort Worth the previous autumn, the honeymoon was a short one.

On March 27, 1901, a man named Oliver Thornton was murdered in Concho County, Texas, which was where the Kilpatrick family lived—in fact, less than a mile away from Oliver and Mamie Thornton. After his stays in Fort Worth and San Antonio, Ben Kilpatrick had returned to the ranch on Planche Spring to continue to lay low. The morning of his murder, Thornton, a thirty-four-year-old schoolteacher who himself had gotten married the previous year—Mamie was also a teacher—walked to the Kilpatrick house. Why, it is not known for sure. Speculation has been that word had reached Concho County of the various rewards for the capture of the members of the Wild Bunch and Thornton, who was carrying a .22-caliber rifle, thought to enhance his modest salary.

He was about fifty yards from the Kilpatrick house, near the family's hogpen, when there was a gunshot. Thornton fell dead. Apparently, no one in the Kilpatrick family felt it prudent to hide the body so it was Mamie, hours later, looking for her missing husband, who found Thornton. Once the county sheriff learned of the shooting, he spread the word to be on the lookout for any of the Kilpatrick boys, especially Ben and George, who were known to have ridden with Butch Cassidy and now, it seems, had fled the area.

It is not known where Ben went—eventually, of course, tying up with Kid Curry and Orlando Hanks—but several days later George Kilpatrick was spotted in Sonora, and with him was Will Carver, who may not have known there was an arrest warrant out on his companion. On the night of April 2, Kilpatrick and Carver were in the Owens Bakery—not, more cinematically, in a rough-edged saloon with a tinkling piano—when Elijah "Lige" Bryant, the sheriff of Sutton County, and two deputies entered.[103]

When the lawmen walked in, they already had guns drawn. Bryant had been wounded by a robbery suspect the year before and was not taking any chances. The sheriff said the two outlaws were under arrest as suspects in the murder of Oliver Thornton. George Kilpatrick made a fumbling motion and Carver's gun never cleared the holster before Bryant and his deputies began firing. Carver was killed, shot six times. Kilpatrick was hit too but survived. Carver's last words were reported to be, "Die game, boys." Bryant would collect a $1,000 reward for Carver's demise. The following year, he did not seek reelection as sheriff, preferring more peaceful pursuits such as serving as a postmaster and later as a county judge. (And he passed away peacefully, at eighty-one, in November 1945.)

Ben Kilpatrick and his two fellow train robbers would not be free men much longer. On October 14, 1901, a young woman entered a Nashville, Tennessee, bank and attempted to exchange a roll of ten-dollar bills for larger bills. A bank employee recognized the bills as ones

---

103 It is fitting that the thirty-seven-year-old Bryant had first come to Texas from Kentucky to take a job as a schoolteacher.

from the Great Northern robbery and called the police. Two Nashville Police detectives, Jack Dwyer and Austin Dickens, responded, and when they arrested the woman, she told them her name was Annie Rogers, up from Texas.

Things got a bit complicated but were fruitful. The new prisoner claimed that the stolen money had been given to her by a man named Bob Nevill with whom she had been traveling. They had arrived in Nashville three days earlier and had been staying at the Lincks Hotel. She also furnished information that led Pinkerton detectives to a Denver photographer where she and Nevill had been photographed in December 1900. When the Pinkertons obtained a copy of the photograph, they recognized Bob Nevill as suspected Great Northern train robber Harvey Logan, alias Kid Curry.

Nearly two weeks later, Detectives Dwyer and Dickens were again called to investigate stolen bills. At about 10:30 on the morning of the twenty-seventh, a man entered the Newman & Company store on North College Street and attempted to make a small purchase with a crisp, new twenty-dollar bill. Mrs. Newman could not make change and sent the bill next door to a drugstore. Alerted by the publicity from the Annie Rogers arrest, a drugstore employee recognized the Bank of Montana bill and called the police. When the detectives arrived and attempted to arrest the man, he resisted. The detectives grabbed hold of him, but he quickly threw them aside and ran from the store.

Once outside, he commandeered an ice wagon and led the police on a dangerous chase through the streets of Nashville. When one of the ice wagon horses broke down, the fugitive forced a man from a buggy and continued his flight. The police followed him for several miles before he abandoned the buggy and disappeared into a large cornfield near the Cumberland River. During the chase, when the police appeared to be about to overtake the escapee, he was seen throwing objects from the buggy. When they returned to the spot, cops found a pocket book and $1,280 in Bank of Montana bills.

At first, the authorities believed that the "ice wagon man" was Butch

Cassidy. But the next day, they showed the witnesses photographs of Cassidy and the other suspects in the Great Northern robbery. The witnesses all agreed that the man they saw was not Cassidy. However, several of them, including Mrs. Newman, thought that the "ice wagon man" looked a lot like Orlando Camillo Hanks.

The next break in the case came on November 5, when a man used four new twenty-dollar bills to purchase a watch at the Globe Loan Agency in St. Louis. When a Globe employee took the bills to a bank, they were recognized as more of the Montana money. Just before midnight, the St. Louis police located the man at Josie Blake's Chestnut Street "resort" and placed him under arrest. When the police searched him, they found $460 of the stolen Montana money and a hotel key. The key was traced to the Laclede Hotel where the suspect and a woman were registered under the name of Mr. and Mrs. J. W. Rose. Luckily, the police arrived in time to arrest Laura Bullion, alias Della Rose, as she was about to leave the hotel. They found another $8,000 in Bank of Montana bills in her luggage.

Attempts were made to identify the tall man who talked like a Texan. At first, it was believed that he was the Sundance Kid, but Great Northern witnesses brought to St. Louis, including Clarence Smith and Mike O'Neil, spoiled such wishful thinking. A photograph of the prisoner had been widely distributed, and on November 13, local lawmen received a reply from Paint Rock, Texas, that the image was "positively identified as being [Ben] Kilpatrick. Raised here and wanted for murder. James E. House, Sheriff Concho County." When confronted with this information, the prisoner reluctantly admitted that he was Ben Kilpatrick.

As if bandits in hiding needed a reminder that brawling in saloons is usually a bad idea, one was given on December 13 in Knoxville, Tennessee. Two police officers responded to a disturbance at a local saloon. When they tried to arrest one of the combatants, he shot and seriously wounded both officers before making his escape. The next day, stolen Bank of Montana bills began to show up around the city.

All of them were traced to the man who had shot the policemen. That day's *Knoxville Sentinel* reported that the fugitive was believed to be "Harry Longabaugh, one of the Montana train robbers still at large." The *Knoxville Journal & Tribune* agreed that this description "tallies very accurately with that of Harry, or 'Kid' Longabaugh, who took part in the robbery of the Great Northern train on July 3rd last."

The newspapers were both right and wrong: the saloon brawler was one of the Great Northern robbers but not the Sundance Kid.

The misidentified suspect was arrested in nearby Jefferson City and returned to Knoxville on December 15. The police found $2,000 of the stolen money on him and another $3,130 in a bag that he had checked at the Southern Railway station. Approximately $4,000 more was gathered up from establishments in Knoxville, bringing the total recovered to more than $9,000. But of the men suspected of the Great Northern robbery, he most closely resembled Harvey Logan. Apparently, his girlfriend being busted did not make Kid Curry more cautious.

To assist them in identifying their prisoner, the authorities asked the Pinkertons to send someone to Knoxville. Two days later, the detective Lowell Spence arrived and identified the man in custody as Harvey Logan. Then three weeks later, Clarence Smith and Mike O'Neil identified Logan as one of the men who had robbed their train.

No one had any idea where Butch Cassidy was, and it pretty much stayed that way. But another member of the bandit gang was not so fortunate. Lawmen were about to learn what happened to the man who had disappeared into that cornfield.

On the night of April 16, 1902—while Kid Curry was still cooling his heels behind bars—a customer at a saloon in San Antonio began flashing a gun and using rough and abusive language. When officers led by Sheriff Pink Taylor entered the saloon, the man jumped to his feet, drew a gun, and fired a bullet that caromed off an officer's belt buckle. While two of the policemen tried to wrestle the gun away from the shooter, Taylor drew his gun and shot the man in the chest and head, killing him instantly.

The dead man was first identified as Wyatt Hanks because of a name found sewn inside his coat. But three days later, Sheriff Thomas Stell of Cuero, Texas, viewed the body and told the authorities that the dead man was Wyatt's brother, Orlando. His twice-widowed mother confirmed the identification the next day when she arrived in San Antonio.[104]

Let's return to Annie Rogers: she remained in the Nashville jail awaiting trial until June 1902. After the defense presented an affidavit from Harvey Logan stating that he had given her the money and that she had no knowledge of the robbery, a jury acquitted her of forging and attempting to pass stolen bank notes.

Following her trial, Rogers returned to Texas, where, without Kid Curry's presence in her life, she probably reverted to being a soiled dove. In the last mention of her in the Pinkerton Agency report, she hocked a diamond ring Curry had given her and told the pawnshop proprietor that she was giving up the brothel life to go work in a department store in St. Louis owned by her mother and a brother. Annie Rogers—whose real name, the Pinkerton reports improbably maintained, was Beulah Phinburg—faded from history after that.

By then, another of the "Wild Bunch women," Laura Bullion, had pleaded guilty to having altered bank notes in her possession and received a five-year sentence. She was released from the Missouri State Penitentiary at Jefferson City in September 1905. She lived the last

---

104 Orlando Hanks would have a form of immortality. In 1979, as part of their "Wild Bunch" collection, the Kenner toy company manufactured a "fast-draw action figure" of Hanks, to be sold in conjunction with the release of the movie *Butch and Sundance: The Early Days*. In it, Hanks was played by the burly actor Brian Dennehy. And another form of mortality: although the perimeter of the Hanks grave site is marked with a concrete border that is about 120 years old, a new marker was installed at the cemetery by the Wild West History Association. A formal dedication of the new marker took place on January 28, 2023. A detailed sixteen-page article titled "O. C. Hanks—Wayward Son" had been published in the September 2021 issue of the *Wild West History Association Journal*.

years of her life in Memphis under the name of Freda Lincoln, claiming to be a World War I widow and working as a seamstress. When Bullion passed away in December 1961 at age eighty-five, she was the last surviving member of the Wild Bunch.

Ben Kilpatrick also pleaded guilty to passing and altering stolen bank notes in December 1901. But the judge showed no mercy to the Tall Texan—he was sentenced to fifteen years at hard labor.[105] Kilpatrick was released from a federal penitentiary in Atlanta in 1911. He apparently had not learned anything from the incarceration experience. On March 12, 1912, Kilpatrick was killed while attempting to hold up a Galveston, Harrisburg, & San Antonio train near Sanderson, Texas.

And finally, it was Kid Curry's turn. When Annie Rogers was arrested, he went to hide out in Birmingham, Alabama, where several railroads intersected, offering the option of a quick escape. After foolishly causing a commotion by threatening to shoot a hotel clerk, Curry was on the move again, this time to Knoxville. There, he befriended a saloon owner named Luther Brady. It was a short-lived friendship, and its end was violent.

A dispute occurred between the two men while they were playing pool. Given Curry's temper, it was no surprise that things escalated quickly: Curry thrust Brady into an empty barrel and began to strangle him. Other patrons of the saloon tried to intervene and chances were that would have prevented further damage, but then two police officers, Robet Saylor and William Dinwiddie, walked in to see what all the fuss was about.

They confronted Curry, who declared that he was defending himself, and he included the officers in that by jerking his gun out and shooting Saylor. The officer managed to get close enough to Curry to hit him in the head with his nightstick, but the outlaw fired again . . . and again and again, until a mortally wounded Saylor was sprawled on

---

105 During his time in prison, Kilpatrick and Laura Bullion exchanged letters, but they never saw each other again.

the foot-worn floor. Dinwiddie also hit Curry in the head, bringing him to his knees, but as he lurched back up, he fired. The bullet struck the second officer in the neck, and he too went down.

Though blood poured from his head, Kid Curry got fully to his feet and ran out the back door of the saloon. A few patrons watched him stagger through a stream bed and then vanish into the night.

Several days later, lawmen were alerted by a tip reporting a man wearing bloody clothing in Jefferson City, thirty miles northeast of Knoxville. Several men carrying shotguns found Kid Curry in a remote area where he had made camp, and he was arrested without further violence. By that evening, he was back in Knoxville.

"The city was electrified by the news that the man who had shot two of their police officers had been captured," reports Gary Wilson. "Despite the cold, wet weather, a large crowd was there to meet Logan when his train arrived in Knoxville." He would wind up in the Knox County jail, held on $20,000 bail, with a trial date set for December 18.

Wilson also describes a festive atmosphere surrounding the outlaw celebrity: "Logan received the daily papers, had clean laundry, and was kept groomed to meet the public. He enjoyed talking with the reporters and reading his own press notices. His visitors now numbered in the many thousands. The sheriff kept parading them through. Only Teddy Roosevelt's visit to town attracted more people. Logan received a pillow from one female visitor, along with a love letter in a scented pink envelope."[106]

After months and months of legal maneuvering, Kid Curry was convicted of counterfeiting, forging, and passing stolen bank notes in November 1902. He remained in the Knoxville jail for months more while his appeal was being considered—until June 27, 1903. On that day, he overpowered a guard and escaped. There really was no more

---

106 The woman's name was Catherine Cross. She claimed that she and the outlaw were soon running away together. She had created a song about him she sang over and over again in a saloon until someone shot and killed her.

Wild Bunch gang to rejoin, but Kid Curry had one more adventure left in him.

For almost a year, he managed to elude lawmen, Pinkerton Agency detectives, and bounty hunters. Then on June 7, 1904, Kid Curry and two other men held up a Denver & Rio Grande express train two miles west of Parachute, Colorado. A posse caught up with them two days later, and during the ensuing shoot-out, Curry was wounded. Members of the posse heard him call to his two accomplices that he was badly hurt and would end it there. Moments later, Curry placed a gun to his head and pulled the trigger.

"Kid" Curry was by then thirty-six years old—the same age as another gunfighter, Doc Holliday, with whom Curry would share the Linwood Cemetery in Glenwood Springs, Colorado.

Only the two refugees from Bandit Heaven were left. They would remain free as long as they stayed far enough away—and kept to their reformed ways.

32

END OF THE TRAIL

The 1969 film *Butch Cassidy and the Sundance Kid* would have the audience believe that it was only a short time in South America before the two expatriates returned to their bandit ways. However, they really did give ranching and domestic normalcy a try. (Well, as normal as two men and a woman with false identities allowed.) As Charles Leerhsen puts it, they "were working toward a common goal of having a more civilized life than Butch and Sundance had known as cowboys up north."

This included, once their house was constructed—with each room having a door leading outside, just in case—furnishings imported from the U.S., enjoying afternoon tea, adhering to dining etiquette, sharing the affections of a springer spaniel, and in other ways living the life of gentlemen planters and farmers.[107] The residents of the surrounding area became friendly neighbors, and the gringos came to be held in such esteem that when Julio Lezana, the province's governor,

---

107 Also, in case they observed or were warned of police on the way, three horses carrying basic provisions were kept saddled and ready to ride.

visited Cholila, he stayed the night with Cassidy, Sundance, and Ethel, even dancing with the latter.

That this domestic bliss did not last can be attributed to their natures as much as circumstances. Bottom line: Butch and Sundance were robbers, not ranchers, and geography could not change that. They were creatures trying and ultimately failing to survive outside their natural habitat.

The first serious indication of restlessness came in February 1902. Only a year after they departed the United States, Sundance and Ethel were on their way back. (Cassidy had bid them farewell in Buenos Aires.) The *Soldier Prince,* a British freighter, took the couple to New York City, where they repeated their experience as tourists. There was a side trip to Atlantic City, where Harry's brother Harvey Longabaugh lived, and at least a day was spent seeing physicians, probably for Sundance's familiar complaints. It is not known what else Mr. and Mrs. Place did, but whatever their activities, they occupied months of their time. It was not until August that they boarded another British freighter, the *Honorious,* to return to Argentina.

Cassidy had kept the home fires burning that fall and winter. There were the routine chores of ranch operations and scouting for additional property. It would seem they still had plenty of funds in the Buenos Aires bank. Less happily, the gregarious Butch learned more than he ever wanted to about loneliness. Sure, there were a handful of ranch hands as card-playing companions and a few local entertainments to attend but Butch had always been a man popular among his peers back in the Mountain West. In Cholila, for all its advantages as a hideout even more remote than Bandit Heaven, he was out of his element living among people he could barely understand.

Maybe that would change when Sundance and Ethel were back. For a time, it did. But something had changed with them too. If they had not returned to the bright lights and cultural attractions and modern amenities of the big city, perhaps they would have continued to acclimate enough to life in Cholila to become content. That the couple had stayed away for five months implies they returned with some reluctance.

But once again, all three tried to make a go of it. And then a Pinkerton detective showed up—in Buenos Aires, not Cholila, but that was disturbing enough.

His name was Frank Dimaio. Based in Philadelphia, he had just finished a job in Brazil. Thanks to spying on Samanna's mail, the agency knew that her brother, Cassidy, and a woman named "Etta" were living in Argentina. Robert Pinkerton had instructed Dimaio to detour to Buenos Aires on his way home to the U.S. and visit George Newbery. The now-infamous "Fort Worth Five" photograph was shown to him, and the dentist confirmed that right in that very office two years earlier he had extolled the virtues of Patagonia to Butch Cassidy and the Sundance Kid (and their lovely companion). Dr. Newbery contended that while outlaws they may have been, in Argentina they were living in a quiet, law-abiding way. Was it really worth such an arduous trip to Cholila to try to arrest them?

No, agreed the Pinkerton op. He left Buenos Aires and steamed to Philadelphia. However, he was not completely done with the expat bandits. Dimaio had a poster created that bore descriptions in Spanish of Butch and Sundance, to be distributed to law enforcement in Argentina. Maybe one would land in the hands of an officer who was ambitious enough.

Robert Pinkerton went a step further. He sought funding, to the tune of $5,000, from several business entities, including the Union Pacific Railroad, to mount an expedition to Patagonia led by Charlie Siringo. When the plan was greeted with a marked lack of enthusiasm, the Pinkerton Agency lost interest. As far as bank and railroad officials were concerned, let those bandits spend the rest of their lives in Argentina—out of sight, out of mind.

The previous year's scenario was repeated in March 1904: Cassidy ran the ranch in Cholila while Sundance and Ethel visited the U.S. St. Louis was one of their stops, to take in the Louisiana Purchase Exposition that had begun the year before to celebrate the centennial of the launching of the Lewis and Clark Corps of Discovery expedition. The couple was completely unaware of trouble back in their new home.

In April, there was a robbery of 5,000 pesos from the Southern Land Company. Though it had taken place six hundred miles to the east, local police arrived at the "Ryan" ranch because one of the thieves was an American named Robert Evans. He had been arrested but then escaped, leaving behind a Colt revolver. There was suspicion that the fine pistol belonged to the man who, rumors abounded, had been a famous bandit back in America. They insisted that Señor Ryan accompany them to Rawson, over four hundred miles away, to make a statement to a judge.

Butch had no choice but to accept the invitation. The trip could turn out to be more than an inconvenience—because he had in fact known Robert Evans, first, as a member of Black Jack Ketchum's gang who frequented Brown's Hole and, more recently, as a visitor who enjoyed the hospitality of the Ryan and Place ranch. Cassidy denied all of this to the judge and was allowed to return home, but the attention of the authorities was worrisome.

Nothing happened, though, until ten months later, in February 1905.

Evans was at it again, this time with another American named William Wilson. The duo robbed the Banco de Tarapaca y Argentino. And it was quite a haul, close to what would be $100,000 in U.S. money. Even though Rio Gallegos, where the bank was located, was seven hundred miles to the south of Cholila, some members of the Argentine law enforcement wondered if Señores Ryan and Place not only knew the Yankee bandits but could have *been* the Yankee bandits.

Things were going downhill. And Cassidy and Sundance's situation would only worsen, with being suspected every time there was a crime committed by an American. Then things got worse a lot faster when a warrant was issued for the arrest of the gringo ranchers. Cassidy and

Sundance caught a break when Eduardo Humphreys, the local police chief, sat on the warrant for two months. He did not want to toss his friends and the beautiful woman in jail. Humphreys suggested this would be an opportune time to relocate before pressure he could not withstand was applied by higher authorities.[108]

The ranchers acted on the suggestion immediately. Clearly, their life of peace and solitude, at least in Cholila, was over. By early May, Cassidy and Sundance had sold off what property and livestock they could in so short a time and, with Ethel in tow, had headed for the hills. When the new police chief showed up to serve the arrest warrant, he found a ranch of empty buildings and corrals.

Where did the trio go? The next stop was Valparaíso in Chile, according to a letter Sundance (signed "H. A. Place") wrote on June 28 to Daniel Gibbon, who, along with John Commodore Perry, had been their closest American neighbors.[109] They were there to wind up business connected to selling their property and decide what to do next and where.

The answer was to split up. It seemed that Cassidy had accepted that he was never going to see the United States again. But Sundance and Ethel could not resist the pull of it, so even though Sundance was still an actively wanted outlaw, they made another trip back, leaving Butch behind in Chile. Perhaps they thought they were out of the Pinkerton Agency dragnet by being in populous San Francisco, where they stayed with another brother, Elwood Longabaugh. The sneaking around and uncertain life was "starting to wear thin" for Ethel, notes Charles Leerhsen. "Sundance, given to long bouts of silence, had never been easy to live with, and lately his drinking had been getting worse."

The alcohol might have affected his judgment—or at least his temper—because upon their return to Chile, Sundance made what could have been a catastrophic mistake. While reuniting with Cassidy

---

108 Chief Humphreys would, in fact, be fired for dragging his feet with the arrest warrant.

109 Ironically, Perry had been the first sheriff of Crockett County in Texas.

in the port city of Antofagasta, Sundance encountered a group of local policemen who kidded him about his resemblance to an illustration on a Spanish-language Pinkerton Agency poster. Instead of going along and laughing it off, Sundance responded with his fists. After the intervention of the American vice-consul and paying a fine, Sundance was let go, with the police not pursuing "Frank Boyd's" real identity.

One can only speculate why, as the end of 1905 neared, Cassidy and Sundance decided the best course of action was to rob a bank. It could simply be their suppressed natures reasserting themselves. A darker answer was they sensed that there was nowhere to go but down. Back to Argentina.

Butch must have remained in contact and maybe hung around with Robert Evans while Sundance and Ethel were away because Evans accompanied them to Villa Mercedes in the center of the country. The target was the Banco de la Nación and the day chosen for the robbery was December 19, a Tuesday. There was a fourth bandit—when Butch, Sundance, and Evans tottered into the bank (they had been drinking at a nearby bar), Ethel remained outside to hold the horses.

It did not seem that the thieves had to chip off any rust because, as bank employees reported, the heist was done efficiently. Two men brandished pistols while the third emptied out the safes. No shots were fired, and the only violence was to the manager, who was struck while attempting to resist. Not a policeman was in sight when the four got up on their horses and took off "in a cloud of dust," one newspaper reported. Another account observed that the female accomplice was "a fine rider" and "is widely admired by Argentines for her skill and natural ability." The bandits made off with 12,000 pesos, or $120,000 in today's dollars.

"The robbery itself was vintage Cassidy: well-planned down to the last detail," notes Richard Patterson. "It was timed to coincide with the town's major monthly cattle sale, which meant the bank's cash drawers would be full, and a clean getaway was assured through relays of fresh horses and supplies stashed along the way."

A handsome haul indeed, but the gang gave up whatever anonymity they had left. Stories circulated about the bandits being Butch Cassidy and the Sundance Kid, with the third man being Kid Curry—although he had died the previous year. In some accounts there was an underpinning of pride that the Wild Bunch had chosen Argentina as the place to be reunited and return to robbery.

Cassidy and Sundance again went their separate ways. The former chose to lie low in Buenos Aires. A pleasant surprise was the appearance of a touring Wild West show that included a few of Cassidy's old cowboy buddies and featuring the rodeo star Bill Pickett.[110] It would be almost a year before he would see the Sundance Kid again.

By the time he did, Ethel Place would be gone. One account has it that she was afflicted with appendicitis and Sundance escorted her back to the States so she could be treated at a hospital in Denver. However, it would seem that such an ailment required more immediate attention. Just as likely, if not more so, is that Ethel finally could not see a future with Harry Longabaugh, being on the run so far from home. Sometime during the first half of 1906, she returned to the U.S. alone.

Remarkably, it was probably coincidence that Butch Cassidy and the Sundance Kid got together again. Back in Argentina, on his own, in late summer 1906, "Enrique Brown" (Sundance) found a job with another American expat who provided mules and horses to firms building railroads. Brown was very handy with the animals and the American boss, Roy Letson, was glad to have him. One assignment was to bring a herd of mules to La Paz in Bolivia. For several weeks, Brown as well as Letson were the trail bosses, and the drive went smoothly as they distributed mules at locations along the way.

While dropping off the last batch of mules at the Concordia tin

---

110 In 1905, then in his midthirties, the African American Pickett, performing as the "Dusky Demon," had joined the 101 Ranch Wild West Show, which at one time or another also included an aging Buffalo Bill Cody and the future silent-screen star Tom Mix. Pickett toured the world in the show, and in places where rodeos were not allowed to have black riders, he was presented as a Comanche. He later went on to be featured in motion pictures, including *The Bull-Dogger* and *The Crimson Skull*. He died in Oklahoma in April 1932 after a bronco kicked him in the head.

mine, Brown encountered "Santiago Maxwell"—and thus, Butch and Sundance were reunited once more. Cassidy, posing as Maxwell, was an administrator at the mine and apparently was content handling payroll and similar clerical duties. His mission completed, Letson returned to Argentina, and Brown stayed on at the Concordia mine as an assistant to Maxwell.

This arrangement worked well enough, and they had a good relationship with the manager of the mine, Percy Seibert. He and his wife would have the fellow Americans to Sunday dinner. It did not take the manager long to figure out who his employees were. That did not stop the socializing, and there was an understanding that Seibert would not reach out to the law; however, if the law came to him, he would not lie.

But late in 1907, this last attempt to stay straight ended. Again, it was Sundance's inability to hold his liquor. In a bar, drunk, he began talking about the bank heist they had committed in Argentina. Cassidy hustled him out the door, but the damage had been done. Too many tongues would be wagging, and local lawmen would not look away. Abandoning the Concordia mine and the Seiberts, they went south to Tupiza, arriving there as George Low and Frank Smith.

This time there was no pretense of leading a law-abiding life. In Tupiza was the Banco Nacional. While Cassidy kept his eye on the building, Sundance roamed the town. This could be the perfect setup. But then Butch was recognized as "Santiago Maxwell" by a Concordia mine acquaintance, which at least gave them pause. Worse, a contingent of Bolivian troops came to stay in the town, so that took away the advantage of scant law enforcement. Time to move on.

The next scheme looked like a sure thing: take the Aramayo y Franke mining company payroll as it was transported by mules through isolated country. If Cassidy and Sundance could stop and rob a train pulled by a steaming locomotive, how difficult could a mule train be?

It turns out, not very difficult at all. On November 4, 1908, the two bandits accosted three men and their mules near Quechisla. The Aramayo official, Carlos Pero, could tell they were "Yankees" even though their faces were covered. That they spoke only English was a giveaway too. Butch and Sundance took a payroll package containing 80,000 bolivianos and one of the three mules. Glad to be alive, the three victims resumed their journey on two mules.

Lying low, the outlaws were staying at a camp belonging to A. G. Francis, who supplied dredges to gold mine operations. One morning, a man known to Francis arrived on a horse to inform the visitors that they were the subject of a bulletin being distributed throughout southern Bolivia and beyond. Police were seeking two Americans who had stolen the mining company payroll. More ominous, the man reported, was that in the town of Salo, where the robbed mule train had stopped, there were as many as a hundred men gathering as a posse.

According to Patterson, "Worried, they made a hasty departure, intending to go north to Uyuni and possibly from there leave Bolivia. At San Vicente, which was on the way to Uyuni, they made a fatal mistake"—deciding to spend the night in the village instead of camping somewhere along the trail.

Butch Cassidy and the Sundance Kid arrived as the sun was setting on November 6. They checked into a boarding house run by Bonifacio Casasola. San Vicente was a bit remote, over fourteen thousand feet up in the Andes Mountains, and with a population of only 350, many of the people were known to each other. Thus, two Americans stood out.

Plus, even there it was known that two gringos were being sought for robbery. And one of them (Butch) was riding a mule with the Aramayo y Franke brand on it. Of all people, it was the mayor, Cleto Bellot, who noted this as he greeted the new arrivals. This task completed, Bellot went directly to another boarding house, this one hosting a tired quartet of soldiers and a policeman who had been searching the area for the thieves.

On being alerted, two of the soldiers and the policeman, clutching rifles, came quietly to the Casasola house. They could see Butch and Sundance sitting at a candlelit table eating dinner. One of the soldiers was an officer named Timoteo Rios. He called through the window for the two gringos to give themselves up. Instead of doing so and taking their chances, the two bandits tried to conceal themselves. But after a few moments, Cassidy emerged from the doorway enough to fire his pistol.

The bullet struck the other soldier, Victor Torres. Though mortally wounded in the neck, he fired his rifle. Then on rubber legs he crossed to another house, fell inside, and died.

There was no sudden appearance of the Bolivian army. What did happen is the remaining two men went back to their boarding house for more ammunition. They returned with enough to perforate the gringos' room. They were joined by another officer, Captain Justo Concha, who directed Mayor Bello to have citizens surround the house to prevent an escape. While the firing was ongoing, screams were heard from inside the room, then gunfire, then silence.

Citizens and soldiers alike kept their distance for the rest of the night. It was not until seven o'clock the next morning that Casasola entered his house and tiptoed to the room he had rented. He found that the Americans were dead. Both had been wounded in the arm, but the wounds in their heads suggested that Butch Cassidy had killed the Sundance Kid by shooting him in the forehead and then had shot himself in the temple.

At an inquest, Pero identified the corpses as those of the thieves who had ambushed him—although all he had ever seen of the masked men were their eyes. But neither Pero nor anyone else ever positively identified the two dead men as Butch Cassidy and the Sundance Kid before their reported burial in an unmarked grave in a San Vicente cemetery. Although descriptions of the deceased bandits bore some resemblance to the legendary robbers, no photographs of the bodies were ever taken to provide proof.

With no conclusive evidence, rumors spread that the pair had once again eluded capture. Reports of sightings of Cassidy and Sundance in South America, Mexico, and the United States continued for decades to come. Cassidy's sister, Lula Parker Betenson, wrote in her 1975 book (when she was 91), *Butch Cassidy, My Brother,* that the outlaw had returned to the family ranch in Circleville, Utah, in 1925 to visit his ailing father and attend a family wedding. Butch told the family that a friend of his had planted the story that one of the men killed in Bolivia was him so that he would no longer be pursued. Betenson claimed her brother lived in the state of Washington under an alias until his death in 1937 and was buried in an unmarked grave in a location that was kept a family secret.

Heroic efforts were made by the husband-and-wife researchers Daniel Buck and Anne Meadows who for decades mined South American archives and police reports to track down the true story of what happened, a saga that Meadows detailed in her book *Digging Up Butch and Sundance.* While the paper trail pointed to their demise in Bolivia, conclusive evidence as to the identities of the bandits killed in San Vicente rested under the ground of the village's cemetery.

The researchers enlisted the help of Clyde Snow, the renowned forensic anthropologist who had conclusively identified the remains of Nazi death camp doctor Josef Mengele. They also received permission from Bolivian authorities to exhume the bandits' bodies. In 1991, guided to their purported grave by an elderly villager whose father claimed to have witnessed the shoot-out, diggers unearthed a skeleton of one man along with a piece of a skull from another. Alas, after a detailed forensic analysis and a comparison of DNA to the relatives of Robert Parker and Harry Longabaugh, Snow found there was no match.

It is possible that the bodies of the legendary desperadoes remain buried elsewhere in the San Vicente cemetery or even outside of its walls. To this day, the ultimate fate of Butch Cassidy and the Sundance Kid remains a mystery.

EPILOGUE

With few outlaws to occupy them, the three hideouts that composed Bandit Heaven became symbols of a Wild West in America that had ended before the lives of Butch and Sundance and Kid Curry did.

Brown's Hole became more familiar to residents and others as less rustic Brown's Park. The assassinations by Tom Horn had indeed proved effective, with enough of the horse and cattle rustlers quitting the area or becoming legitimate ranchers that there was no longer a need for sanctuary. Robbers Roost soon became deserted. During the years Cassidy and Sundance spent in South America, the few outlaws who remained in the Hole-in-the-Wall haven were gradually driven or drifted out by bolder and more numerous lawmen, replaced by ranchers glad for new territory.

Sheriffs and deputies by themselves were not completely responsible for the demise of Bandit Heaven and the Outlaw Trail. As Charles Kelly points out, "Where, in the old days of the Wild Bunch, a hundred grazed knee-deep in grass, a thousand sheep came to tear out by the roots all vegetation. Under such conditions, erosion began its deadly work. After the sheep had passed, even jackrabbits were hard put to it to find a living. Cattle and horses disappeared from the ranges, and rustling died a natural death."

The outlaws who survived did so because they were either in prison and prevented from getting into mortal mischief, or with or without incarceration, they went straight. Matt Warner was one. As noted previously, he married again and served as a justice of the peace, a deputy sheriff, and a detective in Price, Utah, while doing some bootlegging on the side. He died at seventy-four, in 1938.

Elzy Lay had been sentenced to life in the New Mexico State Penitentiary. He served seven years. Not only was he a model prisoner, even being a trustee to the warden, but also during an uprising at the prison, he persuaded inmates to release their two hostages, who were the warden's wife and daughter. Lay was pardoned by Governor Miguel Otero in January 1906. He resumed ranching in Baggs, Wyoming, married, had two children, and later became a geologist who assisted in the creation of the Colorado Aqueduct system in the Imperial Valley of Southern California. He died in 1934, two weeks' shy of his sixty-fifth birthday.

Certainly a frustration for anyone who has written about the Hole-in-the-Wall gangs and the Sundance Kid in particular is the inability to finish the story of Ethel Place. Her fate remains as mysterious as her origins. As the biographer D. J. Herda noted, "When she returned to San Francisco, her newly adopted home, where no one likely knew her and no one ever would, she allegedly left behind the one man she truly loved in Bolivia to die. And so too did Etta Place die."

For decades, researchers and writers have speculated about Ethel's post-Sundance life. Did she marry and live under another name? If she was in San Francisco in April 1906, was she one of the victims of the great earthquake? Did she return to teaching or prostitution, depending on which occupation she had pursued in the first place? Are there people alive today who could be her great-grandchildren?

Herda finally concludes: "Whatever ultimately happened to a woman named Etta Place, she led one hell of a life, and she packed more into a few short years than most women—or *anyone*—could hope to see in a lifetime."

On the other hand, the fate of Brown's Hole assassin Tom Horn is well chronicled. In October 1902, he went on trial for the murder of fourteen-year-old Willie Nickell, supposedly the victim of a feud between cattle and sheep ranchers. The most damaging evidence was a confession the lawman Joe Lefors insisted that a drunken Horn had given him. Horn kept protesting his innocence, but on October 24, the jury found him guilty.

His attorneys took an appeal up to the Wyoming Supreme Court. While waiting in jail, Horn wrote his autobiography, *Life of Tom Horn, Government Scout and Interpreter, Written by Himself.* Writing may have passed the time, but it had no impact on his legal situation—the Wyoming Supreme Court upheld the decision of the District Court and denied a new trial.

Governor Fenimore Chatterton chose not to intervene and execution was set for November 20, 1903. Horn was hanged in Cheyenne and was buried in the Columbia Cemetery in Boulder, Colorado. Loyal to the end, Jim Coble paid for Tom Horn's coffin and a stone to mark his grave.[111]

What of the "cowboy detective"? Decades later on the big screen, bandits had portrayals like *The Wild Bunch* and *Butch Cassidy and the Sundance Kid* with all the bullet-riddled glory, while lawmen like Charlie Siringo, their clothes becoming more threadbare as they grew older, had the simpler, more humble but more virtuous earlier Sam Peckinpah film, *Ride the High Country.* As it ended, Steve Judd, played exquisitely by Joel McCrea, dies alone though being granted his wish: "I want to enter my house justified."

In 1907, after twenty-two years as a Pinkerton National Detective

---

111 Tom Horn was one of the few people in the West to have been hanged by water-powered gallows, known as the Julian gallows. James P. Julian, a Cheyenne architect, had designed the contraption in 1892. The trapdoor was connected to a lever that pulled the plug out of a barrel of water. This would cause a lever with a counterweight to rise, withdrawing a support and opening the trap.

Agency operative, Siringo retired. He had been involved in some of the agency's more sensational cases and overcome considerable risks. Done with dusty trails, he lived on his ranch in New Mexico and wrote more books, beginning with *A Cowboy Detective*. It was not a completely enjoyable experience because the Pinkertons objected to the use of their agency's name and the identities of operatives. Bitter, Siringo wrote and clandestinely published *Two Evil Isms, Pinkertonism and Anarchism*, in 1915. Again, the Pinkerton Agency blocked publication and, this time, attempted to have Siringo prosecuted for libel, asking that he be extradited from his ranch to Chicago. However, the New Mexico governor denied the extradition request.

Restless, in 1916, Siringo began working as a New Mexico Ranger, where his main task was to track rustlers in the southeastern part of the state. After two years, he resigned when his health began to fail. This, coupled with financial difficulties, forced him to abandon his ranch and leave Santa Fe in 1922.

He was not quite done telling stories of the Old West yet. After moving to Los Angeles, Siringo became a minor celebrity thanks to his well-publicized exploits. He worked as an adviser on Western film sets and even took an occasional bit part. In 1927 he released his final book, *Riata and Spurs,* a composite of his first two autobiographies.

The following year, Charlie Siringo died in Altadena, California, in October, age seventy-three. His grave can be found at the Inglewood Park Cemetery in Los Angeles.

At the conclusion of *A Cowboy Detective*, Charlie Siringo wrote something of a lament for lawmen like himself who went the way of the Wild West: "In bidding you adieu I ask if the world has been benefited by my having lived in it? I answer, yes. For have I not planted trees and grass on a sun-kissed desert at the end of the old Santa Fe Trail—at the very spot where once grazed the tired oxen and mules after their journey across the plains?"

ACKNOWLEDGMENTS

Once again I will stress that without the dedicated staffers at various research centers, I would not have a career. This time around, with *Bandit Heaven*, my thanks go to those librarians and curators in Wyoming, Montana, Utah, Colorado, New Mexico, and elsewhere who helped me along the arduous research road and whose unflagging courtesy made the journey an enjoyable one. I am always both delighted and humbled by the expertise and enthusiasm of such research professionals.

In particular, I want to mention Caitlyn Carl, Lisa Cowley, Kellen Cutsforth, Valerie Hanley, Evie Hergenrather, Jessica LaBozetta, Cathy Smith, Suzi Taylor, Gregory Walz, and Mark Wright.

Closer to home, I am also grateful for the efforts of staffers at the John Jermain Memorial Library, especially Susan Mullin, for their long-standing assistance and kindness.

My research included depending on the work of authors who inspired as well as informed me, including members of the Wild West Historical Association and the Western Writers of America. In particular, I would like to cite *True West*, *Wild West*, and other publications devoted to American history whose many articles were valuable sources of information. I am also grateful for the archives of newspapers and their history-in-the-making accounts of events that are included in *Bandit Heaven*.

This book would not have originated let alone been completed without the encouragement and steadfast support of my editor, Marc Resnick. Others at St. Martin's Press who have also made *Bandit Heaven* a happy and productive adventure include Sally Richardson, Andy Martin, Rebecca Lang, Lily Cronig, Mac Nicholas, Rob Grom, Julia Turner, and Steve Wagner. Another "founder" of this book is Nat Sobel, a friend as well as an agent, and I appreciate everything done for me by him and his staff, especially Jenny Lewis.

My dear friends continue to wait for me to not work so much, so we can get together more often. Their support, especially while *Bandit Heaven* was being written, was a big reason why every day still mattered. And finally, my love to Leslie, Katy and James, Vivienne, and Brendan.

SELECTED BIBLIOGRAPHY

Baker, Pearl. *The Wild Bunch at Robbers Roost*. Lincoln: University of Oklahoma Press, 1971.

Ball, Larry D. *Tom Horn: In Life and Legend*. Norman: University of Oklahoma Press, 2014.

Bartholomew, Ed. *Black Jack Ketchum: Last of the Hold-up Kings*. Houston: Frontier Press, 1965.

Barton, Barbara: *Den of Outlaws*. San Angelo, TX: Rangel Printing, 2000.

Burroughs, John R. *Where the Old West Stayed Young*. New York: William Morrow, 1962.

Burton, Doris Karren. *A History of Uintah County: Scratching the Surface*. Uintah County Commission, 1996.

Burton, Jeffrey. *The Deadliest Outlaws: The Ketchum Gang and the Wild Bunch*. Denton: University of North Texas Press, 2012.

Carlson, Chip. *Tom Horn: Blood on the Moon*. Glendo, WY: High Plains Press, 2001.

Coburn, Walt. *Stirrup High*. Lincoln, NE: Bison Books, 1957.

Davis, John W. *The Trial of Tom Horn*. Norman: University of Oklahoma Press, 2016.

Davis, John W. *Wyoming Range War: The Infamous Invasion of Johnson County*. Norman: University of Oklahoma Press, 2010.

DeArment, Robert. *Man-Hunters of the Old West*. Norman: University of Oklahoma Press, 2017.

Dimsdale, Thomas Josiah. *The Vigilantes of Montana*. Whitefish, MT: Kessinger Publishing, 2010.

Eaton, John. *Will Carver, Outlaw*. San Antonio: Anchor Publishing, 1972.

Engebretson, Doug. *Empty Saddles, Forgotten Names: Outlaws of the Black Hills and Wyoming*. Dumas, TX: North Plains Press, 1982.

Ernst, Donna B. *Harvey Logan: Wildest of the Wild Bunch.* Kearney, NE: Morris Publishing, 2003.

Ernst, Donna B. *Sundance, My Uncle* (The Early West). College Station, TX: Creative Publishing, 1992.

Ernst, Donna B. *The Sundance Kid: The Life of Henry Alonzo Longabaugh.* Norman: University of Oklahoma Press, 2009.

Ernst, Donna B. *Women of the Wild Bunch.* Kearney, NE: Morris Publishing, 2004.

Hamilton, W. T. *My Sixty Years on the Plains.* London: Lume Books, 2016.

Hatch, Thom. *The Last Outlaws: The Lives and Legends of Butch Cassidy and the Sundance Kid.* New York: New American Library, 2013.

Horan, James D. *Desperate Men: The James Gang and the Wild Bunch.* Lincoln, NE: Bison Books, 1977.

Horan, James D. *The Outlaws.* New York: Grammercy Books, 1994.

Horan, James D. *The Pinkertons: The Detective Dynasty That Made History.* New York: Crown, 1967.

Horan, James D. *The Wild Bunch.* New York: Signet, 1958.

Horn, Tom. *Life of Tom Horn, Government Scout and Interpreter.* Norman: University of Oklahoma Press, 1964.

Johnson, Pamela Call. *Pioneers and Outlaws: The Settlement of Star Valley, Wyoming, 1889–1896.* Independently published, 2020.

Kelley, Charles. *Outlaw Trail: A History of Butch Cassidy and His Wild Bunch.* New York: Bonanza Books, 1959.

Lamar, Howard R. *Charlie Siringo's West: An Interpretive Biography.* Albuquerque: University of New Mexico Press, 2005.

Lamb, Frank. *Kid Curry: The Life and Times of Harvey Logan and the Wild Bunch.* Boulder, CO: Johnson Books, 1991.

Leerhsen, Charles. *Butch Cassidy: The True Story of an American Outlaw.* New York: Simon and Schuster, 2020.

Lefors, Joe. *Wyoming Peace Officer, an Autobiography.* Whitefish, MT: Literary Licensing, 2011.

Lynch, Sylvia. *Harvey Logan in Knoxville.* East Chanhassen, MN: Creative Publishing, 1998.

McCarty, Tom. *Tom McCarty's Own Story: Autobiography of an Outlaw.* Alberta, Canada: Rocky Mountain House Press, 1986.

Meadows, Anne. *Digging Up Butch and Sundance.* Lincoln, NE: Bison Books, 1996.

Mercer, A. S. *The Banditti of the Plains or the Cattlemen's Invasion of Wyoming in 1892.* Independently published, 2017.

Moulton, Candy. *The Writer's Guide to Everyday Life in the Wild West from 1840–1900.* New York: Penguin, 1999.

Murdock, Harvey Lay. *The Educated Outlaw: The Story of Elzy Lay of the Wild Bunch.* Bloomington, IN: AuthorHouse, 2009.

Nash, Jay Robert. *Encyclopedia of Western Lawmen & Outlaws.* New York: Da Capo Press, 1994.

Patterson, Richard. *Butch Cassidy: A Biography.* Lincoln, NE: Bison Books, 1998.

Patterson, Richard. *The Train Robbery Era: An Encyclopedic History.* Boulder, CO: Pruett Publishing, 1991.

Pingenot, Ben E. *Siringo.* College Station: Texas A&M University Press, 1989.

Pinkerton, William A. *Train Robberies, Train Robbers, and the "Hold-Up" Men.* Wilmington, DE: Legare Street Press, 2022.

Pointer, Larry. *In Search of Butch Cassidy.* Norman: University of Oklahoma Press, 1977.

Rutter, Michael. *Wild Bunch Women.* Guilford, CT: Two Dot, 2003.

Siringo, Charles A. *A Cowboy Detective: A True Story of Twenty-Two Years with a World-Famous Detective Agency.* Mount Pleasant, SC: Arcadia Press, 2017.

Siringo, Charles A. *A Lone Star Cowboy.* London: Forgotten Books, 2018.

Siringo, Charles A. *Riata and Spurs: The Story of a Lifetime Spent in the Saddle as Cowboy and Detective.* Whitefish, MT: Kessinger Publishing, 2010.

Smokov, Mark T. *He Rode with Butch and Sundance: The Story of Harvey "Kid Curry" Logan.* Denton: University of North Texas Press, 2012.

Soule, Arthur. *The Tall Texan: The Story of Ben Kilpatrick.* Deer Lodge, MT: Trail Dust Publishing, 1995.

Waller, Brown. *Last of the Great Train Robbers.* New York: A. S. Barnes, 1968.

Ward, Nathan. *Son of the West: The Odyssey of Charlie Siringo: Cowboy, Detective, Writer of the Wild Frontier.* New York: Grove Atlantic, 2023.

Warner, Matt. *The Last of the Bandit Riders.* New York: Bonanza Books, 1940.

Wilson, Gary A. *The Life and Death of Kid Curry, Tiger of the Wild Bunch.* Guilford, CT: Two Dot, 2016.

Wilson, Gary A. *Outlaw Tales of Montana.* Guilford, CT: Globe Pequot Press, 2003.

INDEX

ABOUT THE AUTHOR

Gordon M. Grant

Tom Clavin is a #1 *New York Times* bestselling author and has worked as a newspaper editor, magazine writer, TV and radio commentator, and reporter for *The New York Times*. He has received awards from the Society of Professional Journalists, the Marine Corps Heritage Foundation, and the National Newspaper Association. His books include the bestselling Frontier Lawmen trilogy—*Wild Bill, Dodge City,* and *Tombstone*—and, with Bob Drury, *Blood and Treasure, The Last Hill,* and *Throne of Grace*. He lives in Sag Harbor, New York.